# Play with a Purpose
## for Under-Sevens
**THIRD EDITION**

Elizabeth Matterson

Penguin Books

PENGUIN BOOKS

Published by the Penguin Group
Penguin Books Ltd, 27 Wrights Lane, London W8 5TZ, England
Penguin Putnam Inc., 375 Hudson Street, New York, New York 10014, USA
Penguin Books Australia Ltd, Ringwood, Victoria, Australia
Penguin Books Canada Ltd, 10 Alcorn Avenue, Toronto, Ontario, Canada M4V 3B2
Penguin Books (NZ) Ltd, Private Bag 102902, NSMC, Auckland, New Zealand

Penguin Books Ltd, Registered Offices: Harmondsworth, Middlesex, England

First published 1965
Reprinted with revisions 1973
Second edition 1975
Third edition 1989
20 19 18 17 16 15 14 13 12 11

Copyright © Elizabeth Matterson, 1965, 1973, 1975, 1989
Illustrations copyright © Andrew Farmer, 1989
All rights reserved

Printed in England by Clays Ltd, St Ives plc
Filmset in Linotron Plantin

# Contents

## Part 2
## Providing for Play

and improvising play materials – Play material in nursery groups
– The quantity and quality of play experience

Getting around – Jumping and bouncing – Balancing and
rocking – Climbing – Riding – Pushing and pulling – Throwing,
catching, kicking and hitting – Building and making – Using
machines and tools – Hand–eye coordination – Cooperating and
combining strength – Specific physical skills (swimming,
gymnastics, dancing lessons, 'soft' rooms, adventure
playgrounds, music and movement sessions)

Family play at home and in the nursery group – Doll play –
Dens and hidey-holes – Hospital play – Playing shops – Puppets
– Dressing up – Scale models – Vehicle play – Animal play

Natural materials – Water play – Nursery group water activities
– Keeping safe and staying dry – Sand – Sand in nursery
groups – Alternatives to sand (or just a change from sand) –
Earth – Clay – Play dough – Other modelling materials – Wood
– Things we eat – Things which live and grow – Planning for
children in the garden – Pets and animals – Making do without
a pet – Books and television – Natural phenomena

What is creativity? – Who is creative? – Painting – Finger-
painting – Pattern- and print-making – Drawing – Collage –
Junk play – Cutting and pasting – Cooking

# Part 3
## Playing Away from Home

# Foreword

This is the third completely new edition of *Play with a Purpose for Under-Sevens* to be published in just under a quarter of a century.

The first edition, published in 1965, was written mainly for parents, while the second edition (1975) was written mainly with nursery groups, particularly playgroups, in mind.

This new third edition is different again. It is speaking for and on behalf of the group most concerned and yet the group least able to speak up for themselves – the children. In spite of what might seem to be a good deal of progress in the last twenty-five years, many children are not getting what they need during their early formative years. For a small minority the situation is intolerable to a degree that would have been unimaginable a few decades ago.

The time is ripe for a 'melting-pot' where everyone puts together what they know in an attempt to work out what it is that children need, rather than just looking at what the separate establishments such as education, social services, voluntary and self-help organizations are able to do for them – to look at what children should have 'as of right', and how those 'rights' can be restored in an age and culture which has done so much to erode and exploit a natural environment.

It is hoped that this book will be a contribution to such a melting-pot, and to this end the jargon of the administrator, the educationalist expert and the computer programmer has been avoided. Jargon and technical terms veil the reality of children as live, growing and developing individuals who have immediate needs. They are not units or statistics or experimental findings which can be worked on at some convenient time in the future – they are individuals who move from one situation to another very fast, and this has to be taken into account.

The professional world is not the only one to use jargon. Parents also have a restricted code, and some of these terms and words have slipped into the manuscript almost unwittingly.

'Proper school', for instance, does not imply that there are also 'improper schools'. It is the term widely used by parents as shorthand for the situation where a child goes to an establishment where he is expected to attend every day whatever is happening at home, where he is 'late' if the bell has gone by the time he gets there, where he is expected to wait for a drink till 'playtime', where he is encouraged not to trot off to the lavatory during 'lesson time', where there is a timetable to be followed, where there are stipulated goals to be attained, and where his mother has to send a note if she doesn't wish him to do something that the other children will be doing (and give a very good reason for it).

In fact it is a very significant piece of 'jargon' – it denotes the point at which parents have to hand over control of what is happening to their child to some outside agency.

Where this and similar 'parent shorthand' terms have occurred, they have been left in. While parents are not necessarily experts who can understand experts' jargon, most experts will be parents and should be able to understand the common language of parents.

The word 'we' has been used not to mean the 'royal we' but to emphasize that adults have a particular place in a child's conception of the world – any adult with whom a child comes in contact is part of the 'them and us' situation as he sees it. Since this book is written for adults to read, this has inevitably translated into 'we' meaning adults and 'they' meaning children.

As to the use of 'he' for children and 'she' for parent, this is what was used some years ago. In the intervening time between the first edition and this new book there have been some interesting moves by writers to use 'she' instead of 'he', or to use both 'he' and 'she' for alternate chapters. The pendulum has now swung the other way, so this edition remains comfortably with 'he' for children and 'she' for parent. If it makes anyone wonder 'Do boys really do that?' or 'Don't girls do this too?' or 'Don't fathers come into it?' the answer is probably yes to all three, but hopefully – because children and families vary – readers will be inspired to go and have a look for themselves.

This book is the result of a good many people doing a good deal of looking for themselves and one person doing a lot of listening. Elizabeth Matterson has drawn on extensive and intensive experience of children in various kinds of nursery group and school situations, a long and wide experience of teaching and tutoring NNEB courses and playgroup courses, and a deep involvement with the Pre-School Playgroups Association as it evolved in its early days – with the intention of reflecting a picture of children, parents and carers as given to her by these individuals themselves. Special thanks are due to Maureen Ellis, who drew on her various connections with the Pre-School Playgroups Association and training committees to contribute some of the information about nursery groups and training opportunities mentioned in Part 3. She also compiled Appendix 1.

That is only two names. There ought to have been two thousand and two because so many people have contributed in various ways even if they did not realize they were doing so at the time.

There is often seen, at the beginning of a book, the statement that 'any resemblance between any character in this narrative and any living person is purely coincidental'. If any reader of this book sees any resemblance between the people who have been used as examples and someone they know, or perhaps even themselves, there is a good reason for that. They were real people in real situations, and there are so many common features in what all children and adults do that it is inevitable that some examples will 'ring a bell'.

This book, therefore, is dedicated in affectionate greeting to the other 2,000 or more contributors: the students who came to be taught but from whom so much was learned, the fellow committee members and tutors who worked alongside as colleagues and friends, the people who gave such a warm welcome to their groups and were so generous with their thoughts and experiences, the children who appreciated what was provided for them and who, on so many occasions, graciously invited an interested observer to play with them.

E. M. M.

# Part 1
# The Children Who Play

All children who play have a great deal in common with every other child, simply because they are children and follow the same developmental pattern of learning with which all children are born.

There can be a great many differences between children who play, because they are all individuals and are born to different families with different life-styles, different cultural priorities.

The following chapters are a blend of the similarities, differences and progress we see in children from 0–7 years.

# Chapter 1

# The Importance of Play

If ten people were asked to define 'play' they would give ten different answers . . .

- Musicians, actors and professional sports players play for a living.
- Adults play for recreation during leisure time.
- Schoolteachers send children out to play as a break from the teaching/learning routine of the classroom.
- A psychiatrist will observe the way a child plays as an aid to diagnosis.
- Mothers tell children to 'stop playing about' when there is a need to hurry.
- A child spends all morning making a garage for his toys, and when he is called to put his coat on to go shopping says, 'But I haven't had time to play with it yet.'

All these uses of the word 'play' mean something quite different from each other. The play referred to in this book is the

PURPOSEFUL,
PRACTICAL,
PROGRESSIVE PROGRAMME of spontaneous activity which every child naturally follows,
PATIENTLY and PERSISTENTLY collecting knowledge at his own
PACE and with very evident
PLEASURE to develop his
POTENTIALITY as an independent
PERSON

In this book the word 'play' is used to mean 'the way children learn'. In modern jargon it would be called 'experiential learning', but that gives no impression of the enjoyment and fun that is such a vital part of what children do. Experience is something that can just happen to us. Children are self-motivated to go seeking after experience. They make things happen.

## What is play?

Play is a vital part of the growth and development process between the stages of being a totally dependent new-born individual and becoming an independent adult.

Babies not only grow in size, they also have to develop and change. These changes go on throughout the whole life-span, but the rate at which development takes place is not always the same. The fastest rate of development is during the first seven years.

The new-born baby can only let us know what he needs by crying, he can't support himself, he has to be carried, he can't feed himself, he knows nothing of the world around him. Without adult care he would die.

At the other end of the scale, when we look at an adult we see a person who walks upright, who uses his body very efficiently, who communicates by talking, writing or drawing, who understands his environment and can manipulate it by adapting it to his needs, or who, if necessary, can adapt himself to what is around him. He can use tools and machines to achieve more than he could with just his body and his mind.

No individual jumps suddenly from being a baby to being an adult – there are stages in between. A 2-year-old stands upright, is starting to communicate with speech, and has begun to decide what he wants to do (or does not want to do!). A 5-year-old has a very efficient body, he knows a good deal about the world he lives in, he can reason and be reasonable for some of the time, he knows a good deal about cause and effect, and he can use a number of tools.

In years a 5-year-old is only a quarter of the way to being an adult, but physically his body is nearly half-way to adult size. This is no surprise because we can see that children grow. What is surprising is the part we cannot see. The 5-year-old has more than three-quarters of the mental capacity he will have as an adult, and this is what enables under-5s to learn faster and more efficiently than they ever will again.

The 5-year-old stage is used as an example not because children stop playing and learning on their fifth birthday but because, in Britain, this is the age at which children have to go to school to be 'taught'. If they are fortunate, the school to which they go will use the play-enjoy-learn principle and provide an environment which is carefully structured to take the most advantage of their natural way of learning.

### Why do children have to play? Why not teach them right from the start?

Children obviously learn and they do it very efficiently – but they have to do it at their own pace and in their own way. There is no way we can teach children something they are not ready to learn or don't wish to learn.

Fortunate babies are born with all their senses, a body which will develop by itself (we don't have to tell it what to do), a brain and a nervous system. They have curiosity, the urge to imitate and repeat. They experiment and gather information. Most importantly, they find this learning rewarding and enjoyable, so that the more they learn the more they want to learn. If the learning process becomes unrewarding then they slow down or stop.

Another part of a baby's good fortune is to be born into a family and a world that encourages this process.

We cannot put young children into a 'direct learning situation'. They would not have the strength or the skill. It would be dangerous and they would be frustrated by constant failure:

- They love playing with water, but we can't make them responsible for washing themselves or their clothes until they have learned by playing and helping us.

- They love mixing things, but we don't give them a bag of groceries and expect them to make their own food.

- We give a toddler a hammer-peg toy rather than a hammer and nails until he has learned how to hammer and aim straight.

5

- We give a 3-year-old a doll rather than a real baby to wheel around in a pram.

- We give a fitting-screwing toy to the 4-year-old rather than an electric plug to wire up.

We could say: 'No hammering or fitting things together, no messing about with water and sticky mixtures until you are old enough to do it properly.' But this would not work either.

Learning and developing skills is a gradual process, and the only way to achievement is practice. Play activities are not for real, and can be repeated safely over and over again. We could call this 'practice' because that is exactly what it is – but since the child chooses to do it, does it at his own pace and enjoys what he is doing we call it 'play'.

## How children play

The way children play will depend on the individual and the stage that has been reached.

The baby who can only just sit up will play with what we give him. We go round the house looking for something he can have. In a few months' time the same child will have learned to get around the house and will help himself to what he wants. We now spend a lot of time preventing him having things.

Different children have different timetables, although they follow the same general pattern. The first baby in the family may play differently from the way a second or third child will play; the child who lives in a restricted space will play differently from one who has plenty of room; the child who does not have enough play material will play differently from one who has.

Play material does not necessarily mean bought toys. There is an absolute wealth of toys and play material on the market for every age and stage. Unfortunately it would require absolute wealth to provide our children with all of these. So long as we don't let lack of money come to mean lack of play material, it doesn't matter. If we look at the toys and work out what children do with them it is often possible to provide a home-made or improvised version, since toys are usually based on what children do naturally.

Most children are interested in anything and everything, but may like some playthings more than others at different times. They may find odd pieces of household equipment much more interesting than what we think of as toys – adult rules and categories mean nothing to them. Some activities which adults would rather not have to do, such as dusting, polishing and digging the garden, are regarded as great fun by the 2-year-old following an adult with a suitable size dustpan and brush, a duster or a little garden spade.

The normal everyday events in the family are important if the child is able to watch, hear and be part of them. He will find a lot to play with by just having a go at anything within his reach that is interesting. This last point is important. Sometimes 'good provision' means removing dangerous or unsuitable material rather than actually providing for him. Sometimes he will need the time and opportunity to stop and look and listen. Giving the time to do this 'nothing' is just as important as 'giving him plenty to do'.

As children develop, their needs change. The role of the adult who is providing for their play also changes. The 'good mother' of the 6-month-old will not be a 'good mother' to the 3-year-old unless she changes in what she is doing and providing. Parents have to learn too.

## Where, when and with whom children play

At the beginning babies play with their mother, or with whoever looks after them, and this is usually in a home situation. Gradually they will play with other members of the family if the play is adapted to the stage the baby is at. They also learn to play alone. It takes quite a while to learn to play with other children on equal terms, and still longer to learn to be a member of a group of children at mixed stages. Like everything else a child learns, this needs opportunity and practice.

A 5-year-old who has never had the opportunity to play with other children has to learn to get on with them very fast (however competent he may be at other skills) when he goes to school. This is one reason why many mothers go to parent and toddler groups, play centres and family centres, and later introduce their children into a nursery group. Here they can, for a few short sessions each week, benefit from becoming part of a group specially geared to their needs.

Cautionary note – perhaps it should be emphasized that the adults who provide the environment in which the play–learn process works best have to work very hard at it:

PARENTS (or parent substitutes) have to
PROVIDE for PROGRESSION in play
PRESENT opportunities for learning
PARTICIPATE by giving the right amount of help at the right time
PROMOTE successful play by taking an interest in what their children are doing and
PRAISE their children for their efforts as well as their success.

But nature is clever. Children derive great pleasure from the hard work of playing, which is why they go on doing it. Providing for, encouraging and watching children play and learn is a most pleasurable activity for adults – which is why they go on doing it too.

# Chapter 2

# The Children Who Play

It helps us to provide for successful play if we know:

- Where the child is now in the pattern of development.
- What he is interested in.
- Which parts of his body he can use, for example how skilful he is with his fingers and whether he can move about and how.

It also helps to know what the next stages are likely to be, as they overlap in a continuous progression. It would be more accurate to say that there is continuous movement between stages, as children may seem to go backwards or stay in the same place for a while. This is because they have to repeat and reinforce what they know and can do – and sometimes want something easy to do, for example if they are tired or not feeling well.

## The personal clock

Just as there is a pattern of development, there are certain times and stages when particular skills and abilities are learned most efficiently. Children seem to have a personal 'clock' which makes them ready to concentrate on a particular activity, and they work at this to the exclusion of almost everything else. At these times they can fail in what they are trying to do over and over again. Sometimes they really hurt themselves, but they go on trying until they can do it because these urges to learn get them over the unpleasant aspects of learning.

All children have this clock but it is different for each child, which means that they reach developmental milestones at slightly different times. Learning to walk is a good example. Once a child wants to walk almost nothing will stop him trying. He bumps himself, falls over, almost bursts with exertion.

It is wise to go along with these natural learning times. If children are not able to learn at the right time for them, they will learn or perhaps be taught later but it will be more difficult and take longer. This applies to adults too (ask any driving instructor or dancing teacher who teaches 'older' students).

At the other end of the scale, we would do better to try to teach a tree than to push a child before he is ready. At least the tree would not lose confidence and be put off learning for good.

## Watching and learning

What children see going on around them inevitably affects their natural play activities, since they watch, imitate and identify with the adults in their lives. There will be differences between children's experience of what adults do depending on the environment into which they are born, since the environment will affect how the adults live, the skills they need and the customs of the society of which they are a part. There are also differences between families living in the same environment.

## Every child's family is different

If there is someone in the family who is interested in gardening, cars, sport, music, swimming, painting or any of a hundred other possibilities:

- Children see this interest.
- They try to take part within their limitations.
- They will be encouraged to develop this interest for themselves by the enthusiast.

It is the keen swimmer who will think of taking the baby to the swimming baths, the parent who enjoyed dancing lessons as a child who looks round for dancing classes for the 4-year-old, the person who reads who will communicate their love of books to a young child, the person who sews who has interesting bits and pieces to give to a child to make a coat for teddy.

These communicated interests may not last into later life.

The valuable factor which will survive is enthusiasm, and this can be transferred to personal interests.

The life-style of the family will make a difference ... Is there a father around at the times when children are awake and playing – or does the baby see only one adult face? Are there other children? Do close friends and relatives help care for the children or is there a nanny? Do the children spend nearly all of their waking time with a childminder or in a nursery away from home?

What matters is that whoever looks after a child has the time, knowledge and inclination to provide opportunities for playing and learning. If a working mother has worked a long day, perhaps with another two hours on top of that getting her child to where he is to be cared for and then going on to work – with the reverse process at night – she will not have a lot of energy left to play with him. He will probably be tired too. The role of the carer should include more than just providing for the bodily needs and safety of the children who are minded.

## Every child's world is different

Even for children born in the same area and to the same family the world can be different, since they are born at different times of the year and therefore at different seasons.

The time a baby spends in his pram can be just a few months. When he develops the idea (or concept) of 'pram' will it include:

■ The muggy atmosphere and near twilight of the raised pram hood, muffled in woollies which cover hands, feet and head?

■ The brightness of a spring day with a breeze tickling his face and moving the pram toy fixed to the hood of the pram?

■ Or the shade of a pram canopy with the air warm on his nearly bare skin?

'Look – tree!' we say to a baby. It may be green – or bare – or have flowers on it.

When he is promoted to a big cot, will it still be daylight when he is put to bed without the familiar security of a little cot, and will the room be bright with sunlight when he wakes up in this strange cage in the morning? . . . Or will the room be dark when his mother leaves him at night and still pitch dark in the morning when he wakes up?

Inevitably the months pass, the seasons come round and he learns that a pram is still a pram, a cot is still a cot, a tree is still a tree.

He is developing so fast as he moves from one stage to another, however, that the three months of a season could cover the time of a complete stage. If more was known about critical periods and imprinting (those times when what individuals see and experience is most important and has a lasting effect), we might see some reason for similarities between people born at different times of the year.

## Some children need special help with their world

There are some children who need extra care and help because their development is hindered or curtailed by what we call a handicap. During their early years they and their family need help to cope with the handicap itself, but they also need help to ensure that the non-handicapped part of this child has the same opportunity to play as other children. The handicap will not blot out the normal needs all children have, and if these are ignored the results may be worse than the handicap itself.

Some children need special help and care because the family into which they are born is deprived:

- Living in the poverty which leads not only to lack of resources and poor health but to the depression which can make a child's demands the last straw.

- Living in poor housing, crowded housing or even no housing.

- Living in a hopeless situation which saps the energy necessary for providing a lively, stimulating, positive environment for children.

- Living in isolation.

- Living in fear.

- Living in a foreign world with a different language, different customs and different values.

What happens to normal children will reflect the values of their immediate family. What happens to these special children will also reflect the values of the community and the State into which they were born.

The next section of the book shows how children play, what they need, how they use their family and the world around them at different times. Each stage has been given a title because there are some strong characteristics which show up at different developmental stages.

There are times when the great efforts and sometimes the frustration of learning new and difficult skills can make a child difficult to live with. Then follows a calmer period while the skills that were learned are practised – until they start on the next difficult skill. For many children the hard work seems to come at the half years, the calmer periods at the full years. The child who blows out birthday candles can be an absolute charmer – tractable and easy to deal with. Six months ago he was really hard work and in another few months he may be 'difficult' again. However, not all children follow this age/stage pattern so neatly. Some are earlier, later or erratic in their progress.

An age range has been suggested, but it should be emphasized that this is only a very rough guide – not a timetable to be checked off. Children vary, their circumstances vary, their pace of learning is uneven and the bounds of normality are very wide.

# Chapter 3

# Introduction to the New World
## (0–3 MONTHS)

It would be interesting to know just how many mothers, showing off their beautiful new baby, have been asked: 'Is he good?' (by which is meant quiet and sleeps a lot) followed by: 'You'll find he's much more interesting in another few months' (in other words he is a bit boring but hopefully will improve). Perhaps these knowledgeable-sounding people have never watched a tiny baby for any length of time, sung to him, patted his feet, gently tickled the side of his face, let him have a little longer in his bath than is strictly necessary because he seemed to be enjoying it. What a lot they have missed and, by the same token, what a lot their babies have missed too.

The new baby has been growing tremendously fast for the nine months before he was born. He couldn't go on growing at that rate (he would be bigger than we are at the age of $2\frac{1}{2}$ if he grew taller at the rate of $2\frac{1}{2}$ inches per month), but he goes on growing very fast in relation to his growth in later years. He sleeps a lot, but the time when he is awake is put to good use.

He has senses and responds to smells, taste, touch, sound and what he sees and he has a healthy body although, because his nervous system is immature, he can't control it. His eyes soon start to focus and he responds to touch. He has a very large brain capacity and a memory – these too need to develop, as does the rest of his body, but this process starts rapidly.

He can cry, which is very useful. He can't look after himself so he has to get someone to do it for him and crying is part of the pattern. He can grasp but doesn't know how to let go. Many babies respond to colour and smell quite early. If we take notice he may respond to one colour more than another. He may be more aware of smells than we are, and we may miss this response except that we know he always knows his mother.

## How he plays and what he learns

At first the parent does the playing and the baby responds. He starts to watch faces intently when people talk to him if he is held at the right distance away (about 10 inches). If we just hold him in our arms naturally and comfortably to look at him, that is the right distance for him to see us. This same distance is right for him to see and watch the playthings we provide. There is no need to wake him up to 'play', but feed times, nappy-changing and bath times, cuddle and sing times get longer. He starts to smile, which is absolutely irresistible, and we start to respond to him.

The furious movements that go with being hungry or uncomfortable or frightened gradually develop into more or-ganized movements of limbs – moving his legs in the bath, waving his arms about when he is changed, pressing his feet against our hand as we feel them to see if they are warm enough. By this means he starts to find out where he leaves off and the rest of the world begins.

He starts to turn his head to listen, then tries to lift it to look. This is no mean task, as his head is large and heavy in relation to the rest of him. It might seem to make more sense if he left learning to control this heaviest part of him till last, but the pattern of development does not work like that. Control of the body develops from top to toes, from head and trunk outwards to the limbs, large movements of shoulders and hips before elbows and knees, out to the finer movements of wrists and ankles, then the really intricate movements of fingers and toes. All this takes years rather than months, but for now he concentrates on control of his head and this is important. His head is where his eyes, ears, nose and mouth are, and when he can control his head he can use these more effectively.

For many months to come his mouth will be a better sense organ than his fingers. He is not necessarily wanting to eat what he puts in his mouth – he may be just trying to feel it. He starts to reach out towards the objects he sees. He doesn't always manage to touch them because he doesn't know how far away they are and he can't control his arm with any degree of

accuracy – so he 'swipes'. Sometimes he misses and sometimes he doesn't.

Gradually, as he starts to recognize faces and sounds and learns to make a noise, he will start to initiate games and the adult responds. Gradually he will 'play' by himself for a little while. He grasps a rattle, waves his hands in front of his face, reaches out to bash his pram beads, watches a mobile or the washing flapping on the line in the garden.

Gradually is the right word to use for this progress, but it does not mean slowly. At this stage babies need a lot of sleep, so the time they have for playing is a relatively short part of their day. They learn a great deal during this short time, so they are actually learning quite fast.

## What the world around offers

This could be a great deal or very little. The baby can't go and find out for himself. His world is restricted to what others provide, but everything is new to him and normal everyday happenings are full of interest – provided he is given the time, space and opportunity to benefit from them. Some babies do not get the time they need if the adult who cares for them has too much to do or is worried or depressed, or over-tired. This prevents them concentrating on and enjoying the baby when he is awake. Sometimes there is not the space to give him a change of viewpoint, nothing much for him to watch. There may be 'nothing' for him to listen to if all sound is blotted out by loud persistent noise from a radio. If his body always has to be encased in clothing because his home is cold and damp, he cannot learn to move his body freely and learn through his skin.

Deprivation of the opportunity to play and learn can start at one month – not at the stage we so often hear about when there is no open space for the games of the eleven-year-olds who instead go around their neighbourhood causing trouble.

## The role of the adult

Adults have to be the baby's link to the world and the people in it. He needs us to provide the love, human contact and companionship to bring forth a response from him and, in turn, to respond to him when he reaches out to us. If we don't notice when he is trying to play with us, or if we ignore him, he will stop trying. He will get the attention he needs in other ways which are not so 'rewarding' for us.

## What he needs

- Something to look at.
- Something to listen to.
- Something to touch . . . and being touched.
- Something to encourage him to play alone for a while.
- Somewhere, some time to be active.
- Someone to play with him.

This short period is the baby's first step to playing and learning. He is ready and able to take that step if he is given the opportunity. These first few months set the pattern for playing both for the baby and for the family around him. Hopefully they all find it rewarding.

# Chapter 4

# Looking, Listening, Learning, Moving
(3–9 MONTHS)

'Ah,' says the knowledgeable friend when she sees the baby at 3 months and he smiles at her, 'getting much more interesting now.' Which indicates that the responses of a 3-month-old to what is going on around him are more obvious to someone who does not know him well. It also means he is now capable of getting a response from people.

### Looking and learning

The baby progresses from being able to hold his head up to trying to pull himself up, and gradually manages a stable sitting up position without support. Once he can do this he can start to reach out.

He will also learn to roll over, and this means new sensations and a different viewpoint. This is how children learn that objects look different depending on where they are – but eventually all these experiences weld into one floor, one ceiling. Once children roll around they will bump into things and start to learn about near and far the hard way. Once they can sit up this frees arms and hands to do more.

### Reaching milestones

Most babies learn to sit up and some learn to crawl towards the end of this period. Some learn to stand up while clinging on to something firm. A few even learn to walk. The difference between individual children can be enormous. It can also be worrying. It always seems to be the mother whose friend's child is walking while hers can only just sit up unaided who does the worrying. Somehow the other mother does not worry that while her child is spending every minute and every ounce of energy walking he is not making progress in other directions. We really do have to accept that children are individuals and develop at different rates.

There is plenty of development going on if we look for it:

- Starting to use hands more, actually being able to hit something rather than just taking a wild swipe, because hands and eyes are working together better and he has some idea of how far away the object is.

- Using eyes and ears more and starting to remember what a sound means – progressing from being pleased to see his cup, to being pleased when he hears the sounds of preparing his drink although he is not able to see what we are doing. He will still get cross if his needs are not met but will wait a little while if he can see his food is coming.

- Using both hands and mouth to gain information. Once a baby starts trying to grab the spoon with which he is being fed he is on the long and messy way towards feeding himself.

A very important stage is reached when he learns to use his fingers and thumb in a pincer movement. Once he can do this he can handle smaller, finer objects, and his favourite ones will be small pieces of food. It means we can give him smaller toys and playthings. It also means he can pick up dangerous objects, so we have to be more careful.

Another milestone is positively learning to let go. The only way to persuade the baby of 3 months to let go of something firmly grasped in his fist (perhaps somebody's hair) is to offer him something more attractive while holding his free hand. He opens his hand to make a grab for whatever we are offering and in doing so lets go of what he has. Once he can deliberately let go, this opens the door to all kinds of play progress. He can put one object into another or put them on top of each other. One of the favourite games is deliberately dropping his playthings when he finds out that someone will pick them up for him. We get tired of this long before he does, so he waits for the next person to come along . . . he is starting to manipulate adults.

A development which should be regarded as a five-mile-stone happens towards the end of this period. He drops a brick

from the tray of his high chair and instead of looking where it was and crying, or just turning to something else on the tray, he leans over to look for it. He has learned 'the constancy of objects' – that something exists and goes on existing even if he can't see it. He may or may not be able to say the word 'gone' but he knows now that 'gone' does not necessarily mean gone for ever. He does not relate this to himself – he thinks he is hidden if he puts his hand over his eyes. For now, if he can't see us he thinks we can't see him – it is going to be a long time before he sorts this out.

A good deal of automatic copying goes on. If we told the baby what to do he wouldn't understand, and he couldn't do it even if he did – but he will copy what we do as far as he is able. We put our tongue out at the baby and he does the same, we clap our hands and he brings his together, we make a noise and he does the same although we may have to wait several seconds.

Copying is a very important part of learning to talk. All babies make noises. They cry, then they coo and gurgle up and down the scale, then they babble – even babies who cannot hear do this. But then they start to imitate the sounds they hear us make.

Nature seems to have programmed us to keep our example simple when we tell the baby what things are. He can usually understand a lot more than he can say, but he has to learn and practise using his voice, lips and tongue to make deliberate sounds and we instinctively make allowances for this. The more the baby learns to 'say' and give back, the more we give him to copy and learn. There are other times when we just chat to him rather than with him, or sing quite a complicated song which he accepts as a whole. This is part of his learning about language too.

Like everything else in the baby's world, he cannot go out and get language experience for himself. We have to bring it to him – and remember that as well as giving we have to let him give back so we have to listen and respond.

One of the developments which is often not specifically mentioned in the 'milestone chart' is that the baby frequently learns to laugh during this period. At 3 months he smiles and gurgles. At nine months he can have a really infectious laugh which has the whole family helpless – not laughing at him but with him.

What causes him to laugh is usually surprise, but it has to be a surprise he can cope with rather than a shock. The noise we make as we clap our hands would make a new-born baby cry – the 7- or 8-month-old can find it hugely amusing, especially if he sees it coming. The pop-up toy which was given a fixed stare or a little jump at 3 months now gives great pleasure. He laughs if someone tickles him rather roughly. The games of peep-bo get more rumbustious. Rumbustious and rough are obviously relative terms . . . the degree will depend on the individual baby. It may also depend on who is doing it to him, as he will feel safer with someone he knows rather than the well-meaning but less familiar adult. This last point is important.

The 3-month-old baby who smiled at everyone may now be a little more choosy about the people he sees and how he responds. He is beginning to learn stranger/non-stranger. The unfamiliar aunt who gets a long stare, then the turned-down mouth and quivering lip, followed by a loud cry may be at the least disappointed. We should be pleased rather than embarrassed . . . another important stage has been reached.

## How they play and what they learn

These babies will play with anything around them that they can reach. They don't have any fixed idea about what is a toy and what is not. What they do will also depend on how much of their body they can control and use.

There is no frustration due to failure, because at this age a baby is not trying to achieve anything particular. He may be cross if we take something from him, but can be distracted by being given something else. For now he is interested in anything and everything, but one thing at a time. He can lose interest quickly, which means he needs a lot of material – but he also forgets, so the same toys are found interesting the next day. The next month they will be interesting because he can do something more with them. Under normal circumstances, i.e. when he is not teething or unwell or just plain tired and hungry, he is easy and cheap to amuse and keep occupied and all his activity is valuable.

Towards the end of this stage he starts to remember a little, so the simple toys which give a reward are useful (the musical toy which needs wobbling, the pattern which moves when he presses a knob, the pop-up toy). A baby mirror is rewarding – the face he sees in there alters as he moves the mirror, if he smiles at it it smiles at him. He is starting to learn about cause and effect and consequences.

## What the world around offers

This is usually limited to his home and outings in his pram. There is plenty of stimulation to be had and learning to be done within his ordinary environment: if we move him around to different viewpoints, different heights, if we provide interesting material to play with, if we push the pram slowly or stop for a while to let him see, he watches intently. As adults we miss a lot of what goes on around us but the 9-month-old takes in a great deal given the chance.

What this kind of learning needs cannot be bought from the toy shop – they don't sell time. We have to give him some of ours.

## The adult's role

We have to provide the material and activities which the baby needs – and remove what could be harmful.

What he needs depends very much on the individual baby, so the other important task is to be aware of what he is actually doing and seeing and experiencing. This means sparing a few minutes to look round at his level or to think, 'What did we do today?'

We can also become 'play-material-minded' and be prepared to put odds and ends in a carrier bag on the back of the kitchen door in case they might interest him another day.

We have to provide the companionship, the conversation, the information, the cuddles and the rough play, and listen and respond when the baby makes his needs known. We have to let him be with us to see what we are doing, and we have to make sure there is time for baby games and singing songs.

We also need to keep an eye on his relationship with brothers and sisters by being tactful – not letting the older children feel neglected or overburdened with too many reminders of 'Mind the baby' or 'He's only little' – sometimes the baby has to come second. Fortunately he is not yet able to take older children's toys or spoil their games, and his smiles and activities amuse them as well as us.

## What they need

- Somewhere safe to be propped up or to sit up.
- Room to move about the floor in comfort and safety.
- More and different objects to handle, look at and put in his mouth.
- Rewarding toys.
- Bath toys.
- Songs and games.
- A safe environment in which to roll, crawl and learn to stand up.
- A doll or teddy or cuddly toy.
- A safety harness with anchorages on all the equipment he will use and could fall from.
- A safety gate now before he needs it, so that both he and we get used to having it in the right place rather than waiting for an accident to remind us that this is something we should use.

# Chapter 5

## Becoming Mobile
### (9–18 MONTHS)

This period can show up the biggest differences in individual timetables – not because there is the biggest variation in time in reaching 'milestones', but because the milestones themselves are such big changes and make a big difference to the rest of the family. Once a child is mobile the whole family have to modify what they do; once he can talk just a little all the family get involved. As far as the baby himself is concerned, he can go and find out for himself instead of having to wait for someone else to do the providing.

### Variations in progress

Some children walk at 9 months (a very few even earlier), almost completely missing out on crawling. Some get around so efficiently by a method other than walking that this seems enough for them – shuffling on their bottom, using both legs in a sort of caterpillar movement, or on their bottom with one leg folded firmly underneath them and the other doing all the work, or doing what can only be called a potty-skate – and proper walking seems delayed.

These fast movers have to wait for a very strong inner urge to change to a slow upright stagger instead of the fast movement they have been doing. It has to become more important to them to stand and walk upright than to get to something they want. Walking becomes the 'something they want'. We see this same singlemindedness in later years, where acquiring the skill itself becomes the goal.

Some children are quite content to develop other areas of ability and delay becoming mobile till much later. Examples of this are all around us if we look:

■ The little girl of 2 years who sat very firmly on the floor – having never shown much interest in crawling or walking – but surrounded by a positive carpet of mixed jigsaw pieces from different puzzles of a standard more usual for a 4-year-old. Over a period of an hour she quietly sorted out and completed six different puzzles – and did this every day.

■ The beautiful child, still with chubby baby limbs, competently and confidently taking her turn (not saying anything but not allowing anyone to push her out of line) to climb up the climbing frame and come down the slide with the other children in the playgroup, then running round to start again – she was 18 months old and she was the youngest of four very active children. She was only in the playgroup because her mother was helping that day.

■ The astonishing little boy playing football with his father and grandfather on the beach – running and stopping the ball with his foot then carefully aiming a kick so that it landed at the feet of each of them in turn. When they were called for a picnic lunch he came to have his nappy changed and was given a bottle of milk with a teat on and baby food from a jar. He was offered, but did not want, his grandfather's sandwich. 'He doesn't eat proper food yet,' his mother said. He was 22 months.

These are just a very few instances which demonstrate that children may pursue one ability at the expense of delaying another for a time.

## How they play and what they learn

This depends on the child himself to a great extent. Once children can move about they have greater freedom to find their own play materials – and this leads to greater hazards. They forget the bumps and hurts and they forget what they have been told, so they need constant supervision. They get cross when adults stop them doing what they want to do. They can be uncooperative when they do not want to do something the adult wants them to do. 'Getting to be quite a handful, isn't he?' says the knowledgeable friend.

They can also give a great deal of pleasure as they give

back so much. They watch, imitate and repeat what we do even more, and happily learn the 'wave bye-bye' games, play peep-bo, enjoy our singing, play the 'Baby have some, Mummy have some' routine with their rusk, listen when we name things for them and show interest in picture books. They want to do what we do and help with household chores. They remember where things belong and point to the cupboard where their cup is kept, or look towards the door or the window or the dog basket when we say 'Where's . . .?'

Skill and control increase. The 9-month-old baby had three or four brightly-coloured bricks to bang or drop or put in a box. He now develops more control over his fingers, and his hand–eye coordination improves, so he learns to put one brick on top of another. Then he knocks them over and laughs. This is a very complicated operation. Look where one brick is, pick up a second one, hold it in the right position in relation to the first brick, very slowly let go to place rather than drop it on to the first brick, and then move the hand away without knocking them over. No doubt he has seen us do it for him many times but we did not explain word by word what to do. He is now doing more than automatic copying.

He learns from any situation or material. If this child spills his food he dabbles in it as he did before, but now he looks at the pattern he is making – then makes it different. If he spills a drink and gets wet he looks at the damp patch on his clothes and points it out to his mother. Before he just wanted another drink. We can see him absorbing information from anything which happens.

He starts to play with a shape-fitting toy – just putting a shape in any hole and pushing hard. It takes time and a lot of practice to work out matching holes and shapes. Even then, unless it is a circle, there is one right position and several wrong ones. Working out how to turn a shape to the right position is another stage to be learned.

The mobile child can start to learn about other children. He may have come across other babies before but he has not known what 'other baby' meant or that they are like him, so he doesn't know that he can hurt them. Once he can move and get at them he can do some damage, but it is curiosity rather than aggression which causes the trouble and the mutual tears. He is just as frightened and upset as the injured party and needs just as much comforting. It could easily be his turn to be 'attacked' the next time they meet. More vigilance and at least a veneer of politeness on the part of the adults who have to deal with this will be needed for some time yet. Fortunately the hitting back reaction is some time away, by which time babies will know more about retreating strategically to the adult's feet.

## What the world offers

Hopefully it offers space – without it he cannot move freely, discover what distance is, what ordinary objects look like from different angles or how near and far objects are. For children in restricted homes, the space they use will have to be outside the home.

Equally it must give time – time to go at this new, slow pace of walking, time to watch and imitate.

It may contain hostile and negative elements that are new. On the whole everyone is nice to small babies who sit still (people who don't like babies tend to keep away from them), but now he finds adults won't let him have everything he wants, and brothers and sisters get annoyed if he takes their toys and spoils their games. He is awake for longer so will take a larger share of attention, and other family members may resent this. He still gets a lot of attention but not necessarily as much as he is demanding.

Outings are important, as they offer more information to be collected, more 'things' which have a name.

He finds that 'doggie' can mean different-looking animals that are not at all like the one in his picture book, which is different again from the cuddly toy sitting in the corner of his cot. 'Car' may be something red, blue, green, moving or standing still, making a loud noise or a little noise or no noise at all. It may be small enough to put in his mouth if it is a toy car, huge if it is a real one.

He starts to learn so efficiently and naturally that we do not notice how clever he is being – but he can't do it unless he has the information to work on.

The world also becomes dangerous – not because it has changed but because the mobile child has.

## The role of the adult

Perhaps the most important element a child needs in his world at this stage is sensible organizing of his environment by the adults who care for him – gates across stairs, dangerous chemicals put away, sharp tools out of sight as well as out of reach, older children keeping small items and playthings off the floor or away from where he can get at them. He is quick, curious, not really devious, but inevitably we have our back turned when he manages to do something dangerous, otherwise we would have stopped him. He is effectively disobedient because he forgets rather than because he defies. We have to be his 'common sense' because he hasn't got any yet.

The adult involved with caring for the crawler/toddler may well have an older child still at home for most of the time. There has to be a real balancing act between the worlds of the two different stages, since the older child still only has the common sense of the 4–5-year-old. The natural activities of older children and the materials they can use because of increased skill can be dangerous for the younger one, and some restricting is going to be necessary. This usually means a playpen, which is equally useful for both children – there are times when the older child plays there just to be away from the little one (and it is not unknown for adults to use it as a retreat sometimes).

Adults have to take the positive role of being the provider – of play materials, words, songs and games and good quality experience (it is the way we use outings rather than the length or cost that matters). Adults also have to play a passive role – in that they accept the mess and the mistakes and sometimes let this child try by himself before giving the help we think he needs. If we leave him a little he may come up with an answer of his own. It may not be the same one we were thinking of but that doesn't matter. There are plenty of things that really do matter about which we have to be firm, and just occasionally he needs to work things out for himself.

We also have to be careful not to overestimate his capacity. He is getting capable and clever but he can't keep it up all the time. He gets tired, and needs to regress sometimes to the quiet cuddle and just sitting being quiet.

The adult needs to be provider/enabler/cooperator/

sharer/information source/bodyguard/arbitrator/comfortable, comforting lap. Perhaps the knowledgeable friend was right this time. He is quite a handful. Add a 4-year-old and we have both hands full.

## What they need

- Safety.
- Something to aid balance and movement.
- Noise makers.
- Put in – take out material.
- Something to build with.
- Something to look at.
- Somewhere to keep quiet.
- Experience of natural materials, water play, etc.
- Opportunities to develop household and personal care skills.
- Fitting, matching, grading material.
- Encouragement to talk . . . outings, songs, games, conversation.

# Chapter 6

# The Stirrings of Independence
(18 MONTHS–2 YEARS)

What children do now will depend on what happened during the last period. If they have learned to walk they progress to walking well and faster. They start to climb if they have not already done so, and they try to jump. Having got the huge effort of walking out of the way, other skills and abilities develop fast, particularly language.

The children who did not walk at 18 months will most likely start to do so now and will learn fast. Since they spent all the time when they were not walking practising other skills such as talking, there can be a 'levelling out' effect by the age of 2.

### Learning more

During this stage these toddlers use what they have already gained in order to gain more. Once they can talk they can ask for information. We gave information before, but it was what we wanted to give rather than what they wanted to receive. This chapter could just as well have been entitled 'The "What dat?" stage'.

When they can use their hands confidently they can concentrate on what they want their hands to do rather than just getting them to work. At 9 months they copied adults without really knowing what they were doing. Now they watch carefully, remember and imitate. Their pleasure is in the doing, and they are not self-conscious or self-critical therefore they are not frustrated by failure.

They can remember simple sequences and concentrate more, so they can play alone without our help for a little longer.

They use old materials in new ways and regard anything they find as new play material.

They try very hard to do what everyone else does; thus the 'stirrings of independence' of the chapter title relates to trying to conform rather than to rebellion. They say 'Me do it' and push away our helping hand – not to be naughty but because doing things for themselves is the next inner urge, just as learning to walk was a month or two ago. The wise adult will go along with this as far as possible. If this stage is missed it could be a long time before they are willing to spend so much time and energy on their struggles again.

## Being awkward

Now that they know and remember more they can start to make choices. A few months ago they resisted being dressed because they did not want to be dressed. Now they resist because they want to wear red trousers instead of the blue ones, or a pink dress instead of the white one we try to put on them. They reject food because they prefer something else. Half the time we feel they are 'being awkward for the sake of being awkward', which has more than a grain of truth in it, but this is a big step forward. It involves remembering the items that make up a choice even if they cannot see them at that moment, thinking about them in a split second, making a decision, delaying immediate gratification by waiting for another kind of food rather than satisfying hunger by eating what is in front of them, using energy to insist even in the face of adult disapproval when they really want approval.

This can be inconvenient, not to say infuriating, for the adult, depending on what is going on at the time. However, the individual who grows to be an adult without having learned to make judgements and choices and take decisions and who does not have the energy and stamina to pursue goals is not going to get very far.

An important point about making choices at any age is that we have chosen one thing rather than another and have thus accepted that we can't have both.

Fortunately, learning to reason and compromise will come later. For now it is sensible to create simple choice situations for a child which are not inconvenient for us – which piece of apple,

which mug, milk or orange juice, even red or blue trousers so long as both are clean and ready to put on.

## How they play and what they learn

These children really work at their play – and regard as play what we might call work:

- They help with everything we do, know where things go, know what tools to use and have some idea of how to use them.

- They start to use toys which require more effort on their part. We can add a wooden spanner or screwdriver to their fitting toy. We can offer beads which thread on a lace instead of drilled blocks to slide on to a rod because they are starting to use both hands at the same time, with each making different movements. Old playthings are used in a different, more complicated way.

They link what they have seen with their play materials. Toy cars are brrrmmm-brrmmmed round the floor and parked under the hearth rug, dolls are washed with a wet sock then dragged around in a cardboard-box pram covered with an old jumper. A little hoard of playthings is carried around in an old shopping bag and favourite places found to keep small treasures safe.

They use their bodies more skilfully and confidently:

- We may have supported them on a 'paddle' trike and steered for them. Now they will push our hands from the handlebar so that they can steer. When they can do this reasonably well they shrug off our supporting hand from their back. Some children at this age have learned the manoeuvre of the three point turn, others get themselves out of a tight corner by standing up and turning their trike round bodily. Both solutions are equally effective, but this is a good demonstration of how children can differ in their approach to a problem even at this age.

- They start to climb stairs but can't always get down, so we show them how to do it safely by coming down lying on their fronts so that they are as near to the stairs as possible.

- They learn to run but have difficulty in stopping or

avoiding something in their way, so they need a clear space to practise.

We can see and hear how they use their minds. They enjoy naming familiar objects in picture books, so they are learning words. It will take a while for them to grasp the idea that a 'car' may also be 'green', an apple is not a car but it is green, their jumper is neither a car nor an apple but it is green. We can provide the opportunity to learn by naming colours as casually as we name other things for them. We know they have learned when we say, 'Where's the green one?' and they deliberately point to something red and roll about with laughter at this trick they are playing on us. If they were not sure, they would have been hesitant and looked at us for confirmation of their choice.

They start to learn about parts of things belonging together and do very simple jigsaw puzzles – often choosing one particular piece to start from. They learn about 'sameness' and match similar objects and pictures. They notice very tiny incidental details – 'Birdie', they say, looking at a picture of lambs in a field. Sure enough there is a tiny little bird in one corner which we had missed because we were too busy looking at the lambs. Children do not always see what we expect them to because their vision is very wide and the obvious (to us) main feature is not particularly important to them – because everything is important to them.

## The world as a learning situation

What a child experiences is a total learning situation. The more there is in his world the more he will learn. There will not be understanding – that comes later – but this age group is collecting knowledge everywhere. They don't need exotic, expensive or sophisticated materials and outings but they do need variety. They also need some basic consistency so that they can establish patterns and procedures.

The world one toddler lives in can be very different from that of another. If we consider just one very ordinary part of the daily round such as shopping:

■ Is it something that happens every day, once a week, before or after dinner, how many adults go with him?

- Does he walk, go in his pushchair, on a bus, in a car?

- Does the adult with him stop to talk to friends on the way?

- Does she have to ask for what she wants in the shop or does she help herself?

- Is he taken into several different shops or just one? Do they have a special smell or is it the anonymous odour of the supermarket he remembers?

- Can he see what is on the shelves or does some mysterious business get carried out over his head?

- Does he walk round or is he carried, or is he put in a big basket on wheels – can he get at the packets and have a sly little nibble at the wrappings?

- What happens when his mother comes to pay – do they have to wait, does the basket have to be emptied out and then filled again? And is this the most likely time for him to be given a sharp little tap on the hand and an exasperated 'No' if he touches something while he waits?

- Does the shopping go home on top of him, squashing his legs, or underneath him in a pushchair tray or in a big cardboard box in the car boot, or does he have to walk and be pulled along when he would much rather be carried?

- What happens to the shopping when he gets home?

The possibility for variation is wide in just this one aspect of children's experience. Multiply this by all the other activities that go on in a home and we can see why children vary in what they know and do.

## Meeting other children

A child's experience during this period may well include going to a mother and toddler group or other places where he sees small children. If older brothers or sisters go to a nursery group and his mother helps occasionally, he may see play activities there even if he does not join in. This can be a very useful learning situation. All children have a special place in the home because it is their home. We allow their toys to be special to them because they have to learn 'That is mine and you can't have it' before they can learn 'And that is yours so I mustn't touch it.' In the group situation everything is there to be shared, which can be very different.

It also makes a pleasant change for a mother to have the company of other adults. She will be responsible for her child, but hopefully it will be someone else's turn to make cups of tea and put the toys away for once.

## Experience away from home

If a child spends most of his day for most of the week with a childminder, it may or may not be like being at home depending on how many children are being cared for and what their ages are.

The childminder may try to get all her housework done before the children come or after they leave, so what the child sees is different from the usual home routine. She may have to share her time between more children and that will make a difference. Because the children may not be at the same age gaps to be found in a family, the examples a child sees may be different from what he sees with brothers and sisters.

In a day nursery the responsibility is to look after a much larger number of children in a narrower age band than is found in a family. There are no beds to make, no family meals to prepare. The cook will do that in the kitchen, which may be out of bounds, so no nibbling of carrots as they are being scraped, no cleaning out the bowl or having a piece of pastry to play with. There will be no cleaning because the cleaner does that, no family washing to peg out on the line. There will be other things to do instead. The children will still watch and imitate but it will be the skills of the nursery nurse rather than those of a mother which they learn.

Children will still be at home in the evenings and at weekends but there may not be the time and opportunity to let them help with ordinary everyday activities – unless we deliberately make the time.

As for the children who have no home, no space to play, no toys to use because there is nowhere to keep them, no one to watch doing the normal everyday business of a household – who can say how this will affect them? These are the 'deprived family' children. They have been deprived at every stage but the deprivation is even deeper for the mobile children.

## The role of the adult caring for toddlers

We have to be tolerant with their mistakes, generous with our time and belongings and understanding about what they are trying to do. We still have to be their common sense because their own will be a long time developing yet.

Since children are very observant and imitate, we have to be careful about how we treat them and other members of the family. They pick up our attitudes without understanding, just as they copy what we do. In twenty years' time we will see a grown-up son or daughter peeling potatoes or digging the garden in the same way we dug it or peeled them when they were 2. They will probably also be just as kind/unkind, patient/impatient, tolerant/intolerant, considerate/inconsiderate as they learned from us at the same time as they watched how to hold a potato peeler or use a garden fork.

We are role models, as the sociologists would say. Children's concepts of morality may not develop till a much later age, but habits and attitudes start here:

- We can praise success rather than criticize failure. Whatever it was the child did is done and our words are not going to make it better or worse, but it might make a difference to what he achieves next time – to his attitude to trying again – and it might encourage a habit of generosity of comment to other people.

- We can say: 'Yes, you can do that in a minute/after lunch/tomorrow' or whenever we know he can do it, rather than 'No, you can't do it now.' We were not going to let him do whatever it was right now anyway, but we have made an alternative suggestion for a positive solution.

- 'Your sister will want to sit in that chair when she comes home from school,' we say as we move all his toys – or 'We must save some for . . .' when he wants more pudding. We were going to move his toys anyway, and we always save a share of favourite food for an absent member of the family – but we are giving a simple explanation which suggests that other people have needs and rights.

- The rhythm of taking turns will be learned in the simple games like 'One for teddy, one for me'. As yet he has no notion of shares or fairness but he gets the mechanics right.

This is usually a happy, busy period because the toddler wants to do what we do. 'What a good child,' says the knowledgeable friend, 'a real little Mummy's help.' She is not there long enough to see what hard work it can be for the adult, who would love to get on with the cleaning or hanging out the washing without the hindrance of a helping hand, but progress is very obvious and the long journey to independence has started.

These children use their bodies well and have tremendous energy. They are fast movers without much idea of speed and distance or danger. They want to be like others and do what everyone else does, but so far they only know the 'what', are a bit hazy on the 'how', and will not understand 'why' for some time. They can vary between being loudly uncooperative and a 'wrecker' (with the best of intentions) and being a loving, responsible, rewarding companion – all in the space of half an hour.

They can also regress very quickly to baby behaviour. They are still only two years old, after all.

### What they need

- What they had before plus more bricks, more books (try the library), more materials to explore, more small versions of household equipment, more opportunity to borrow what they need but with vetting and supervision.

- Some means of being active – climbing, sliding, perhaps a ride-on toy or a pedal trike if they did not have one before.

- More means of developing skill – jigsaws, fitting toys with tools, threading beads, matching and sorting material.

- Sand (under supervision), more water play toys, a piece of play-dough of their very own.

- More home-play material – dolls, very simple doll's clothes and doll's pram, tea-set and saucepans, a fastener toy plus more opportunity to help with what we do.

- More vocabulary and explanation from adults, more songs and finger play, playing simple games.

- Opportunities for making a choice.

- A safe environment.
- Simple outings.
- Experience of real live animals.

If there is a local toy library it may be possible to borrow some toys and equipment.

# Chapter 7

## Act Now, Learn Later
### (2–2½ YEARS)

Children now start to use what they have previously learned. They think they know what to do because they saw other people doing it and copied. They didn't make too many mistakes because they took the lead from others, so they were in the right place at the right time and were supervised. They weren't concerned about the end result so they did not get frustrated. The 'why' may have been explained many times but they did not really understand. They were too busy with the 'how'.

### Making mistakes

There now comes the point when children want to carry out the activities they have seen for themselves and by themselves, not just because someone else is doing it. They make inconvenient mistakes and these show just how little they did understand.

They know cooking is mixing things together, putting them in some kind of receptacle and putting this receptacle somewhere special. Sometimes you have to stir. Nothing wrong so far. They want to cook by themselves, so they go off to the bathroom, mix talcum powder and shampoo in a tooth mug, stir it with a toothbrush, pour the mixture into their potty and put it to cook in the linen basket.

They know water comes from a tap. Sometimes it comes when they hear the word 'bath time', sometimes when their mother touches the tap, sometimes when someone holds the kettle to the tap. They experiment until they find that if they grasp the tap and twist it the water will come out. So far, so good. But they don't know that they have to turn the tap off, or that water can fill the sink completely and that if the water comes right up to the top it will overflow.

The adult who has to clear up the mess has some justification for being exasperated, but neither right nor reason to think of this as naughtiness. These children have a great deal more learning to do and most of it will be done by learning from mistakes, so they need patient, firm, simple explanation. They also need tactful provision of alternative activities and materials – a set of pans and a wooden spoon of their own, for example, an 'oven' even it is only a strong cardboard box with a door cut in and black rings painted on the top, sand and water to mix – an opportunity to play with water where they can learn about 'overflow' and 'slosh over the side' without doing any damage.

### Saying 'no'

We all want the same result – for children to become independent. Part of developing independence is doing things for and by themselves. Another part of the same process is refusing to do what we want them to do. Before they were just uncooperative. Now they turn round and say 'no'. 'That child needs a firm hand,' mutters the knowledgeable friend (what she really means is a good smack).

'No' is just a word like any other, but this crystallization of their attitude into something they can say can seem quite a challenge to the adults who care for them. If we think about it we realize that 'no' is a word we use quite frequently to them, and although we have excellent reasons for saying it they too can regard it as a challenge. They don't understand all the good reasons.

This is all part of growing up, and if we can avoid too much confrontation this helps:

- Say: 'We are going shopping in five minutes', rather than 'Get your coat on this minute.'

- Or take their refusal calmly: 'We won't have time to see the ducks if we don't go soon.'

- Or, if we were only going out to give them a little outing, we can give way and say: 'We'll go tomorrow then.' Quite often this works best of all and they fall over themselves to get their coat on.

We can also help by saying 'no' as little as possible, saving it for the times that really matter, because it can become just as much a habit for adults to say 'no' to children as it can become for them to say it to us. We should be consistent. If we say 'no' today we should say it tomorrow too. So should the other adults in the household. There will come a time when our children should be allowed to learn to negotiate and compromise, but for now they feel safer in their kicking against authority if they have something firm and stable to kick against.

We can also help by being just as firm and quick about saying 'yes' as we are about saying 'no'. They need us to be decisive at this time – it is a stage for us just as much as it is for the children. Sometimes we say 'Oh, all right then' or 'I suppose so', plus a long-suffering sigh when they ask for something. This rather implies that they have worn us down, so they try to wear us down the next time. 'We'll see' is an answer which will infuriate an adult, let alone a small child, and it doesn't solve the situation, merely perpetuates it.

## The stage of the tantrum

Part of the stable framework children need is our approval and affection. Learning to be independent and needing approval do not go together well, and this can be a trying time for everyone. We may get the exhausting, frightening, sometimes embarrassing temper tantrum when muddled feelings overcome a child. It is frightening and exhausting for the child too, because he doesn't know why he is lying on the floor kicking and making a dreadful noise. He has lost control of himself just as we have lost control over him. Not every child goes through this phase, nor is it always the full-blown screaming, sobbing, kicking on the floor in the supermarket affair, but it is common. It is only a stage, rather like a snake struggling to get out of its skin so that it can grow larger, and it will not last long. 'I wouldn't let him show me up like that,' says the knowledgeable friend. 'Oh,' we answer back for once, 'he'll soon grow out of it.' And, of course, he does. If it has to happen at all it is better to happen at the age of 2. Adults who have never had to learn to cope with disappointment and frustration can have a temper tantrum at 22 or 32 or 42 which is much worse.

We can help children through this stage by letting them

channel their frustration into socially acceptable behaviour through their play. This is a very grand phrase which boils down to letting children bash their teddy or a lump of dough or clay rather than hitting the baby, by providing for and allowing destructive play with indestructable materials, for example a large cardboard box to kick instead of kicking the furniture. Sometimes we can divert them from making a scene by making them laugh if they are the laughing type of child. Some are and some are not.

### How they play and what they learn

Physically they are very active and become more capable. They could run before but now learn to run faster and to stop and avoid obstacles. They negotiate stairs carefully and slowly on their feet, rather than going up on all fours and coming down on their tummy as they did before; try to ride a tricycle with pedals instead of pushing themselves along with their feet; learn to kick and catch a large ball, and try to walk along a low plank or 'stepping stones', which shows that their control and balance is improving.

All their skills and knowledge start to come together:

■ They hammer efficiently, use screw toys and a wooden screwdriver, complete a simple jigsaw with a little support and encouragement, build a tower of bricks and try, but not necessarily manage, to use a small suitable pair of scissors – or unsuitable ones if that is all they can find.

■ They start to match and sort objects and develop ideas about large and small, heavy and light, which is all useful language experience.

■ They can start to pour their own drink from a small jug, and have a good try at putting on socks and pants and a loose T-shirt. Taking clothes off is easier than putting them on. A teddy or a doll is dressed and undressed if there are simple garments on them.

■ They will play for longer, which means getting further with the game each time. They will also go back to unfinished games and start again if we can leave the material as it is until they are ready to come back.

- They enjoyed songs and finger rhymes before but now they join in and do the actions.

- They still watch carefully, not necessarily imitating immediately but remembering and doing later as much as they can of what they *thought* they saw (sometimes they misunderstand what they see). They watch people, sometimes looking at strangers so intently and unselfconsciously that it is almost a rude stare.

- They may also start to use a small space as a den where they can feel they are in charge, such as a particular corner of a room, under a table, on a landing half-way up the stairs.

Their language develops as they start to use the words they have with the extra words which make short sentences. Sometimes they get the tense wrong and word endings wrong – 'Daddy goed out', 'Mummy comed in', but these mistakes can be quite reasonable – the English language has some very odd rules. They can involve adults in their play more because they can communicate more efficiently. 'Cup of tea?' they ask their mother. 'Yes, please,' she says and they come back with a cup of sand. 'Say thank you,' they tell her. They can remember and carry simple messages from one adult to another. 'Dinner ready?' they come to ask an adult in the kitchen and go back with the answer, 'Five minutes.'

Previously their interest in colour and texture arose accidentally from the materials themselves. Now they enjoy using chalks, crayons, or a large brush for painting. They will try finger-painting, given the opportunity. They deliberately make marks or impressions and experiment rather than create.

## Left hand, right hand

This may be the time when 'handedness' becomes apparent, although most under-5s can use both hands. When they start carrying out activities requiring some precision in the use of one hand, such as using a spoon, crayons, paintbrushes, it may become obvious which one a young child is going to use as his fine activity hand. This is not a personal whim on his part. It happens because that is the way his brain control area for hands is working. Most adults have a preferred eye and preferred foot in addition to a preferred hand.

Ten per cent of the population is left-handed, and more boys (and men) than girls (and women) have this particular characteristic. There are various arguments for and against persuading children to use the right hand. Different experts have different opinions, and different children react in individual ways to this situation.

There can be no doubt that for the most part this is a right-handed culture we live in and left-handers have to meet more difficulties to achieve the same object as right-handers. We read from left to right, write from the left, tools are made for right-handed use (although it is possible to find some items such as scissors for left-handed people). There can equally be no doubt that left-handers survive perfectly well and can often use both hands better than right-handers can use both.

If parents are worried or if a child is worried about left-handedness, then seeking advice could be helpful. Some children do adapt – indeed, people who have lost limbs or the use of limbs learn to adapt, even to using feet and toes rather than hands and fingers. It has to be an individual decision taken in the light of how strongly an individual child can and will cooperate. There is more involved than a pair of hands, after all.

## Moving up in the family

This may be the time for a 2-year-old's life to change a great deal if a brother or sister is born. It will make a difference to the amount of attention he gets and it could affect the quality of attention, but it will also add a new dimension to the information with which he is presented. Fortunately he is beginning to be more independent, and the very need for him to be so may speed up this process.

Unfortunately his common sense does not double overnight just because there is a new baby, and he still needs supervision as he experiments to learn more. There are more home accidents to children between the ages of 2 and 3 years than in any other age range (see Chapter 21, page 218). This is a dangerous age, and whatever else we have to do we have to watch this age group.

The new baby may be a great source of interest, and 2-year-olds can be a genuine help in fetching and carrying. Their play will reflect their interest, and dolly bathing and feeding may come high on the list of play activities.

Nevertheless, this new baby can be a great disappointment. 'You'll have a brother or sister to play with,' they were told. Then when 'it' comes it is pretty useless. It won't play with them, they can watch but are not allowed to play with it, and the people who used to make a fuss of them are more interested in what is in the pram than in listening properly to what they have to say. Still – they learn. They soon know exactly how the baby is cared for because they watch every detail.

The routine of the household will inevitably change and the 2-year-old learns to adapt. Adapting is a very necessary skill/ability which everyone has to learn sooner or later.

The children who have an older brother or sister will learn to adapt when the older child goes to school and they 'move up' to being the oldest child at home for most of the day during the week. The only child is going to have to rely on playmates – and learning to adapt may not come until he goes to school unless there are other children to play with in a pre-school group.

## Using the world around

The world outside the family may be much the same as it ever was, but as they become more confident and competent this age group begin to use it in a different way – they make things happen in addition to watching things happen. They deliberately add water to the sandpit rather than playing with the small area their drink spilled on. They stop their pull-along toy as they come to a step and lift it up rather than just pulling harder on the string.

They are learning to control things. They also learn that things can control them:

■ It doesn't matter how much they kick the door, it will not open until they use the knob properly.

■ If they want to get their trike past the table leg they have to manoeuvre the trike – the table leg is not going to move over for them.

■ If they overload a truck with bricks some will fall off as they pull it along.

This consistency of inanimate objects, which is non-personal and quite unmalicious, offers the first steps in learning self-discipline. They can say 'please' and get cross or shout (which may or may not work with people), but with objects it is the same every time. They have to conform to get the result they want.

If 2-year-olds meet with other strange children they watch them but are fairly neutral unless their space or possessions are threatened. They are not ready to share but they may take what other children have and will be quite surprised if the other children make a fuss. They are not yet ready for the 'How would you feel if . . .' which is said to older children.

## The role of the adult

We have to understand the turbulence of the 2-year-old. There are many ways in which we can help support them:

- By making sure the challenges they face are not totally beyond them (they don't know that the jigsaw which belongs to an older brother or sister is too difficult, so we find them an easier one).

- By providng easy, stretchy clothes with large openings and simple fasteners. If they want to use the big lavatory we can give them a box to stand on. If they cannot see out of the window we can put simple but effective bars up and provide a low stool to stand on.

- By reassuring them that we love them even if we do have to say 'no' and show our disapproval of their actions.

We have to watch our attitude to the 2-year-old, since it may be affected by where he comes in the family. 'Give the baby his first,' we say to an older brother or sister – referring to the 2-year-old as the baby. If there is a new baby we say to the 2-year-old: 'You are a big boy/girl now and you'll have to wait till I've given the baby his food.' Both these 2-year-olds are at the same stage but our expectations vary and this is unreasonable on our part. It is our good luck that on the whole children tend to meet our expectations, but if things are going badly wrong perhaps we should stop and think about why this is happening.

If we can weather the storms of the 'no', the tantrums and the messy experimenting, in a few months' time there can be a change to real sunshine. Children become calmer, more tractable, more affectionate, helpful, skilful and knowledgeable. Increased ability and independence leads to even faster progress. Within the family they can hold a simple conversation, tell a very simple sequence of events, they listen and understand a great deal and follow one or two instructions if these are carefully given one at a time.

Just as important, there can start to be the hint of a change in us. For the first time we begin to feel that this child will not only 'grow up' but he will also 'grow away'. We are beginning to see the child as an individual.

### What they need

- More opportunity to be active.
- Creative materials.
- Construction materials.
- Model play.
- Opportunity for home play.
- More books, more puzzles, music to listen to.
- Provision for or permission to keep a special little place for their play.
- Some experience of other children the same age . . . perhaps a parent and toddler group.
- Easy fastenings on their clothes, simple clothes for dolls and teddies.

# Chapter 8

# The Home as a Stepping Stone
($2\frac{1}{2}$–3 YEARS)

Children of this age vary in what they can do and how they play, but this tends to be another levelling-out and catching-up period. We see them developing more skill, controlling and using their bodies, becoming more capable at personal tasks.

What they can already do they do better and for longer. The new learning which takes place is achieved more quickly for several reasons:

- They have some skill and information on to which they can hook the new knowledge.

- They have more time because they sleep less.

- They can concentrate for longer.

- They can ask for help.

Each child started as a 'me-only' who only recognized his own needs. He may now be a 'me-first', recognizing that other people have needs too, but to him his are still more important. 'Goodness, that child's grown up a lot,' says the knowledgeable friend as he spontaneously offers the plate of biscuits to her. She didn't see him carefully take his favourite biscuit off the plate for himself before he offered it to her – but a year ago he would not have thought of it or been able to hold out the plate for her while she chose. 'Yes, he has,' we say firmly.

### Learning faster, needing more

Because these children sleep less, they play longer and play with or at a greater number of activities during a day. This can be hard going for the adult who has to spend ten minutes finding the materials and ten minutes clearing up for ten minutes' worth of play. It also takes a good deal of space for both using and storing materials. They want to do more difficult tasks, but they can only do this with our help so they can be quite demanding. They also become concerned with someone else's opinion of what they have done, so long as it is favourable. 'That's clever. I'm clever aren't I?' They keep on until they get an answer. They are starting to make personal judgements about what they achieve and how well they do it. Some of this may be a way of getting attention, but there is the hint of self-assessment there.

Some idea of time begins to develop – not the time a clock tells but the 'after dinner', 'bath time', 'shopping day', 'tomorrow when I wake up' personal timetable that is far more meaningful to them than the symbols we use to regulate our activities.

Although they sleep less they need quiet activities for a rest, so looking at picture books, listening to music or using younger play material because it is easy become part of the daily programme.

They may enjoy some television programmes for under-5s and remember the characters and music. If they don't like it they will switch themselves off. The best thing about short TV programmes is that hopefully someone sits with the child to have a rest themselves. This means someone is there to answer questions and discuss this shared experience if that is what the child wants.

Pets and animals become great sources of enjoyment – but the situation where the child and the animal actually come together needs some supervision. The $2\frac{1}{2}$-year-old still has a lot to learn about animals and his inexpert handling or inappropriate treatment can cause the most docile of family pets to retaliate.

## What the world around offers

When children stay awake longer and go to bed later they may see more of adults who work outside the home. This means more contact with the world outside even if it is at second hand. When they are clean and reasonably dry outings can be longer and further, so they see more at first hand.

The type of neighbourhood will make more difference to children approaching 3 years than it did to the baby of 3 months but, whatever their world offers, they will be able to take advantage of it only if someone will take them, as they certainly cannot go alone. Fortunately they are willing and able to learn from anything and everything. The vehicles they see may be cars or trains or tractors, the animals they know about may be cows and pigs in a field or dogs in the park. They will become familiar with the sights and sounds, tastes and smells, comings and goings of their world as they see it, and all this experience is absorbed.

Every area, every situation has something of interest to offer this age group provided it is available. The child in a high-rise flat who doesn't get out often, the child in a large family or group where there is so much to be done for so many, the child with no one to take him out and give him time to look or give him words for what he sees, can be cut off from this necessary part of learning.

## Playing with other children

Brothers and sisters are a good start for learning about other children but they are not always compatible playmates. There may be only a short difference in years but there can be a big difference in the stages they have reached.

If we have enough space and there are close neighbours with children of the same age, perhaps they could come to play. It is even better if our child can go there sometimes to see someone else's home and toys. The situation where adjacent back gardens have a gate in the fence and there can be an easy coming and going of children of the same age would be ideal. The children could choose when to play together, go back to their own garden when they got fed up with each other and come back five minutes later when the quarrel had been forgotten. Unfortunately, learning to resolve quarrels gradually because there is the option of walking away is all too rare these days. If we have to make elaborate arrangements to take or fetch children because of traffic hazards, we cannot let them go rushing back home alone, and it would be time-consuming and embarrassing to take them back before the time arranged.

The parent and toddler group, drop-in centre or play centre with which these children may be familiar has provided them with an opportunity to play alongside other children with their mother's supervision. They are now ready for learning to 'play with' other children and this can lead to problems. The groups have wider needs to meet than just those of nearly-3-year-olds and may not be able to provide the extra space, activities and materials this age group needs without depriving other adults and children who use the group. If the nearly-3 just goes ahead and takes what he needs from younger children these little ones get distressed. If he interferes with older children they may hit him or push him away and then he gets distressed. It may seem to be time to move on.

## The role of the adult

Paradoxically our role becomes more difficult and more tiring rather than less as these children become more capable. We have to:

- Enable them to experience more both inside and outside the home.

- Extend their knowledge by giving information when they ask for it.

- Enrich their experience by providing more material by borrowing, making, improvising if we are not in a position to buy it.

- Sit back a little when they get into difficulties and see if they can work their way through them – and give just enough help if they get really frustrated.

- Let them experiment with paper, paint, crayons and other art and craft materials without rushing in to show how.

- Let them pretend 'cook' by themselves, not just have a share in our food preparation.

- Give choices so that they can learn to make up their own mind.

- Provide simple dressing-up clothes and props or, more usually, allow them to keep what they have found for themselves.

- Play simple games of matching and grouping at their level.

- Laugh with them, let them play their little tricks on us, help them make up silly songs.

- Read a book with them or tell them a simple story at bedtime.

- Perform a balancing act between trying to give them what they need without depriving younger and older members of the family of what they need . . . and still try to have some sort of life for ourselves.

Both inside and outside the home their world contains danger . . . they have no idea how fast vehicles move, they forget what they have been told and they are very single-minded so they can only attend to one thing at a time. Indoors their curiosity, speed and ability can get the better of all our precautions. They are still in the 'high incidence' range of accidents and need constant watching. Having spent all day with them, we find our precious off-duty time taken up doing jobs that are safer to do out of the sight and reach of a 3-year-old.

Even in his own garden the nearly-3-year-old needs protection. Garden fences and gates need to be adequate and secure. Fish ponds and pools need fencing or, better still, filling in. Large outdoor equipment is going to get hard use and needs regular checking and immediate attention if repairs are necessary. Climbing frames and swings need a soft or special surface underneath to absorb the impact if a child falls off (see Appendix 4, page 305).

## Thinking about a nursery group

This is the time at which the phrase 'nursery group' seems to be plucked out of the air, and just looking back at this section we can see why the possibility of group play may be considered:

- These children are more self-sufficient as regards personal needs.

- They need more time, more space, more material than they have had before and yet our resources are already fully stretched.

- They can get along with people who make allowances for them but they don't make too many allowances for other people, so perhaps it is time they came across children of their own age and stage so that they find their own level.

There may be a playgroup attached to the group that mother and toddler attend together, or a mother may have met other mothers who have children in a nursery group, or a health visitor may have mentioned it, so the idea doesn't really just come out of the blue.

The possibility of a child joining a nursery group has to be carefully considered:

■ To decide whether or not a group would be helpful. Not every child goes to a nursery group and it is certainly not compulsory as school education is. It is wise to work out what the child and his family will lose as well as what they will gain (see Chapter 9, page 62).

■ To work out which type of group would suit the child and family best (see Chapter 9, page 62).

■ To find out more about what choices are available, whether what is needed actually exists in the neighbourhood, and if it does whether there are places for every child who needs one (see Chapter 23, page 249).

If we do decide to let our child go to a nursery group it will have to be with our help and support. We would not dream of pushing a nearly-3-year-old into a strange railway station, telling him one of the porters will look after him along with all the other people there, that we will collect him when the 3.30 to Edinburgh leaves, then firmly waving goodbye. Yet a completely strange nursery group can be just as frightening for a child.

The home has to be first a bridge and then a stepping stone to this new experience, so that these children can have a foot in both worlds, using us as a link. This allows them to progress at the pace which suits them, but it can only happen if both the family and the group are flexible.

The 3-year-old may have a good deal of knowledge to bring to the group with him if he has been to a parent toddler group with his mother:

■ He knows a little about other children.

■ He will have some idea that different places have different rules.

■ He may have had to share group playthings.

- He may know there will be trouble if he attacks other people and that he has to keep a wary eye on what is his.

- He may have reached the stage of playing alongside other children.

- He knows other adults look after small children because he has seen them doing it.

In a strange situation, however, he may forget all this and become distressed or make mistakes. This is not necessarily 'babyish' behaviour. Adults, too, can get a bit flustered and forget what they know in an unfamiliar situation. They seek advice and support if they have to make an unfamiliar journey, take a friend along for company when they attend a hospital outpatients clinic.

If the 3-year-old is to take steps to the outside world he too needs a 'friend' to give reassuring, supportive help.

## Getting used to nursery group

Adults who work in a nursery group call it the 'settling-in' process when the group with which they are familiar absorbs another new child. There have been other new children before so they know the ropes. From the child's point of view it could be called 'branching out'. Very little of it will be familiar to him and he doesn't know the ropes.

If the new child's mother takes him for just a short part of the group session to begin with he will watch, listen and remember a little of what goes on. If he goes for different parts of the session he will start to realize that there is a pattern to the morning or afternoon just as there is at home.

He sees his mother accept the new adults so, gradually, he does too. They know his name and he learns theirs. His mother is given a cup of coffee and he is given milk but he sees that all the other children have their milk together at a table. First he may be willing to put his empty mug on the table where all the other mugs are and then, given the choice, he may eventually decide he is going to have his milk with the other children rather than sitting by his mother. When they all sing songs or listen to a story his mother joins in so he does too. His mother takes him to the lavatory and he hears what other children say and do when they want to go there.

Gradually, each time he goes to nursery group, he will leave his mother for longer and longer periods, going further and further away before coming back to where he knows she is. Then he appears to forget her – but he soon remembers her if something upsets him.

Since his mother goes to the group she knows what goes on and can talk to him about it at home, so this new experience of nursery group is not limited to the half hours he spends there.

If he is introduced to the idea of playgroup at about 2 years 9 months, then by the age of 3 he may be ready to stay alone for a short time – or he may not. It depends on the individual child. What we are aiming for is a situation in which the child lets his mother go rather than her leaving him. Different groups have different procedures. The staff may say: 'You know your own child best, so you decide when he is ready to be left here alone.' That is quite true – we do know our child better than they do – but this is a new situation to us too, so perhaps in this case the child himself is the one who knows best.

Whatever age a child is, and wherever he goes, this settling in is an essential part of developing independence in the new situation. It is important that it is successful and pleasurable, just as any other play learning has to be successful, otherwise there is a halt in the progress.

### What they need

■ Opportunity for physical activity – raise the board they balance on, put the slide up higher, ball games with adults or older children doing the 'hard work'.

■ Materials for pretend play – a big box or a den to hide in, dressing-up clothes, puppets (simple hand and finger) (see Part 2, pages 157–67).

■ More water and sand – more complicated water and sand tools (see Part 2, pages 170–74).

■ More jigsaws, books, music – more at the stage they are at now to provide variety, more at the next stage (try the library and toy library).

■ More sorting and matching material, particularly colours and shapes.

- Creative materials plus glue, paint, construction material – and space to use them (see Part 2, pages 185–97).
- Simple train set/dolls house/traffic layout.
- Story and reading times.
- Pictures of animals, pets, time to look at wildlife.
- Outings.
- 'Suitable' TV programmes.
- Freedom to sit and think or just relax quietly.
- See Part 2, page 137.

# Chapter 9

# Getting on with People – Learning to be a Follower
(3–4 YEARS)

### Differences between 3-year-olds

Differences between individual babies and toddlers have been obvious up to this stage, but this is the year in which differences in children are most marked – they vary in height, build, ability, behaviour, speech and conversation, in what they can do and what they like doing, and in how they react and behave with other adults and children. Some 3-year-olds are shy and timid, others are outgoing and daring.

So far it has been possible to say that differences between babies and toddlers will 'even out' in time. Many of the differences between children of 3 years may even out too – but some do not. It is possible to see family likenesses and characteristics which will not change all that much as children grow older. The characteristics which were inherited are there for ever. Those which have been learned from the family will be reinforced over and over again before the children are fully grown.

### How they play and what they learn

For children of 3–4 years in general this is a very valuable learning period, one might even say training period – hence the phrase 'learning to be a follower' in the chapter title.

They want to learn. The toddler may have said 'Me do it' and pushed us away when we tried to button his coat. The 3-year-old just gets on with what he wants to do and asks 'Show me' when he gets stuck.

They want to please. This makes things easier for everyone, because children who positively respond to praise can be shown/

taught with far less effort than the child who says 'Don't want to' and only responds to negative comments such as 'No', 'Don't touch', 'That's naughty.'

They watch and copy. They want to do what we do and what other children do. They remember better than they did a year ago, which means they can start to learn and remember a whole sequence of actions. Three-year-olds will fetch the spoons, or forks or knives, when we start to set the table for a meal. By 4 they know that everything has to be taken off the table, and the cloth or mats fetched from a drawer and laid on the table, that the knives, forks and spoons come from another drawer and that there have to be enough for everyone, that plates come from somewhere else and have to be carried carefully, that salt and pepper go in the middle of the table, that butter comes from the fridge, that there has to be a chair for everyone – depending upon their experience. We take this simple sequence for granted and can do it automatically while keeping one eye on the clock and the other watching to see the potatoes don't boil over. Three- and 4-year-olds have to think about each separate item. If they get knives and forks the wrong way round it really doesn't matter too much. There is plenty they do get right which we can praise. Later we can suggest that they might like to change them round. Once they know there is a right way they will ask us if they have got it right.

A good deal of what 3–4-year-olds enjoy doing at home may seem to us to be more like work – but since these activities are done with pleasure and by choice then they regard them as play – and we can regard them as purposeful play. Three-year-olds happily absorb from us information, skills and processes which would be very tedious for us to teach and boring to learn for an older child who would much rather be off doing something else.

These children also spend a good deal of time asking questions and chattering, which may also be regarded as play activity since they enjoy it. It is a valuable source of information, and good practice in one of the ways in which we all 'find out' and communicate with each other. The toddler asked simple questions and got simple answers because that was all he could take in. The answers may not have been all that he wanted, but he did not have the ability to ask for more. Three-year-olds usually have a good vocabulary and use it well to get the information they want. They are persistent and go on asking in slightly different ways until they find out what they want to know. Then they go on asking until they are sure the answer is going to be the same each time – or until they have understood it. This can only happen if the adult or adults they are with have the time and the patience to cope with this.

If children have to 'wait a minute' or 'ask someone else when they come home', or are ignored completely, then they forget and lose interest and go on to something else. If this happens often enough they stop asking questions. The high ratio of adults to children in the home means that 3-year-olds can get a good deal of information there 'on demand'. However skilful a teacher or group leader is, she has more children to cope with than a mother. Her time has to be shared, so there is less opportunity for each child to get information as and when he needs it.

## Progressive play

The 3-year-old knows a good deal about toys and playthings. Most of his waking time since he was born has been spent 'playing'. He now starts to use his knowledge and skill to impose his will and ideas on the material or toys he is using instead of materials limiting what he can do:

- He starts to experiment. He may have got very cross and frustrated when the too dry sand he put in his little bucket would not turn out into a sand pie. Now he adds water because he is beginning to learn about 'too dry'. He may get it wrong and find out about 'too wet' but will be interested in, rather than cross with, the result.

- He starts to carry out definite ideas and this leads to what we call 'activity play'. The buildings produced with a set of building blocks are something quite specific – not just the tower of bricks which was all the toddler tried to make. The toddler learned about what happens if the bottom brick of a tower is taken away – the 3-year-old learns how to build a structure which will not fall down even if there is a gap in the bottom layer.

- He starts to play pretend games. Dolls are tenderly tucked up in a cot (which may be just an old tomato tray to us) and have to have a mattress, cover and pillow. Teddy is sat up at a table (the same tray turned upside down) and spooned imaginary food. He plays at shopping and pedals off to the corner of a room or the garden to get imaginary eggs or sugar.

■ He can concentrate for longer so he can get further with each game and activity. It takes less time and fewer tries to learn something new. This means he progresses further each time and this leads to more skill and knowledge.

## First steps to playing with others

Three-year-olds are very interested in other children and want to learn to play with them. Just as they forgot the bumps and hurts when learning to walk because their urge to do so was very strong, they are now willing to accept the upsets and frustrations that arise between children. Two minutes after some incident that may cause a storm of tears or a quick retreat back to a familiar adult, they are back ready to play again.

There may be neighbours' children to play with or they may have been settled in to a nursery group (see page 59). They may have the confidence positively to manage without their mothers for a short time, providing the place they go to contains both adults they know and trust, and interesting things to do. The child who is introduced to a nursery group after the age of 3 may well settle in more quickly than he would have done three months earlier but this process is still necessary.

Playing with other children is a skill which has to be learned. There are stages, just as there were for learning other skills, and these follow a pattern:

■ There will come a time when two children at more or less the same stage are playing with the same material close to each other but their two games, though similar, are separate. If we watch closely we see they are not actually looking at each other but they each sneak little looks when the other is not watching. This is 'parallel play' – they are working on the same lines but the lines do not come together.

■ There comes a moment when one child's play takes up

some of the other child's space, and the other child draws back a little but doesn't say anything. Then the other child also takes a bit more space so that the two games start to interweave. They are 'weaving a pattern of avoidance'. They are aware of each other but take care not to actually interfere with each other's game.

■ This may go on for quite a while, or on several occasions, until at some point one child will quietly add some of his material to what the other one is doing, or will gently take some of the other child's collection. Nothing is said, but they have a little look at each other, as if they are deciding whether or not to object – and then carry on playing. Gradually the two children will start playing with all the material. They cooperate and use it to build or create a much larger result than either could have achieved separately. They have taken the first steps to 'playing with'.

Given time and opportunity, play can develop into sharing ideas, and if two children contribute ideas their progress goes faster and further than just the sum of two children playing separately.

This is rather different from the situation when two children of different ages and stages play together. Then the older or more advanced child takes the lead and the younger child just watches or does as he is told – or the older child deliberately plays at the younger child's level and plays 'for' him rather than 'with' him (or he may just take most of the material and let the younger one have only what he doesn't want for himself).

## The benefits of nursery group

The most usual reason for letting a child attend a nursery group is to play with other children. It is probably the most important benefit the group can offer:

■ With a larger number of children in a nursery group than the home, there is usually some compatible playmate. Some 3s are more like 2s, some 5s are more like 7-year-olds, so in a group of 3–5s the ability range can vary from 2 to 7 years.

■ With a natural flow of children coming in as others grow older and leave the group to go to school, the 3-year-old has the opportunity to grow and be one of the older ones.

- The 3-year-old who naturally watches, copies and wants to please gains a great deal from having older children to watch, and he spends a lot of time doing this. The benefits are mutual because 4–5s are at the stage of wanting to lead and be top dog – a tractable 3-year-old willing to be the baby in family play, or the underdog who gets 'shot', or just simply accepts being ordered around and does as he is told, can be a very useful asset. When it all gets too much for the 3-year-old he can retire to some of the less demanding activities at his own level.

If the group consists of only 3–4-year-olds, this watch and learn element is missing. It takes the 3-year-olds longer to develop their play and it does not progress so far.

There are other advantages to be gained from nursery groups:

- The child who attends a group two or three times a week for a few hours should find the space, time and activities which may not be possible at home.

- Because the group's only function is to provide for play within a limited age range, it can provide a variety of suitable equipment and activities which are available all the time. A very expensive climbing frame may be out of the question at home. There are other people and age ranges there whose needs have to be met, and all that money, space and the time spent supervising the child who wants to climb may mean another family member has to go without what they need. In the nursery group the same climbing frame could be in constant use over a period of twenty years by as many as 500 different children.

- There are more children to be supervised in a group but there are more adults to do this, so that more than one activity can be under someone's supervision.

- Adults will be in charge at a group just as mothers are at home, but their attitude, while loving and supportive, is different. They can be truly impartial about the conflicting needs of children. Any rules will apply to all the children.

- Taking turns and sharing group toys is much easier to learn with non-personal possessions.

One benefit which should not be overlooked concerns the family of the child who goes to the nursery group:

■ Just for a short time, several times a week, whoever normally looks after him can be relieved of the distraction of being responsible for the 3-year-old. This period of relaxation is good for the adult, and anything which is good for the adult is good for the child.

■ The new experience of nursery group is something extra for the 3-year-old to talk about and learn to explain to someone who was not there. This stretches his language ability.

■ He gains ideas which can be used at home, so his play progresses there too.

■ Any gaining of independence and confidence within the group means that the 3-year-old is less demanding at home.

■ Parents who become involved with the group see their children in relation to others of the same age. This can be quite a surprise for the parent who has not been able to do this before. The child they thought was forward (or backward), large (or small), slow to talk (or a never-ending chatterbox), very independent (or too inclined to sit back and let everything be done for him) may (or may not) turn out to be all of those – but it becomes obvious that there are other children of the same age there who are just the same. Their child is really quite normal because the bounds of normality are very wide.

## Sorting out the pros and cons of nursery groups

The reasons for parents deciding to let their child attend a particular nursery group are many and varied (see Chapter 23, page 249). There is more to be considered than the simple question of whether or not he will benefit from going to a group where he will eventually stay alone:

■ The question of at what age, for how long, how many times each week and over how many months has to be decided (see page 272).

■ Full-time attendance at a nursery group means that the child misses out on very valuable home experience.

■ Spending all his time at home may mean a child does not have the opportunity to play with other children and learn to get on with a non-family group.

■ We have to take some time and care in choosing a group. The only place available may be in a group which would not be suitable. The child from a restricted home, perhaps a high-rise flat, needs space and opportunity for physical play. A group with limited premises and a 'sit still and finish your crayoning' routine is not able to offer him what he needs.

■ A place in a very young group, where the speech and conversation is not well developed, may not be suitable for a very articulate 3-year-old who talks and behaves more like a 5-year-old. It is not only not stimulating for him but may lead to difficulties. (He goes around the group saying very politely, 'Please may I have a go with the bicycle when you have been round the garden two more times,' and the younger children, who have not yet learned to use or accept speech as a means of negotiating, respond with 'Get off' and a hefty shove – so he hits them back.) They are not at the same stage or using the same language.

With children who would naturally speak a foreign language and have to learn a 'second language' in the group, at least one of the adults there ought to be able to communicate with them. These children can and do make surprising progress, but there are times when they need the comfort and help of their own language. (Think of us as adults being in hospital in a foreign country. Because no one can understand us, or make us understand them, we feel ten times worse.) If there is no one to help a child at these times his mother needs to stay longer. If there is more than one child with the same 'home' language perhaps their mothers could take turns to stay.

It may take six months of part-time attendance at a group for a child to learn to play with a small group of other children. Perhaps it is worth saying that two months' full-time attendance would not speed up this learning – there is what might be thought of as the 'casserole effect'. A successful casserole is cooked at gas mark 2 for four hours. Using gas mark 4 for two hours or gas mark 8 for one hour is not the same thing at all – and the result leads to indigestion. Exactly the same point would apply to adults and their learning or training. Experience takes time to sink in.

Children who go to one group as a stop-gap until another place is available have to start all over again with this new group. Children who are taken to several different groups on successive days may become confused (just as adults who do several jobs at the same time get tired and confused).

Some balance has to be achieved in what children gain and lose, and we should not lose sight of the benefits of what children learn at home. We tend to think that education only happens at school, yet there is plenty of evidence to show that the quality and quantity of the learning which goes on at home in the very early years shows up as beneficial at every later stage.

## The 'I don't want to go' situation

Sometimes there is a disappointing and puzzling set-back in children's attitude to the nursery group when they have been there a few months. It doesn't happen with every child but is common enough to be mentioned.

They seem to have settled down well and to be enjoying it immensely, when suddenly there are tears and they don't want to go or they want their mother to stay with them again. The adults in the nursery group are disappointed, the 'knowledgeable friend' does some muttering in the background, and the child's mother feels embarrassed as well as concerned – not knowing whether to keep him at home, move him to another group, or take what seems to be the regressive step of staying with him again.

If we think of it from the child's point of view and how he behaves, it is not so surprising. In his first few months at the group he spends a lot of time just watching what goes on from the safety of the sand tray or the water trough, or somewhere where his hands can be busy but leaving his eyes free to watch. He will wait to have his turn at some activity until older children move away. At group times the adult staff will keep an eye on him because he is new and needs support. His behaviour does not trouble anyone.

As his confidence and knowledge increase he becomes bolder and starts trying to join in. He knows what he wants to do and goes straight for it. Although this is exactly what we would hope for, it can lead to him coming into conflict with other older children. It may also mean he breaks rules that he didn't know existed, so an adult checks him.

Every group has to have some minor rules, even if it is only about not throwing sand and water. These are not written down and displayed; no group sits all the children down at the start of a session to recite what they must or must not do. The only way a child finds out about rules is by breaking them – and then he is 'told' about it. The adults who are supervising probably have a new intake of children to look out for by this time and they regard him as one of the older children who should know better – so they use a much firmer tone than they would have done when he was 'new'.

It is not surprising that branching out can lead to a touchy period. If the adults concerned all work together to restore his confidence, if his mother can stay with him again for a few sessions, or if he can go back to coming late and leaving early, this miserable time for everyone clears up quite quickly and he is again very happy in the playgroup.

This sequence is not confined to young children – think of how we all behave in a new situation such as a new job, a new neighbourhood, a new group or even a new partnership. For a while we tread very carefully, not saying or doing too much until we have 'sussed out' this new situation. Then, when we think we know what is what and who is who, we start making decisions and join in conversations or discussions. As with the children, this is the time we inadvertently 'tread on someone's toes' and feel embarrassed or hurt or humiliated when it goes wrong. We don't cry and stamp our feet and say we are not going any more – instead we develop terrible and genuine headaches, dread waking up in the morning because we have to go to work or see someone, lose all our confidence and double check on everything we do. The older and more experienced we become at coping with new situations the more often we realize that this is not the first time this has happened to us – nor will it be the last. What we do know is that we will come through it. The 3-year-old doesn't know this yet, and it can be very painful for him.

## The world of the 3–4-year-old

■ We can let him share in what we do. This may be housework, shopping (he can help make the shopping list and choose from the shelves), cooking, and it can include our hobbies and interests. Other members of the family, neighbours and friends who are willing to let the 3–4-year-old watch, ask questions and 'hold this a minute' or 'pass the spanner' or 'beat up this egg for me' can be useful.

■ If he goes to a group this can provide experience, time and opportunity which is not available at home.

■ He can gain more from stories and books than he did a year ago. Some children gain from suitable TV programmes (for example, the nearly-4-year-old who kept a whole carriage full of eavesdropping adults enthralled for an hour's journey between railway stations explaining to his grandfather exactly how mother crocodiles carry their babies, what they eat, where they live – then went on to the life history of the hermit crab and finished with an account of the sea-horse. He may not have remembered everything from the TV programme he had seen, and he may not have got it all correct, but there can be no doubt it had provided a unique experience for him).

Unfortunately there is still a good deal of danger in the world of the 3–4-year-old. Even when all the common-sense precautions are taken and the necessary warning given, they still forget and their experimenting can lead to situations we had not realized could arise.

Sometimes the 3–4s (indeed the 3s to any age) deliberately do something they know perfectly well they should not do. An experienced observer sees them give that sly little look to see if we are watching before they do something 'naughty'. This is now a two-part problem. First, they are doing something dangerous, second, they are deliberately disobeying a perfectly reasonable and understood rule. Swift action is usually necessary to avert the danger and there is not time to think 'How should an adult react to the situation?' Adults are just as individual as children and react in different ways, so we may all say and do different things – but at least we need to be consistent. If we say something is naughty or dangerous one day, it is confusing for the child if we just laugh at it the next day.

## The role of the adult

The role of the adult is:

- To be a provider of materials.
- To listen and encourage conversation.
- To provide information.
- To be a playmate when invited to join pretend games and let the children tell us what to do rather than taking over their game.
- To be a partner in real games (board and card games, taking turns games).
- To provide sensible graded challenges and variety.
- To provide outings (not necessarily expensive ones) and to allow time to look, notice and comment on what is seen.
- To read books, tell stories, sing songs.
- To be receptive to experimental ideas ('Can we have green rice for dinner? blue cakes for tea?').
- To help and support the 3–4-year-old in his efforts to mix with other children and adults.
- To support the child who goes to nursery group, and support the group.
- To offer more time and opportunities for play to the child who does not go to a group.

If we are involved in caring for other people's 3–4-year-olds we have to remember that the appearance of 3-year-olds can be deceptive:

- They can be as tall as a 5-year-old but that doesn't mean they can behave like a 5-year-old.
- They may talk very well but may not be equally capable at other skills.
- They need room and opportunity to regress as well as progress.

- They learn rules by breaking them.

- Different families, cultures and ethnic groups vary, and our rules may not be the same as their parents' rules. It is important not to confuse children. We should not encourage them to do something their parents have forbidden (such as playing in mud or with paint which might get their clothes dirty, or eating particular foods) unless we have discussed the matter with their parents and reached a mutual compromise.

## What they need

- Space, time and opportunity to play.

- Time and opportunity to watch and help adults.

- All the materials they had before plus more to provide variety.

- More difficult games, puzzles, construction and sorting/matching materials, more opportunity for physical activity, materials for pretend play, opportunities for activity play (see Part 2, page 137).

- Other children to learn to play with, older children to watch.

- Opportunity to manage alone for a short while and get used to other adults.

- Approval for their efforts – and to be trusted to do a 'real' job in the household or nursery group.

- Adequate and consistent 'safety' training (see Chapter 21, page 218).

# Chapter 10

# Big Boys and Little Madams
# – Learning to be a Leader
## (4–5 YEARS)

In the family 4–5-year-olds are competent, knowledgeable and companionable. They are less demanding in many ways than younger children – they feed themselves, most can dress themselves provided clothing and shoes have easy fastenings, many can manage by themselves in the lavatory, and some make a reasonable attempt at bathing and drying themselves. They play for longer and will struggle with a difficult problem before they ask for help. They can be selfish and thoughtless at times, but equally they can show great concern and care for smaller children or anyone (or any animal) who is hurt. They know the rules (even if they do break them) and are quick to notice and comment loudly if other people break them. The 'knowledgeable friend' may be told, 'Mummy doesn't do it like that,' or 'Well, my Daddy lets me,' in a tone that implies 'So there!'

### Learning to lead

With other children they have learned to be a follower, and for a short time they can be a member of a small group. Given the necessary opportunity, i.e. being an older one in a group with younger children who are willing to obey just so that they will be allowed to play, they are now ready to learn to be leaders.

If the 4–5-year-old is in a group only with children older than himself, he may have to go on being a follower, and this opportunity to learn to lead while he has the urge to do so may be quite lost. At school he will have to wait to be a top class Infant or even a top class Junior before the chance comes again.

If we watch closely, we can often see a difference in the way boys and girls achieve leadership. Boys tend to rely on physical size and ability and on saying enthusiastically, 'Let's go and do . . .' and their friends say 'Yeah' equally enthusiastically and they go and do it. Girls tend to be good organizers and use language to instruct other children what to do, which makes them appear very 'bossy'. 'Big boys', 'little madams' or 'bossy boots' are terms any parent or adult working in a nursery group will recognize. The child who has a better command of language, the child who has more ideas, the child who has more confidence and competence is more likely to become a leader.

The usual pattern in an average-sized nursery group with a 3–5-year age range is for the 4–5s to alternate roles of being the leader and the led. The group moves from one activity to another, and whoever is most competent tends to dominate. The 3-year-olds will join these groups gradually – providing they do as they are told.

## How they play and what they learn

The 4–5s, given the opportunity, play really well. All the skills and knowledge they have learned seem to come together so that they are confident with play materials and activities:

- They can plan and then carry out an activity.

- They restart games from where they left off last time.

- In a group they use everyone's skills and knowledge so that they achieve (whether with real or pretend materials) a very complicated game.

- They use tools and materials well. They know colours and shapes and can match and sort them.

- The 3-year-old was happy just using paint or banging a piece of wood with a hammer or cutting paper with scissors. The 4-year-olds are past this stage of wanting to 'do'. They now want to 'make'.

- Physically they are very competent. On a tricycle they are fast and efficient, on a climbing frame they are confident, and on a suitable assault course they show great stamina and determination. Given the opportunity, somewhere flat, and either stabilizers or a willing adult to help with the first stages, many are good enough at balancing to learn to ride a two-wheeler bicycle.

■ In ball games most of them can kick, catch and throw a ball, although not many can use a bat to hit a ball. Some of them may start to play a ball game with friends, but it doesn't last very long as the more able children become frustrated by the unsuccessful efforts of the less able. However good anyone is at hitting a ball with a bat, there has to be someone else who can get the ball near enough to them before they can hit it.

■ They can cooperate with other children, so they can use two-person equipment such as rockers and seesaws or carry heavy items between them. They have learned that if they want a ride in a truck someone has to push them and, since this someone will want his turn at riding, they will have to do some pushing later on. They not only accept taking turns, they learn to organize this for themselves.

## Learning the rules

This age group have been familiar with rules for some years – what they are or are not allowed to do or have or touch or play with. In a group situation they begin to realize that rules can work to their advantage. Rules become part of their language and play:

■ Children who can cooperate on two-children activities have accepted that they have to work together and share the easy parts and the hard parts.

■ Younger children say: 'Let me have it.' The 4-year-old says: 'Let me have a go.' He knows that just as someone hands over the tricycle or doll's pram (or whatever it is) to him, he will, in his turn, have to hand it back or let someone else have a go.

■ They are starting to learn that rules only make sense if everyone obeys them, and we hear 'That's not fair', 'That's not allowed'.

■ In group games they make up their own rules. The leader of the group will make sure everyone in the game obeys the rules, and he will be quick to alter a rule if he finds it does not work to his personal advantage.

■ Being able to understand, accept and keep to the rules means they can start to play proper games. Three-year-olds playing 'Snap' are happy just to match pictures. Four-year-olds insist on a strict order for having turns and woe betide anyone who tries anything that does not fit in with the accepted pattern.

Once children have a firm idea of rules we can start safety training – letting them check with us that the climbing frame is safe before they go on it, that doors and gates which should be shut are shut, what we have to do before we cross a road. They still act on impulse and forget, but these children are at a receptive stage and hopefully, if they know the rules and procedures, they will remember when they are old enough to look after themselves a little more.

## Rivalry

Rivalry is a feature which may be seen both at home and within the group – the 3-year-old, seeing another child being praised, says, 'I did it too,' or 'I can do it too,' implying that he is just as capable. The 4–5-year-old in the same situation chips in with 'I did it better,' 'Mine's better (or bigger) than yours.' This rivalry on a personal level goes on for a long time.

All children need to be able to do something well, but 4–5-year-olds need to excel at something. The child who never succeeds or excels develops a poor opinion of himself as he sees others triumph yet his turn never seems to come. This may lead to seeking attention in other ways – perhaps boasting or being aggressive. The tactful adult has to think of ways of helping this child by finding something he can do well and drawing everyone's attention to this, or by giving him some special job to do. If it is something the other children would like to do, so much the better.

The attention-seeker will get the attention he craves one way or another. We might as well let him achieve it in a way that is pleasant for him and everyone else, rather than by anti-social behaviour. Anti-social behaviour can become a long-standing habit which lasts far longer than the age range we are considering.

### Special interests

The 4–5s may be interested in everything but they often have a particular interest. This may or may not persist in later life, but its value is that children who have learned to take a deep interest in one subject often go on to develop other special interests as they grow older. Their special subject may have started within the family because an adult or an older child has a special hobby or ability, it may be the result of group influence when a particular 'craze' started, or it may just seem to come from nowhere. It may enter into everything they do. If it is cars they play with cars, build garages with bricks, make car parks in the sand, make cars with clay or dough, hammer 'wheels' to a block of wood, paint and draw cars, look at pictures and books showing cars, do car jigsaws, and 'brum-brum', 'peep-peep' their way around the house or group. They spend more time taking their tricycle or pedal car to pieces than they do riding in it or on it, they talk about cars, ask questions about cars. It could just as easily be an interest in animals, birds, gardening, dolls' houses, nursing, teaching, dinosaurs, fossils.

### Using language

Language is a very important part of learning and playing for the 4–5s. They use it:

■ To ask complicated questions and understand complicated answers.

■ To explain what they are doing to other people so that others can cooperate with them.

■ To persuade others to do what they want done: 'If you let me have all the bricks we can build a den. That will be better, won't it?'

■ To negotiate: 'I'll let you have two goes of my scooter tomorrow if you'll let me have a ride on your bike now.'

■ To instruct: 'You lie down there and be the baby and I'm going to be Mummy and get your dinner, and then you get up to the table to eat your dinner and then you've got to be good because I'm going to do the ironing.'

■ To clarify: 'I don't want that colour – I want the purply

colour that I had yesterday that was blue with red in it, and it looked like the colour of your jumper.'

■ To communicate abstract ideas: 'I need some of your sand because I haven't got enough and you've got too much, and your barrow is too full and my barrow is nearly empty' (and when this didn't work) 'and if you don't give me some, that's not fair because we have to share' (and when this didn't work) 'and anyway your barrow will be too heavy and it will all spill out and be wasted' (then threateningly) 'and anyway, you're mean and I shall tell on you' (and as a last resort) 'and you're not my friend any more!' All this was recorded in a playgroup between two 4-year-olds. Two 3-year-olds playing later in the same sandpit were gaining the practical experience that is needed before they could even start to understand and use phrases like 'not enough', 'too much', 'nearly empty', 'too full', 'too heavy', 'spill out and be wasted'.

■ To be aggressive (see page 81).

■ For fantasy and make-believe play. The 3-year-old did some pretend playing with rather limited material. The 4–5-year-olds can add language to pretend play so that the game reaches a new level where props are not so important. Their games may reflect something they have seen or heard or what they thought they saw or heard, something which is bothering them, something which has frightened them, or they may be trying on for size the role of the adult – seeing what it feels like to be someone else. This can be the stage of the imaginary playmate, or at least it can be the stage at which we realize there is an imaginary playmate because the articulate 4-year-old talks about him.

### Special language

Their language and vocabulary development may include using swear words, since they copy and imitate and what they say and how they say it reflects what they have heard. Every parent and adult has his or her own views on children swearing. How they react when their children do this is an individual matter. Some adults deliberately ignore it, others try to get children to substitute other words, some treat it as naughty behaviour which has to be stopped.

We all tend to use the language, the special words, even the dialect of the group or groups we belong to. It is part of accepting and being accepted by the group. Most adults have a different language and vocabulary for home and work – even a special language to use with strangers (most of us have a 'telephone' voice for instance). Different professions develop different jargon and vocabularies. Children usually resolve the matter for themselves in time – they develop a different language for home and for nursery group, or for home and for school, or even for home, for school and for playing outside.

In a nursery group situation with different children who have different parents with different views, this can be difficult. Group discussions with parents may help to achieve a consistent attitude on the part of the staff, but they have to be held regularly as new parents join the group. This usually comes down to: 'We don't use that word (those words) here because a lot of people don't like it (them)', which children can accept along with all the other rules they learn.

## Aggression in play

Some 4-year-olds can be very aggressive virtually all the time, and most of them have times when they can be aggressive in different ways:

- Well-adjusted 4-year-olds who have learned to play with others and are able to communicate well with other children can usually solve their problems without hitting, pushing or snatching, unless they are faced with a situation such as having tried everything else first without success.

- They may become aggressive if they are tired or hungry or too hot. Research shows that most friction in the family or group happens at these times, and adults, too, have similar times when they are more likely to become irritable or lose their temper.

- It may be that violent children have not learned that others will hit back. If they are physically large and powerful they may not learn this until they are bullied by children bigger than themselves.

- Verbal aggression may take the place of physical violence.

Shouting at others, calling names, poking fun can lead to just as many tears and as much hurt, even if it is bloodless.

■ There can be the non-violent, non-verbal aggression of face-pulling, putting out tongues, rude gestures or sniggering behind someone's back.

■ Displaced aggression can be seen at this age, and often it is the smaller, less dominant child who shows it. Nothing is done to the offending person, but another child or doll or teddy or 'thing' is attacked viciously.

■ 'Telling tales' can be used as an indirect aggressive tactic in the hope that someone else will deal with the offender. This can be confusing, as there could be a perfectly good reason for a child informing an adult about someone who is breaking rules. They may tell the adult because they think the adult should know – or they are checking whether or not the rule is a firm one and applies to everyone – or they may be genuinely concerned for the other child's safety.

The 3-year-old forgets a quarrel after a matter of minutes. The 4–5-year-old does not forget so quickly and is not always ready to forgive. 'I'm not playing with you any more' and 'I'm not your friend' can go on for several days. Sometimes other children are brought into the quarrel. 'Let's not play with him' is suggested to a group of children and then the chant becomes 'You can't play with us.'

Temporary exclusion of children from a group can be distressing, yet the excluded child may have done it to someone else only a few days ago. It happens to every child at some time. The 4–5s are not yet at the gang stage but they are taking the first clumsy steps towards it. They are practising by creating small, temporary groups which have an invisible barrier of group approval and acceptance around them.

## Rising-5

As they approach their fifth birthday children are usually competent in language, skilful with tools, confident in using their body, imaginative in their activities, able to play in a small group of children which they organize for themselves, play games following simple rules, decide first what they are going to do and then do it – and they can get 'bored' if they don't have enough to do. Although they use younger children they can be very irritated by them. Bored and irritable children are miserable children, and they make everyone else miserable.

This has probably always been the case, but with the growth of playgroups more people who were concerned with groups of children of nearly 5 years came together for discussion and training and this particular age group became one of the most frequent topics of discussion. They were given a name – 'the rising-5s' – and this was usually said either with apprehension or a long-suffering sigh.

Playgroup staff considering this problem of rising-5s came up with some useful suggestions:

■ Children who had been in the group for a period of two years with the same equipment were tired of it. They needed more variation and additional material, or special materials for 'big children only'.

■ If the activities of younger children spoiled their much more complicated game, then they needed at least some space and time free of the little ones.

■ Duplicating material ensured that the young children could play as they wished without depriving the older children of their longer, more advanced game.

■ Longer stories, which would have been too complicated for 3-year-olds, could be something special for the older group.

Children who do not attend groups show the same characteristics. They seem to need more than the home can give, and parents tend to use a common phrase, 'ready for school'. This is quite reasonable. Children in this country do have to go to school at 5 years (many are offered a place before then), and if they really are ready for it so much the better – but sometimes the parent who says this really means, 'I am ready for my child to go to school.'

If adults who care for 'rising-5s' either at home or in groups are asked to say why they think 'proper school' would be good for their children, top of their lists always come:

■ Having to sit still.
■ Having to do as they are told.

- Being taught to read, write and do sums.
- Having to concentrate on things they don't want to do.

After all the positive efforts which have been made to encourage children in purposeful play and enable them to develop at their own pace, these seem to be very negative aims. Either these adults have lost confidence in their children's ability to learn – in spite of the fact that the personal in-built programme of development children are born with has worked pretty well so far – or they have lost confidence in themselves and in their ability to contribute any further to their children's learning.

Some of the loss of confidence by parents in their own ability to 'teach' children has its roots in educational history. We take compulsory education (which in this country starts at 5 years) for granted, but it has not been with us all that long (since 1870) and it was introduced into a very different world from the one we live in today. Certainly from the time of the Industrial Revolution and even before then young children were exploited – 5-year-olds working in mines and factories, small boys being sent up chimneys. 'Slave' labour existed in this country just as much as in other areas of the world. By making education compulsory the authorities improved this situation, but it also implied that parents were not adequate to provide education and training for their own children.

Reading and writing were taught in school and were seen as something only schools could teach, and at that time that was true. Very few parents could read and write – many would have been unable even to write their name, and there would have been no books, except perhaps a Bible, in the vast majority of homes, so there was no question of children learning for themselves. Inevitably it had to be a teacher rather than a parent doing the teaching. This is certainly not the situation today.

Whatever may be the reasons for parents to have this loss of confidence in their children or themselves, it is a pity. It is also damaging, as research indicates that both early and later involvement of parents in their children's education is extremely valuable and shows up as beneficial at every stage of school life.

## Reading, writing and arithmetic

Reading, writing and doing sums are skills everyone sees as desirable. Since infant school covers the age range of 5–7 years, which is the age when most children do start to acquire these skills, we still think of them as being taught by teachers rather than being learned at home.

There are many different views of how these subjects should be taught, many schemes to be followed by teachers, and some schemes to be followed by parents even before children go to school. Every parent and teacher has to make up her own mind about these, but teaching and teachers involve learning and learners. Some regard has to be paid to the individual child.

If children and parents enjoy early reading scheme activities then that is fine. If what these schemes do is bring forward worrying about a child learning to read by a couple of years, then that is not fine. If they put pressure on the child so that he has difficulty in pre-reading activities and attaches the label 'failure' to himself at the age of 3, then that is the worst situation of all. The child who is a 'failure' at 3 will fail to learn a good many other things apart from reading.

As with every other kind of learning, children vary in when they learn to read and write. Some children at the age of 3 ask us, 'What does that say?' or 'Show me how to write that.' If these children are ready to ask, they are ready to learn. If they asked us to show them how to fasten buttons or wash themselves or use scissors, we would do so without a second thought. If a young child asks us to show him (more often it is a her) how to read and write and we refuse on the grounds that we don't know how to teach them, we miss out on that desire to achieve a particular task – that precious time when children are willing to spend time and effort on gaining a new skill. We also imply that learning to read and write is something very special and difficult to do, so when they do go to school this attitude goes with them.

There are necessary stages in learning to 'read, write and do sums'. When these children were learning to walk it was not a case of lying flat until one day they got up and ran. In the same way there has to be practice in the many different abilities that are needed before all these skills come together and enable a child to read and write and understand numbers. Often we do not recognize how some of what a young child is doing when sitting and watching, looking and playing, is leading to 'readiness'. (See 'Pre-learning skills', page 214.)

Some children are not 'ready to learn' to read and write until perhaps 7 or 8. This does not matter in itself, but special care needs to be taken that they do not come to think of themselves as failures. The failure attitude can be transferred to any new learning and will be a handicap long after learning to read and write has been accomplished – rather like a subconscious limp that goes on long after a broken leg has mended.

## What the world around offers the 4–5-year-old

Hopefully it offers space, time, other children, materials for play, a family who enjoy and encourage progress, and an opportunity, for a short time, to learn to manage alone in a peer group without too much adult intervention. Children also need freedom of choice, but it has to be a real choice from a variety of activities. The freedom to choose from either one thing or nothing is not true choice.

This is a good time for learning and teaching about safety rules, not only what not to do but also what can be done to keep safe. Children of this age are still in danger because they forget, and forgetting takes only fractions of a second. Remembering to check and take precautions takes time and the ability to learn procedures, but the 4–5-year-old is good at this. We can show children how to lock gates, handle tools, test equipment and set them a good example.

## Going to school

The most important change in the world of the 4–5s is being offered a place at school. Education authorities have different policies and different situations. When our children are offered a place is going to depend on a number of factors – falling numbers may mean that a school has to fill otherwise empty places and classrooms, too few places mean overcrowding and having barely enough space for those children who have reached 5. Whatever the reason a child is offered a place, and when he is offered a place, it is not going to have anything to do with what that individual child needs.

School places may be offered to children of 4 years and 1 day, and there are subtle pressures on the parent to accept. Just some of the reasons parents might accept the places are: to ensure a place in that particular school at 5; because all the other children are going to go at this age; to give the child a 'good start'; because their children might miss out if the local nursery groups are losing this age group to school and their child will be the only 4–5-year-old left behind; because if the local school does not have its full number of children the school may be closed down; in families where English is a second language, perhaps the sooner the child goes to 'proper' school the better he will learn English. Many parents do accept school places for under-5s – see Chapter 23, page 249.

For parents who have to make a decision about accepting a school place for their child, there are three basic questions to consider:

**1** Does this child have to go to school now? (The legal age for starting school is during the term after which they become 5.) If the answer is 'yes', then legally he has to attend school but there may be a choice of schools. It is also possible to educate children at home provided certain requirements are met, and a very few parents take this option. Some parents opt for private education.

**2** If this child does not legally have to be in school, does the place being offered suit him at the stage he is now? Will the routine, the environment, the ratio of adults to children, give him what he needs? Are only full-time, everyday places offered, and if so, what will this child lose, or gain? We tend to underestimate what 4-year-olds learn at home and how much individual attention they get there.

**3** If the neighbourhood has nothing else to offer the child except a place in a school class for which it is considered he is not ready, or which is not geared to his needs, can anything be done about this? Over the past two decades parents have gained knowledge, ability and, not least, respect by providing for their children what is otherwise unobtainable.

## The role of the adult

The adult's role will be much as it was during the previous year, but it is also necessary to:

- Deal with rivalry if it goes too far and be an arbitrator if appealed to.

- Give opportunities to extend play (which boils down to space, time and materials).

- Adopt a calm attitude of acceptance towards boasting and exaggerating, and accept fantasy play without spoiling the game by adding adult ideas.

- Create a situation which is safe enough for children to play without constant, close supervision.

- Start safety training.

- Encourage clearing up by providing storage space which is accessible to children (the top of the wardrobe won't do).

- Encourage children to take part in sensible conversations with older people so long as they observe the normal 'good manners' rules.

- Make considered decisions about children starting school, and be prepared to accept that in the early days of school children may come home tired, thirsty, hungry and irritable (just as we often do after a long day).

- Support the child who starts school by walking the narrow path between taking an interest and prying information from children who don't want to tell us anything.

- Deal with the 'I want . . .' because 'I've seen it on TV . . . my friend's got one' situation when we know this desired object is not going to be of lasting value. This can be difficult. We all want things at times, and we all know the disappointment of the sensible, unwanted present. Perhaps Christmas and birthdays are so special that we can relax the 'It won't last two minutes', 'It's a waste of money', 'You won't play with it if I do buy it' attitudes just at these times – if we can.

- Investigate what opportunities there are in our area for this age group (perhaps story sessions in the library, swimming, etc., see Chapter 15, page 147).

- Give more time to books, stories, music, sharing our own interests with them.

### What they need

- Other children to play with.
- Sometimes freedom from younger children.
- To be treated with the same respect as an adult while they are behaving in a mature, sensible adult manner.
- Private space to keep toys and treasures.
- Encouragement to throw away their own rubbish rather than us 'having a clear-out' when they are not around.
- Simple print books to add to their collection of books.
- Someone to spend time reading with them.
- Preparation for school, which is best achieved by a settling-in period just as they had for nursery group, except that this time it will not take quite so long.
- Lots of opportunity for activity play (see Part 2, page 137).

# Chapter 11

## The Wider World – Here I Come, Ready or Not
### (5–7 YEARS)

The vast majority of children in this country will already be attending school or a group of some kind by the time their fifth birthday comes around (see Chapter 23, page 258).

In areas where schools are overcrowded, full-time education may be delayed till a few weeks after their fifth birthday, but the delay will not be very long.

### Full-time school

Going to school full-time makes a tremendous difference to children – it is intended to, after all – but they still spend more waking time at home than at school if we count up the hours.

Home, parents and family are still very important. Some parents see the school as quite different from home, and feel that what goes on there has little to do with them. Some schools would take the same attitude. The 5–7-year-old is still the same child whether he is at home or at school, and the best results happen when parents and teachers consider themselves to be partners who have an interest in each other as well as in the child who moves between the two.

Schools and parents who achieve a happy working relationship are fortunate, and even more fortunate if they both become part of the local community. This does not happen by accident (see page 276).

### The task of the 5–7-year-old

The natural developmental task of this age group, who have learned to walk, to talk, to play alone and with others, to copy and imitate adults and who have become self-sufficient enough to manage without constant attention and support, is to develop independence, to learn to become members of a peer group of age-mates, and to learn more about the world outside the family for themselves.

Not so many years ago this age group could have been encouraged to go to a park alone, to run errands, or to go to school with another 5-year-old or a brother or sister. Few parents are willing to allow their infant-school children to do this now. There are traffic hazards, and the possibility of being molested or even of being attacked for the sake of a few coins in their pocket. As a community, a culture, a generation, we are not able to allow the 'inner urge' of developing independence in the outside world to take its natural course. The least we ought to do is provide supervised outside adventure playgrounds and allow for natural spontaneous group play in a place near where children live and where what goes on can be unobtrusively overlooked by responsible adults.

School – which our children are legally obliged to attend – provides some opportunity for this natural development. It also demands learning which is not part of the in-built pattern of development of skills with which our children are born. Learning to read and write and develop mathematical skills is part of our culture rather than part of our in-born inheritance, unlike learning to walk and run and talk and provide ourselves with food, so there is no specific inner time clock for them.

To teach and learn these extra skills means having to rely on the natural urges children have to copy and imitate, to gain adult skills generally, the desire to achieve and gain praise and the need to be part of a group. Thus we have to take more part in the teaching – and we have to take account of whether a child is capable of the basic skills needed for these cultural tasks we ask him to undertake. There is no point in applying pressure to learn if the child is not yet physically capable of these complicated tasks.

## Starting work

For the first time we have to consider the word 'work'. The work children do in the infant class may be very similar to what we previously called play, but they have to follow activities at someone else's direction and adhere to the timetable of a group. They may enjoy enormously what they do, but because it is not self-directed it is 'work'.

There is not only the factor of what teachers expect children to achieve – there is also the group situation, which means that the rate at which the child is under pressure to achieve is the pace of the group. Inevitably for some children this is too fast, and for others too slow. Even in schools where the curriculum and practice allows for individual progress, the children are going to achieve at different rates – and since they are not stupid they soon realize that others are faster than they are and become disheartened – or that others are slower and that they are having to wait for the group to catch up. Learning to accept these situations is just as important as learning to read and write.

The 5–7-year-olds have to learn to conform with as much of the outside world as affects them. This situation is not new. They have already learned to conform within the family, or take the consequences of not doing so. It may, however, lead to a stormy period of 'settling down', 'having corners rubbed off', and this age group may need support and encouragement which we had not expected to have to provide after the happy confidence of the 4–5 period.

Many parents get their first inkling of this on the first day of school – their 5-year-old, who looked so large and competent in the nursery group, suddenly no longer looks so big alongside the 7-year-olds in the playground. The school clothes bought to allow for growth, still smart and a bit stiff, seem too large and heavy – and a whole day before we collect him again seems a very long time.

The new 5-year-old in the school playground looks smaller and different from the 7-year-olds because he *is* smaller and different. Apart from just growing during those two years, the body shape and proportions change. Limbs become proportionately longer. Faces alter in shape, the rounded chubbiness disappears, baby teeth start to come out. There are other changes in the body structure which we cannot see, but they are evident in how the 7-year-old moves and uses his body:

- Maturing of some of the body tissues, particularly the nerves which control muscles, means the 7-year-old can stay still and control his body in more difficult postures. The 7-year-old has grown into being able to sit still and concentrate for longer, rather than being taught to do so.

■ Seven-year-olds move gracefully and economically and they are stronger than 5-year-olds. They have more control of their hands.

■ They start elaborating on the physical skills they have learned so far, doing clever tricks on their bicycle, doing daring acrobatics on anything they can climb on, jump off or swing on, and their balance is good enough to allow them to walk along the tops of walls or other dangerous heights when our backs are turned.

■ They have more stamina and play harder for longer.

In another two years the 5-year-old will have developed the same characteristics as the 7-year-old without anyone doing too much about it. This is the natural pattern of development.

The new influence of school affects children differently in how they play at home after a school day:

■ Some will want to carry on at home with new ideas learned at school. Others want to do something entirely different.

■ Some children come home very tired and seem to need a winding-down period. They have just about enough energy to rush to the lavatory, have a drink and something to eat, then sit quietly watching television or doing some rather mechanical, undemanding activity. If we ask questions they reply reluctantly or 'can't remember' and become irritable.

■ Other children rush out of school needing to let off steam. They shout and chatter and we get a non-stop account of the doings of the day. Once home they get out all their toys and play vigorously or speed round the garden on a tricycle.

All these reactions to school are common and do not necessarily reflect how these children behave in school. Many parents and teachers, after talking together at a parents' evening or having an informal chat after school, wonder if they are talking about the same child – so these exchanges of information are useful to both parent and teacher and can only be of benefit to the child.

Homes still have to provide for play and activity after school, at weekends and during holidays, so the 5–7-year-old still needs his share of family space, time and finance. He may be less demanding of adult attention, but he still has to be taken to and from school, to an outside play space and to any other activities he is able to join in. The mother who decides to return to work on the grounds that she will be free once the 5-year-old goes to school can find herself very hard pushed trying to be in three places at once.

Five-year-olds have enough vocabulary and conversation skills to make themselves understood and to understand given normal development and circumstances. What they may not have in a new situation is the confidence to say so if they have not understood something. This last point is particularly important for children with language or hearing difficulties, whatever the cause of them may be. It is almost impossible for a teacher with a large group of children not to have all her time taken up by the children who do ask for help – and the child who does not understand or hear, and does not ask (and keep on asking) for help, gets further and further behind and less and less confident. Small groups and/or extra adults are of great benefit to such children. Failing that, most parents would willingly be of more help if they knew what their children were supposed to be doing. They can't help unless they do know. No child is going to come home and say: 'Well, today I did not understand . . .' because first, he does not understand what it was he did not understand, and second, this is the age when children become embarrassed by failure and they try to avoid situations where others may comment on it.

## The language of the 5–7-year-old

Language and conversation are an evident feature of a child's personality right from the first sounds he makes, but a peer group of age mates is not going to make allowances for him as his family did.

What is being said, and how it is being said, is just as important as making people understand. The child who continually boasts, criticizes and has a derogatory attitude to others is not going to be liked – yet being rejected will make him do it even more. He needs help just as much as the child with a speech difficulty. He may be reflecting a family or regional cultural pattern and it is no more than a habit, but it is a very costly one when a child has to mix with others. Another child with exactly the same language ability may use it to be pleasant and friendly. The results from the point of view of social reward are much greater.

The child who pokes fun at others, laughs at their mistakes or mishaps, criticizes, points out their failures, becomes the child who is afraid of being laughed at, doesn't try new things in case he fails. If he can't admit that anything could possibly be his fault then he can't say 'Sorry'. If he can't say 'Sorry' the other person can't say 'That's quite all right – never mind', and he is left with the guilt feeling.

The child who is sympathetic and appreciative towards others is not afraid of being laughed at. It doesn't occur to him that he may be, since he doesn't show this behaviour to others. All adults can do is provide an example and a social climate where respect and concern for others is the norm, where failure is acknowledged but not blamed, where we laugh at our own mishaps, not other people's – and where we say 'Sorry' and the apology is accepted.

The spoken word is used by this age group to negotiate and bargain but it is also enjoyed for itself:

■ Silly verses, funny words, catch phrases, slightly naughty rhymes are hugely enjoyed (any poem with the word 'knickers' in it is guaranteed to amuse them).

■ They start to tell word jokes which depend on double meanings, on puns and on the emphasis given to particular words in a phrase ('Why does a fireman wear red braces?' they ask, and we frantically think of all sorts of reason why the braces should be red. 'To keep their trousers up,' they tell us).

■ The pretend play of the 3-year-old and the fantasy play of the 4–5s now develops to fantasy using only words to convey ideas – telling stories, exaggerating. Two children can be heard working out a complicated sequence of events in words. They can communicate and convey ideas without the need for props or mime.

## Reading and writing

The written word – reading and writing – becomes important at this stage as skills which society expects children to master at some time during these two years rather than as a means of communication.

A few children will be able to read and write before they start school, many will learn during the infant school years, and some may take longer. The ability to read fluently opens up a whole new world of books, information, enjoyment, escape and independence. The child who can read can live in someone else's world for a while, he can get the answers he needs without waiting for an adult to give them.

We tend to lump reading and writing together, yet they are very different. One involves recognition and interpretation. The other demands the ability to recall and copy plus enough skill and control to use a pencil.

The basic skills which are necessary before children can learn to read are usually developed through natural play activities (see page 214).

The efforts involved in learning to read and write can be a great source of worry to parents and children alike – though not, of course, to the parents whose children learn easily and naturally at the age at which they are expected to do so. It is the parents of children who experience difficulty who sometimes allow this slowness in achieving this one goal to blot out appreciation of all the other things their slow learner can do. This is the same reaction as that of parents with children who are slow to walk (see page 19).

There is a wide variation in when children will learn. Some children are slower than others in reaching all the milestones, some children come from a family where other members were slow to read. There can also be a wide variation in the degree of skill they will attain. Even among adults there are some for whom reading is tedious and slow and for whom it is not something they do for pleasure.

The worst thing that can happen to a child who takes longer or starts later or even does not learn to read at all is none of these things. It is the sense of being a failure which can develop which does the damage. Some non-readers learn to live with this, some hide this failure very well and learn to compensate. Many, however, find that 'I can't do it' affects them greatly, and they fear they are going to fail at learning other things – so they do. In an education system which relies almost exclusively on literacy, as ours does, these children have a double handicap. Fortunately, more is known about some of the specific reading difficulties experienced than used to be the case, and more help for those who could benefit is available.

## Working with numbers

Learning to deal with numbers is the other important subject that we associate with going to school. Some children have difficulty but it doesn't seem to cause such widespread problems as learning to read and write. The play activities of young children have all been good for pre-number work – the everyday routines of one-to-one (one chair, one plate, one cup for each person, two socks because we have two feet), putting things in order of size, sorting things into groups, are all part and parcel of our daily living. Many children can count quite well by the time they start school. They have probably practised on Smarties or biscuits or pieces of apple, just making sure who got what.

The number work done in infant classes is very practical, with plenty of handling of materials. Tackling abstract ideas of number and working in one's head is usually left until later years in school. Modern methods of teaching mathematics have taken some of the sting out of the subject.

## Rewards and encouragement

Because success can be a long time coming and many goals are long term, infant-school children appreciate having some indication of immediate reward. Many schools use a star or merit system. Even the everyday ticks and crosses on their work give pleasure to this age group. At home they ask for approval. At both school and home, large tasks can be broken down into stages so that progress can be noticed and rewarded.

Some children do not succeed and they can become very disheartened. They need to be rewarded for effort as well as achievement – they also need a bit of tactful help. It is the least able child who needs the best scissors, the strongest piece of cardboard, the sharpest pencil, yet so often it is the most capable child who gets there first and takes the best things. (As many adults would agree, this doesn't apply just to this age group. It happens to us too.)

These less confident, less able children can be helped by having some 'fail-safe' activities or pre-fabricated projects (see page 190). Their skills will not improve if they are given too much help, but to give them enough support to gain confidence and enjoy the pride and pleasure of achievement that may not come naturally pays big dividends.

## Groups, gangs and competition

As children progress from 5 to 6 to 7 years, they usually become less aggressive in their approach to others and this helps them to play in a larger group. They become protective and competitive on behalf of their gang or team, and this de-personalizes aggression to a degree that other children accept – and indeed see as loyalty. Adults and society as a whole encourage this in school, in sport, in commerce, in politics, because this characteristic benefits these institutions. Aggression is still there but has become socially acceptable because it is socially useful – unless it leads to extreme behaviour such as football hooliganism and racial riots.

The 'gang/group' influence can be a strong incentive to achieve in school and at play – indeed, if children cannot do what the rest of the group do they will not last long as a member of it. These groups can be the source of opting out from some activities in the school playground or playing field or play centre. 'We don't want to do that, do we?' says the leader of a little group of boys when he can't do something, and the rest of the gang agree with him. One or two of the children who trail after him may really want to do whatever it is, but they don't dare to disagree if it means leaving the group. 'That's silly, isn't that silly?' the leader of a group of girls appeals to her bosom friends of the moment, and they all walk away very disdainfully. Tomorrow that very same activity may be what they all do because the leader suggests it as her own idea.

Groups can also be a source of coercion – even 6-year-olds dare each other to do things they know would not be approved of or are dangerous. Excluding someone from a group is easy. If the child who wants to join can do everything the others do, they simply change the rules. 'We don't allow people with red hair, or freckles, or blue shoes.'

Some children seem content not to be accepted as a member of the group. They get on quietly with what they want to do without making any special effort either to be in or out. It may be due to quiet confidence, it may be a lack of sensitivity, or they may be at a different stage. They may win a grudging respect from their peers or they may be ignored.

Other children who are not accepted by the group become very distressed. They may try to 'bribe' their way in with sweets or toys. They may submit to any indignity or unfairness to be allowed to remain on the fringes of the group. Yet others become nervous and depressed, eager to please yet aware that their efforts are more likely to fail than succeed. Some become the clown of the group and make a place for themselves by making or letting the others laugh at them.

On the whole these group influences do not lead children too far astray at the 5–7 stage, when they are mostly under adult supervision. If these influences persist at later stages then children really can get into difficulties with the outside world unless there is some acceptable outlet for their activities.

## Special play

Play activities may show the effect of the 'craze'. Suddenly all the children want to have or do specific things. While it lasts it is very important to children to be part of it. We may blame TV advertising, quite rightly, for the great pressure it puts on children by exploiting their need to be part of the 'in-thing', but crazes existed long before television was available. They are recorded in stories of children generations ago – marbles and whips and tops, hoops, hopscotch, skipping-rope games, playing sixes against a wall with two balls, snobs (or jacks or other regional names), conkers all appeared at different times of year. The exploitation factor nowadays is the money that is necessary to enable this generation to take part, since most of the crazes involve simply owning manufactured goods rather than having skill with inexpensive materials.

There are other skills which belong to the adult world which children are ready to develop as they approach their seventh birthday, and these may be learned at home or taught at school, or both:

- Cooking usually appeals to boys and girls alike.

- Girls and some boys may show interest in knitting and sewing. Obviously the tools and materials they are given should be appropriate, and the simpler the design the better. Interesting colours and fabrics look good even if they are stapled together rather than stitched.

- Woodwork and clay activities now lead to a specific result rather than experimenting with basic materials and tools, and they ask for help and say 'Show me'.

- Model-making is often a favourite pastime. The materials used may be pre-fabricated (sets such as Lego and Meccano) or a special kit, but many children enjoy using everyday objects to create a model. TV programmes aimed at this group rely heavily on this interest, yet children can be disappointed with the results of copying the demonstrations they watch with such attention. It may be that the skill level required is too high for them – measuring accurately, cutting meticulously, very neat folding and handling. In this case it may be argued that at least children are being encouraged to practise these skills. More often the failure is due to the children using inadequate materials and tools. 'You could use a cereal box/newspaper/powder paint/wallpaper paste,' suggest the presenters, as they quickly assemble pre-prepared items and use good, stiff cardboard/cartridge paper/pre-mixed acrylic paint/quick-drying strong adhesives. 'Don't use Mummy's best scissors,' they warn – yet we don't see them using the blunt, awkward scissors usually sold for use by children.

- The children's paintings and drawings change as they use the same materials with which they used to experiment. Because they have more hand control they can create smaller, more detailed, more representational drawings and pictures. They need smaller brushes and materials suitable for finer work. A small proportion of this age group will progress to free and imaginative work and ART becomes one of their favourite and most satisfying activities.

- The majority of children of this age are knowledgeable about shapes and colours, and are interested in designs and techniques. This can become an enriching part of every individual's life, leading eventually to creating pleasing home colour schemes, mixing and matching colours and fabrics in clothing, planning meals so that the result is colourful and attractively presented, planning a garden that is a pleasure to look at. This may not be regarded as ART but it is everyday creativity which affects the quality of life every day.

■ The changing patterns and colours made by light and shadow, the effects of distance and perspective – these are all experiences which give pleasure and cost nothing if we have a seeing eye. It is often during the 5–7 stage that this seeing eye can be developed and encouraged by adults who point out and share and discuss their own appreciation with children. The habit of appreciation is infectious.

■ Interest in nature study and science is another feature of this age group which can be encouraged and fostered at home and school. They enjoy watching living creatures and finding out about them. Turn over just one square foot of earth in the most unpromising location and there is usually something of interest there. Simple experiments with magnets, batteries, magnifying glasses, pulleys, cog-wheels and gears, properties of liquids, can add to the knowledge they gained by playing with natural materials.

■ The 5–7-year period can be the time when children develop an interest in collecting. This may or may not carry into later life as an obsessive hobby – for now it is part of their curiosity, setting themselves goals, trying to complete things.

■ Interest in music may become specific – they like a particular kind of music or instrument and we start to wonder about music lessons for them when they are a little older.

■ Playing with toys and using them for imaginative games or as the focal point of a complex layout is probably at its height during these two years. They like things that are accurate and which work. Since their hand control improves they can manage smaller, more intricate mechanisms – smaller construction sets, proper tools, efficient adhesives, kits to make up.

## Practising sport

Physically the 5–7s are strong and efficient. Given the opportunity, they enjoy gymnastics, riding bicycles, swimming, climbing, obstacle courses. Their skill with ball games begins to improve with practice.

One of the most sensible developments in the teaching of games skills has occurred relatively recently. In the old style lessons the system of playing formal games gave most practice to those who were competent and none at all to the individual who was out first go or carefully put in a position where his lack of skill did not spoil the game for others. In the new system, where everyone has an equal number of opportunities to hit a ball, catch a ball, have a go at scoring a goal, the less naturally able child should benefit enormously. This system suits 5–7-year-olds very well. They are not yet ready for the group spirit and loyalty required for inter-team competition if they have no chance to be part of the team.

Board games and card games demand a different kind of skill and concentration. These children can now follow rules without an adult, as the more dominant or knowledgeable child will take on the leader role. The players need to be reasonably well matched, as a child who loses all the time soon loses interest. The more able 5–7-year-old is not yet experienced enough to work out that it is sometimes sensible to let the other person win if you want him to go on playing with you.

## 'Why can't I have?'

This age range can become great wanters, and they can make themselves and their parents very miserable with their demands. As small children they played with what we gave them and made the most of whatever opportunities they had. Toys borrowed from a toy library or shared within the family or nursery group were very much enjoyed just as toys. Now they want their own things and unfortunately they tend to want what all their school friends have – or what advertising campaigns suggest to them. Furthermore, they want the latest version, not realizing that this latest version will inevitably be supplanted just as earlier versions were. The vast majority of parents cannot afford to meet these demands and wouldn't do so even if they could – but this still leaves the child unhappy and resentful and at 5, 6, 7 he doesn't forget.

There is nothing wrong with wanting. It is a very useful part of the human nature. If we were content just to satisfy basic human needs for survival we could lead a very simple life – and we would be very simple people. Human beings are capable of more than that, and it is 'wanting' to do things, 'wanting' to know things, 'wanting' to have things that provides the drive and energy to work, learn, explore and find out. If, however, what we want costs money rather than personal effort, there are going to be many occasions when we are not going to get what we want, and we have to learn to cope with this for our own benefit and, for obvious reasons, for the benefit of the society we live in. Unfortunately, individuals and groups simply taking what they want – from others – seems to have become a depressing part of life.

The 5–7s need our help to learn to cope with disappointment when they can't have what they want:

■ Hopefully, they were encouraged to make choices at an early age.

■ They should have learned about having to wait.

■ They should be able to reason a little and listen to reasons, so rather than just saying 'No', we can try to explain why not. We can make bargains and encourage them to make decisions by giving them pocket money, letting them choose a birthday or Christmas present with a price limit in mind.

It may help children to take a wider view if we let them see that we, too, have disappointments. Obviously they couldn't cope with something really devastating, but we can introduce the idea on a day-to-day basis: 'I would have liked to buy . . . this week but I really don't think I can,' 'We really ought to decorate the kitchen but it would cost too much to be able to do it this year – perhaps a really good clean would make it look better,' 'I was looking forward to . . . but I shan't be able to save up enough money. Never mind, perhaps I can go another time.' These are all things we say to ourselves many times, but the children are not aware of them unless we say them out loud.

## The world of the 5–7-year-old

What the world offers these children now is a certain constraint. They are ready to move out into the environment around them but unfortunately it is not safe for them to do so alone.

School offers a new experience but also brings limitations. The child who does not like a particular subject cannot opt out of that session. Equally, the child who is deeply interested in what he is doing has to stop whether he wants to or not at the end of the lesson. Children become aware that certain achievements are expected of them and that what they achieve is going to be measured and compared against others. This new part of their life offers advantages as well as drawbacks. A varied timetable ensures new experience and regular practice – being made aware of a standard of achievement can lead to pleasure and confidence and create a challenge or goal for them to aim for. After all, how do we know we have got there if we don't know where we are supposed to be going? Provided the system has a safety net for the slow or non-achiever, most children enjoy infant school and this age-group, given adequate educational resources, can be a joy to teach.

Out-of-school experience will depend on the environment. Virtually all primary schools are neighbourhood schools, so the children attending will come from similar backgrounds. Their world may not widen as much as we think it does. The child who goes to a crowded, perhaps run-down, drab and depressed school will almost certainly live in a similar locality. In country areas there is more space but there are fewer people, so children may be bussed to school. The friends they make and the groups they belong to may not be available during the holidays and weekends.

While the physical world of the child is not going to change dramatically when he goes to school, one area of experience which does increase is getting to know other adults. There will be head teachers, teachers, assistants, school caretakers, dinner ladies, welfare assistants, volunteers who come in to help with activities, school bus drivers, 'lollipop-crossing' wardens. All these people are important, as children use them to develop their ideas of how adults behave.

The local authority or statutory organizations or voluntary organizations may provide playgrounds, swimming baths, libraries, parks and playing fields, and there may be private gym clubs, dancing and other sports opportunities. Social Services departments often have lists of what is available in their area; there may be lists in schools and libraries. Once children reach 7 there may be Cubs, Brownies, youth clubs and other organizations they can join.

It is clear that parents still have to do a great deal of finding out and fetching and carrying – and all too often they have to do the paying, too, if their child is to benefit from what is available. Many parents also have to spend time and energy to provide, or persuade others to provide, what is not.

### Watching television

Television is by no means new to this age group, but they may be influenced by it much more than previously. They probably watch for longer and concentrate more, there are more programmes for this age group at home and at school, and they are more likely to see some adult choice programmes.

Whether or not this is a good influence depends on what they watch and how it affects them. It may provide common experience for them to talk about with friends at school, it may give them information and interest they would never otherwise gain and, for better or worse, it provides powerful role models.

The habit of watching television is going to be part of a family pattern. The 7-year-old who lives in a household where television is always on will expect to watch a good deal, and his parents are not likely to object to this. The parents who do not watch very much are going to be the ones who ration and choose and make rules about when their children watch. If we do find children who watch too much television it is probably because there is nothing better to do, or they have no play space. Perhaps we should turn our attention to this rather than nagging at the children.

### The role of the adult

... is changing rather than becoming less important and time-consuming. Parents are still very much needed:

- To fetch and carry.

- To find out where extra activities are.

- To give support with any problems arising from starting school, and help with school tasks brought home to do.

- To encourage reading by helping the child to read, but also by still reading to him and by choosing and providing books which are interesting.

- To make sure there is time for conversation and answering questions – in school there may be less opportunity for children to talk and get the information they want when they want it than they had as pre-schoolers.

- To allow time and opportunity for concentration on a long project and to find space to keep half-finished materials safe until next time.

- To have patience and sympathy with the 'I want' as well as firmness.

- To develop tolerance with the 'Well, my teacher says!' situations.

- To listen carefully to what children say when things are going wrong or when they seem upset.

- To give more responsibility to children who are ready for this but to bear in mind that this age group still have accidents – not so much in the home but outside and on the roads.

- To bear road safety in mind all the time, and make sure the children do too.

- To give them the cuddles and affection they still need when they are tired, irritable, not feeling well.

- To support the child's school, to take an interest in what goes on there and to find time to give whatever practical help is necessary.

## What the 5–7s need

- Encouragement, praise or anything else which will help them to be self confident.

- Graded challenges and acknowledgement of effort as well as success.

- More and better tools, art materials.

- Space to play and space to store half completed games safely.

- Opportunity, space and equipment to be active and develop physical skills.

- Opportunity to feel free of adult direction and intervention, at the same time as being adequately supervised.

- Special outings and help with 'collecting'.

- Access to books which suit their taste and ability (even comics and joke books in big print, if that is what they are prepared to try to read), plus books for someone to read to them.

- More and different safety training. This age group shows a marked reduction in the number of accidents they have at home, but they are now reaching the age, stage and activities to have accidents on the road and in playgrounds. Parents can't reduce their efforts in the field of safety training yet. 'Road sense' is the great protector – and it has to be taught.

### Tail piece

Having come to the end of our chosen age range it makes sense to wonder why we stop with the 7-year-old – after all, we all go on playing for one purpose or another for decades to come.

It may seem ridiculous to say we are stopping here because the 7-year-old is losing his baby teeth and growing new ones – but that very obvious change in a child denotes other changes. He has grown, developed and matured, and has more in common with an adult than with the new-born baby he was only a relatively short time ago. He can use his hands, body, senses and brain, communicate, cooperate and learn. The personality he has developed will go on developing but it is not likely to change radically. What he needs now is experience and practice.

The tiny teeth that are put under the pillow do not leave an empty jaw behind – they have left a good foundation, and the big adult teeth waiting to come through should last the rest of the child's life. Our children's early playing/learning experience has similarly left a good strong foundation for the next stages of development and the rest of the life span.

# Chapter 12

## The Special Child

All children are special – but some are more special than others because they have a handicap or a disability. Some have a special gift. There are times when we have to make special arrangements for every child because they are ill or injured.

### The sick child

For children who are not well, whether they are confined to bed or sitting rather droopily around the house, there are some common factors to be borne in mind (in fact they apply just as much to adults). Being really ill causes loss of energy and concentration and a general lack of interest in anything. Children need soothing rather than entertaining at this time. The most welcome comfort may be someone's quiet presence and a dear old teddy to cuddle up to. They have almost gone back to baby needs.

Getting better but still not feeling well enough to do much is boring and frustrating, so this is when children need to be kept amused.

- Concentration goes, so any activity needs to be short (or put away half-finished).

- Easy rewards which don't require much effort are needed. For children this can mean going back to playthings and activities that were favourites a year or two back, mobiles, wind chimes, story tapes they know well, and a new book which takes little effort or, better still, someone to read it.

- Most of all, children need someone to be with them.

This is the time for a mother to close her eyes to anything that is not absolutely essential, and spend as much time as possible with a child who may seem to have gone back a year or two in his behaviour as well as in his ability to play. The recuperating child behaves like a toddler. It is a good idea to move an armchair to where the child is. Even if it is not possible to spend every minute sitting in it, 'I'll be back in a minute' carries more conviction if the armchair is there as evidence that we mean it. Moving the child to someone else's bed during the day can offer a change of scene and a chance to freshen up the sick-room. A cot or day-bed in the living-room for short periods is another possibility.

Sometimes children feel perfectly well but have to stay immobile to allow a broken bone to mend. This is different altogether from being ill. Boredom and frustration become conditions in their own right, and ingenuity is needed to allow these children to play at their normal level but from a fixed position.

Some children will spend time in hospital. For most it is likely to be a short stay, but for a few it may be a very long stay indeed. In both cases, hopefully, the hospital will recognize that these children are still children in spite of the fact that they need treatment.

There has been a revolution in children's hospital wards over the last two decades. Play is now accepted to be therapeutic (i.e. a positive healing agent which contributes to the 'making better'), and the majority of hospitals have play-rooms and play-ladies who are experts in providing suitable activities. Children confined to bed may even be given the opportunity to play with water and sand or to cook or take part in messy activities – which would have been unthought of not so very long ago. The quantity and quality of the play activity in hospitals will vary, probably for no better reason than the degree of commitment of consultants and senior nursing staff to the promotion of this aspect of healing and, of course, how suitable the actual premises are for this approach. This is another field in which parent concern and pressure, notably the National Association for the Welfare of Children in Hospital (Action for Sick Children, see Appendix 1, page 291) has played a large part.

No one would actually choose to go into hospital, but adults can accept that there is a need for treatment and that if hospital is the only place where we can be treated then we must go there. It is difficult to explain to children why they have to go to a strange place and have nasty things done to them by people they don't know. In other circumstances this would be called kidnapping and carry a criminal penalty. Preparation in the form of carefully thought-out play activities can be useful, as it gives the opportunity to talk about what a hospital is for, what goes on there, why people wear funny clothes and smell different. Action for Sick Children (see above) produces a special parents' pack which contains advice.

These same play activities can also be useful when children come home from hospital. Their illness may have been cured, but being away from home may have left some after-effects which need after attention. Adults cope with their experience by talking (sometimes endlessly) about their operation. Children 'play it out' rather than 'talk it out'. Teddy bears are bandaged, dolls are injected, and everything is wheeled round on a makeshift trolley for quite a long time after they come home.

## The child with a handicap

Parents and carers who look after handicapped and disabled children may feel that what has been read so far is not of specific benefit to them – that the needs of their children have been ignored or glossed over. This is a common, natural (and often justified) feeling on their part, and relates to far more than the information in this book.

Rightly or, less often, wrongly they feel that no one really understands the stress and strain, their continuing disappointment on behalf of their child rather than because of their child, that society as a whole expects them to bear. There may be plenty of lip service and generosity in the form of full collecting tins on special occasions – but far less day-to-day practical help and consideration from the general public, and far fewer resources made available by authority in its various forms than they need.

In fact, everything that has been read so far does apply to 'special' children – because they are 'children'. They have the same needs as normal (whatever that is) children of 0–7 years.

Just to prove the point – if we go back to the beginning of the book and work through from Chapter 1 to Chapter 11, marking with a bright, thick pen anything that is relevant to a handicapped child, the odds are that there will be very few pages which do not have coloured marks.

## Similarities

The similarities between 'special' children and their peers are far greater than their differences at this age.

Opportunity groups, where children with special needs play alongside ordinary children, vary, but a passer-by casually glancing through the window of a typical one would just see a group of children playing as they would in any nursery group. If the passer-by came to the door and watched for a while she would notice that one child was blind, one had two hearing aids, another had callipers on his legs, one had a slightly runny nose and an open mouth which dribbled a bit, yet another had the features which go with Down's syndrome, one child looked rather large to be sitting on an adult's lap.

If, instead of walking away at this point, this passer-by came right in and stayed to play for a while, she would realize that the little blind girl was playing with finger paint, the 4-year-old boy with the hearing aids was absorbed in playing with chime bars, and the little chap with the callipers was laboriously climbing up a stairway of shallow wooden boxes to come down the low slide – while the rest of the children in the queue waited patiently for him. His shrieks of pleasure were just as loud as theirs, and he proudly looked round for approval just as they did. The smiling child with Down's syndrome and the dear little boy whose illness had left him with the problems of the runny nose and the need to breathe through his mouth were joining in anything that happened around them, including squirting everyone with water from a squeezy bottle, and they were reprimanded just like the rest of the children. The child on the adult's lap was laughing with delight as he watched. In other words, that first impression when glancing through the window had been right. It was indeed just another group of children playing.

For handicapped children development may be slower, and in some areas (perhaps speech or physical ability or mental ability, or maybe all of these and more) there may be a limit to what can be hoped for in the way of achievement – play materials and activities may have to be structured – intense and continued effort on the part of adults may be necessary. Nevertheless the play–enjoy–reward–learn sequence still holds good.

## Differences

Inevitably there are differences between handicapped and 'normal' children. However, not only is every handicapped child different from normal children, he is different from every other handicapped child simply because all children are individuals. Handicaps vary. Specific handicaps vary in severity. Their effect may vary at different ages and stages. Individual children need individual treatment, even if they share a common label.

Some very hopeful things have happened over the last two decades which should help handicapped children a good deal:

- Parents of children who have similar problems have formed local support groups. They are thus able to benefit from being helped by – or helping – others who really do understand the stresses and strains because they actually share them.

- There has been an increase in the number of national associations which support parents and children with specific problems. By using the weight of their numbers they can campaign more effectively for what they need than an individual parent could – or than an association which had an interest in several handicap problems would (see Appendix 1, page 291).

- There has been new legislation (the 1981 Education Act which came into force in 1983), based on a four-year study of children with special needs by the Warnock Inquiry into Special Education.

## The new approach to handicap

The new approach which should result from the 1981 Education Act is a much more sensitive and sensible one than previous procedures. It recognizes that lumping children together under one named handicap does not necessarily identify all the needs of these children as individuals.

One change which should take place is that when children are looked at individually to see what extra help they need, this will lead to more children getting help even if they are not classified as having a specific handicap. It is estimated that 20 per cent of our children may be found to need some kind of special help (even such simple help as enabling a child who is slow to talk to attend a mother and toddler group, providing physiotherapy at home for a child with a movement problem, or showing a parent whose child appears to have learning difficulties how she can help her child). Since the number of children previously classed as handicapped was only 2 per cent, this can only be good news for those children whose need may not have been identified, let alone met, under the old system.

Another large and very welcome change is that parents are to be consulted more and involved more in the decisions made about what help their children need and what help they actually get. This should bring twofold benefits. The parents should feel happier and more confident about their child's future, which is very important, and also their intimate knowledge of their own child can be considered. Children can behave very differently at home from the way they do when being examined or tested, and there is no point in treating just the child as he appears in the examination room.

Perhaps the most important change which will affect handicapped and disabled children is that the policy will be for 'special needs' to be met in an ordinary, normal setting if

(a) it is in the best interests of the child
(b) it will not be against the interests of the other children.

Children should not be excluded from their peer group because of the severity of their handicap. If the parents of a handicapped child wish him to attend a local school, they may have to persuade the local education authority to put in ramps, provide extra care in the form of an extra helper, or arrange for suitable toilet facilities. They may have to be pretty persistent with their persuading, but they have the right to try.

The new system will work by using *assessments* and *statements*.

'Assessment' means investigation of a child's problems by experts in various fields, including doctors, teachers and other specialists, and including what the child's parents have to say.

'Statement' is the term used for the recommendations, made in the light of the assessment, as to what is needed for that particular child. Once this has been done the Local Education

Authority has a duty to provide the necessary help even though that child may not have reached school age.

*For children under 2:*

- The Local Education Authority (who may have been informed by the Health Authority that a particular child may have special needs) must ask parents' permission to assess a child's need.

- Parents who think their child may have a special need can ask the Local Education Authority to make an *assessment* of their child's difficulties.

This may result in quite simple help. The vital factor is that if relevant help is provided at an early stage, that is when it can do most good.

*For children of 2–5 years and upwards:*

- Local Education Authorities have a duty to place as many children as possible in ordinary schools in spite of handicaps and to provide the special help needed within the normal school setting.

The process of *assessment* and *statement* is done in stages and can take some time:

- Parents are involved at each stage, and if they disagree with an assessment by a particular expert they can ask to meet him and discuss the report.

- If parents do not agree with the final statement which indicates how the Local Education Authority sees their child's special needs, they can appeal against it.

*Statements* have to be reviewed every twelve months, so that children should continually get the treatment most appropriate to the stage they are at now. At last the sticky label situation, where a child may have been labelled once and for all (without any regard being paid to the fact that successful treatment may lead to 'no special treatment' being the most appropriate treatment of all) has gone.

This is good news. The bad news will be if resources are not made available to ensure that the spirit as well as the letter of the Warnock Inquiry into Special Education is observed. All too often when resources are inadequate it is the needs of under-

5s which are the first to be disregarded, as no one has a particular responsibility for this age group. Apart from any question of justice, this is a very false economy. The earlier necessary help is given to a child the less likely he is to need more costly help later on. This very obvious point seems to be a very hard one to get over to the people who make the rules, interpret the rules and allocate the available funds.

## The child with a special gift

Gifted children may seem to present rather different problems from handicapped children. Once the term 'handicapped' is translated to mean 'having special needs' we can see that the problems are common. Gifted children also have special needs in addition to the normal needs of 'normal' children. Parents of gifted children could also take a coloured pen and mark up anything relevant to their child in Chapters 1 to 11. They too would see that everything that applies to normal children applies to gifted children.

Gifts vary, as do handicaps:

- Some children show special abilities at an early age which reflect the gifts and interests of a member of their family.

- Others show a talent which seems to come from nowhere.

- Sometimes what appeared to be special gifts seem to disappear. This can be because these children were ahead of their peer group and then all the other children caught up. Or it may be that the child becomes an excellent all-rounder and is simply going to be good at everything.

- Sometimes special gifts only appear after the age of 7, because the ability is associated with developmental stages (such as very fine hand or body control) which come later than the early years.

- Sometimes a 'gift' is not necessarily exclusive. All children can do it or have it, but the 'gifted' child has much greater ability than the others. In this case recognition only becomes possible when a child goes to school or joins a class where measurement and comparison in relation to others of the same age shows up how much better this particular child is.

It would be encouraging to think that the same policy would be implemented for gifted children as for handicapped children:

■ That appropriate provision would be made for a gifted child after a wide consideration of his total needs.

■ That every child would have his gifts considered and his needs met – in addition to those who show outstanding ability.

A child-centred approach to assessing the needs of a gifted child, rather than just providing opportunity to develop the gift, could lead to much the same recommendation as for a handicapped child – the vital need to be in a normal situation:

■ A very young child with a special ability will pursue it for himself. This may lead to spending so much time on it that development in other directions is hindered. This child's special need may be to be encouraged to do other things too, rather than to be encouraged to concentrate even more on one ability. Concentrating exclusively on something that is not shared by the rest of a child's peer group can lead to missing a great deal in the early years which cannot be recovered at a later stage.

■ There is a difference between enabling a young child to pursue an interest at his own pace and positively pushing him in this direction. Too much emphasis on one ability can lead to parent and child assuming too much. It is usually the comparative element (how much better this child is than others) that is used as the measure of success. Using this yardstick can lead to disappointment, even a sense of failure at a later date, if other children start to catch up and the gap narrows.

Enabling a child to pursue a special interest or gift is usually not too difficult in the 0–7 age range. Most parents, groups and schools can keep up with the under-7s by using local resources. At later stages, when extra help and advice is needed, other parents who have had similar experience can be helpful. There may be a local group – or a local teacher – who has information. Finding out more from the National Association for Gifted Children would be a good start (see Appendix 1, page 291).

Taking an all-round view, the outlook for children with 'special needs' has improved, mainly because it has been recognized that they have 'normal needs' too:

■ As for the attitude of authorities who provide money and other resources, the door has been opened for them to change their priorities and their practice.

■ As for that tremendous group of society known as the general public, it may take another generation while children who have met, played with and worked with handicapped children in school grow up – but eventually, hopefully, everyone will come to realize that handicap is only one part of human personality.

■ And, not least, parents who have already learned just how powerful an influence they can be when they help each other and campaign together have been given the right for their views to be considered when provision is planned for their own 'special' child's 'special needs'.

## Deprived and socially disadvantaged children

Unfortunately there is another huge group of children who have 'special' needs, simply because their 'normal' needs are not being met:

■ The children who live in deprived families.

■ The children who live in deprived areas.

■ The children who live in inadequate housing.

■ The children who live in bed and breakfast accommodation and have no home.

■ The children who live in one-parent families, which so often become virtually no-parent families as the single parent struggles desperately to be mother, father and breadwinner.

■ The children removed from a family situation where they are abused and put into a non-family situation where they are abused.

■ The children who do not get the medical attention they need when they need it.

Perhaps it is time we stopped tinkering with isolated areas of deprivation. Stopping up gaps means that some casualties have occurred before the gap was noticed. Defining areas of specific deprivation involves creating boundaries, and where there are boundaries there will always be individuals on the borderline who lose out.

We need some definition of every child's rights, and we need one single authority to implement it. The short-term benefits to every individual, whatever label they are given, would be great. The long-term benefit to society would be inestimable.

# Chapter 13

## Tidy Thinking about Development

In spite of all that has been said so far about children developing at different rates, being individuals with different personalities, likes and dislikes, abilities and disabilities, there are times when we have to consider children in larger categories and groups.

In groups providing alternative care, or in mother and baby groups, parent and toddler groups and in nursery groups, we have to think in terms of providing for all the children who will be there even if what we have planned is not used by, or does not affect, some of the individual children.

The following figures should be helpful as a quick checklist to remind us about age-group characteristics.

**Figure 1** *Age-group characteristics at 0–3 months*

| Physical development<br>*Growing and developing* | Intellectual development<br>*Learning and remembering using information* |
| --- | --- |
| ■ grows fast and sleeps a good deal<br>■ becomes alert while awake<br>■ changes from being rather floppy to holding up head when carried<br>■ starts to wave arms about<br>■ starts to kick<br>■ learns to roll from side to back<br>■ holds a suitably shaped rattle in either hand<br>■ reaches out to hit things<br>■ starts to lift head and tries to pull up when hands are held<br>■ from seeing best at a distance of 10 inches, starts to watch intently things which are further away<br>■ responds to touch, grasps adult's fingers, wiggles toes when his feet are held | ■ soon learns to know his mother and if distressed will not respond easily to anyone else<br>■ learns familiar voices and stops crying when he hears them<br>■ becomes aware of other sounds and turns towards them<br>■ becomes aware of different smells<br>■ puts everything to his mouth<br>■ notices and looks intently at things which move<br>■ may respond to some colours, particularly bright ones, more than others<br>■ starts to make noises other than crying |

**HE NEEDS**
■ love, attention, security, stimulation, opportunity to play and exercise
■ something to watch, hear, touch

| Social development<br>*Adjusting to others, getting on with people* | Emotional development<br>*Feeling and expressing feelings* |
|---|---|
| ■ cries because he is hungry, cross, uncomfortable, frightened but then develops different cries which mothers can distinguish<br><br>■ will stop crying to listen<br><br>■ starts to make cooing noises<br><br>■ responds to a smile from someone else then starts to smile first. At 3 months, smiles at everyone happily<br><br>■ responds to strange adults unless very distressed<br><br>■ starts to enjoy being handled and relaxes at bath times<br><br>■ enjoys music and being sung to | ■ can get very frightened, very cross and can also glow with happiness. This is a time of extreme reaction which can change quickly<br><br>■ becomes very attached to his mother |

**HE NEEDS**
- someone to smile back at him and respond to his noise
- warmth and a safe place to kick with no clothes on

**Figure 2** *Age-group characteristics at 3–9 months*

| Physical development | Intellectual development |
| --- | --- |
| ■ progresses through sitting firmly when held to gradually supporting his own back and sitting up | ■ starts to know people as individuals and recognizes family names but can't say them |
| ■ learns to pull himself up to sitting | ■ is interested in everything but has some favourite playthings and books |
| ■ progresses through turning from side to back to rolling over easily and crawling | ■ enjoys looking at books and pictures and will point with finger |
| ■ goes from kicking vigorously to taking some weight on his feet to standing with support | ■ remembers what familiar 'action' toys do and laughs before they pop up or make a noise |
| ■ learns to hold things more efficiently then masters picking things up with thumb and forefinger. Hands grow larger as well as stronger and more skilful | ■ responds to peep-bo games and may start the game himself |
| | ■ looks for things which are dropped or have been hidden |
| ■ learns to 'let go' and drop things deliberately | ■ watches carefully when taken out for a walk |
| ■ uses both hands separately and together for holding | ■ starts to learn about near and far, hard and soft when he becomes mobile |
| ■ copies first automatically then deliberately what others do – particularly facial expressions | ■ deliberately splashes with hands in the bath |
| ■ puts things in containers then takes them out | |

**HE NEEDS**
- ■ time from adults to play, talk, sing, laugh with him
- ■ lots of slow walks with time to watch
- ■ many simple playthings – bricks, containers, noise makers, books

| Social development | Emotional development |
|---|---|
| ■ begins to respond and play with all members of the family but may become wary of strangers towards the end of this period | ■ shows rage and disapproval by stiffening his body and trying to throw himself backwards |
| ■ has 'conversations' by making a noise, waiting for a response then making a noise again | ■ pushes away anything he doesn't want or doesn't like |
| ■ 'calls' people by making a noise | ■ frowns while he is deciding whether or not to cry or object to something or someone |
| ■ tries to copy sounds | ■ gets cross if something is taken from him but can be distracted |
| ■ starts to really rock with laughter which makes other people laugh | ■ shows tremendous pleasure while playing or being played with |
| ■ copies simple actions like clapping or waving | ■ can be frightened by sudden loud noises or nasty surprises |
| ■ knows his own name when it is said | ■ may become distressed if other people are cross or speak sharply – not necessarily to him |
| ■ understands simple words and will look towards where the object is | |

■ **HE NEEDS**

■ somewhere safe to learn to pull himself up to standing and for crawling

■ lots of time to play in the bath

■ straps or harness, safety gates and guards for the other people in the home to get used to using them

**Figure 3** *Age-group characteristics at 9–18 months*

| Physical development | Intellectual development |
|---|---|
| ■ learns to crawl or get around the floor if he has not already done so | ■ once moving about learns more at first hand by touching and bumping into things, having a closer look |
| ■ learns to walk and uses furniture or something to hold on to or push | ■ watches and imitates and tries to do what the adult does |
| ■ may start to go upstairs on his front but will have difficulty coming down | ■ does not understand about too large, too small when fitting objects in containers – uses trial and error methods |
| ■ tries to climb up on furniture | ■ starts to have preferences |
| ■ gets up from a lying position to standing without adult help but may flop down on his bottom | ■ notices tiny little details |
| ■ puts things in containers and takes them out | ■ learns that 'things' have group names |
| ■ spends a long time fingering things and looking closely at them | ■ has little idea about cause and effect – why things happen and how to make them happen |
| ■ still puts things in his mouth | ■ does not concentrate for long |
| ■ has a good try at feeding himself and holding a cup | ■ forgets |
| ■ places one brick on top of another – maybe more – to make a tower | ■ has no idea of danger |
| | ■ learns to say a few words but understands many more |
| ■ scribbles with a crayon and dabbles in food | ■ may slow down talking while learning to walk but still quietly absorbs what is said to him. When he does start to talk he will start using all these 'absorbed' words |
| ■ watches for a ball rolled to him and tries to push it back. Crawls after a ball | |

**HE NEEDS**
- ■ a safe environment; a playpen is useful, safety gates essential
- ■ more words, more conversation from adults, even if he does not give back yet
- ■ encouragement and praise
- ■ more books and songs

| Social development | Emotional development |
|---|---|
| ■ may understand simple instructions: 'Give it to Mummy', 'Put your foot out' | ■ can get into a great rage if adults stop him doing something he wants to do |
| ■ may use some words. This varies a good deal. Average would be about ten | ■ can be cooperative about being dressed if he wants to be – and very uncooperative if he does not |
| ■ plays with people by throwing things down to be picked up | ■ can have quite a little tantrum if he is not given what he wants or something is taken from him – but soon forgets |
| ■ offers things to people and expects a simple 'thank you' in return – also expects to get back what he gave | ■ may show fear and distress in some situations – sudden loud noises, large noisy animals, noisy places |
| ■ may seem aggressive with other children but does not mean to be | ■ can be surprised and distressed when people say 'No' – and is puzzled because he doesn't know why |
| ■ has no idea of mine and yours and takes other people's things | |
| ■ can wait a little while for attention but expects to get it before other children | ■ looks towards his mother when he needs reassurance or information |
| ■ may find adults and other children are stopping him doing things, speaking firmly and saying 'No' and this is a new experience | ■ is surprised and distressed if something he does makes another child cry |
| ■ in a strange situation looks to his mother for reassurance and does not go far away from her even when mobile | |

**HE NEEDS**
- long leisurely outings
- opportunity to see other children
- more adult-type toys – telephone, dustpan and brush

*Figure 4 Age-group characteristics at 18 months–2 years*

| Physical development | Intellectual development |
| --- | --- |
| ■ can walk well and tries to trot – most children are flat-footed and walk fast rather than run – has difficulty in stopping | ■ language is becoming an important tool. Starts to ask 'what dat?' |
| ■ bends down well to pick things up | ■ repeats words adult says |
| ■ comes downstairs on his tummy with help and supervision | ■ uses a good many words and short sentences |
| ■ becomes efficient at using push and pull toys | ■ understands a great deal of what is said to him |
| ■ learns to push a pedal-less tricycle or trundle toy with his feet | ■ picks out objects which adult names |
| ■ throws a ball but does not aim very well. Has difficulty catching a ball | ■ recognizes objects from pictures and books |
| ■ makes heavier scribbles | ■ may match colours but does not name them |
| ■ tries to take off screw lids and uses screw toys | ■ may learn to do or help with a simple jigsaw |
| ■ works very hard at his play and uses more energy than is strictly necessary | ■ looks for something which he knows is hidden |
| ■ builds a small tower of bricks | ■ starts to match holes and shapes |
| ■ is learning to be 'clean' but may have more difficulty in keeping dry | ■ curious about everything but does not concentrate for long |
| | ■ starts to make choices and show preferences |

**HE NEEDS**
- a good deal of companionship and attention
- lots of words, conversation and being listened to patiently

| Social development | Emotional development |
|---|---|
| ■ starts using more words to get information and attention. By two years has perhaps as many as 200 words | ■ wants to do things for himself and gets very cross if not allowed to do so |
| ■ chatters to himself while he plays | ■ may get cross but can be loving and affectionate |
| ■ plays in the company of other children rather than with them and needs careful supervision | ■ may be independent one day and dependent the next |
| ■ enjoys the company of his family | ■ may show some fears and cry, hide his face or hide behind an object or person |
| ■ enjoys 'rough' games with a competent, trusted adult | ■ takes great pleasure in 'doing' and is not too concerned about failure |
| ■ listens carefully to what is going on around him and observes how others behave | ■ can be very distressed if other children hurt him |
| ■ uses language to attract attention but if this does not work will grab at the person he wants attention from | ■ can be very distressed when other children cry because he has hurt them |
| ■ may interfere with older children's games and their attitude to him may change | ■ may 'explore' in an unfamiliar situation, but returns to his mother frequently then goes off again |
| ■ fetches things for other people when asked | |
| ■ follows very simple instruction: 'Fetch your shoes', 'Sit in your chair for a drink' | |
| ■ favourite activity becomes 'helping' adults | |

**HE NEEDS**
- household work and routines to be slowed up so that he can help
- encouragement to do things for himself – which usually means allowing time for this

**Figure 5** *Age-group characteristics at 2–3 years*

| Physical development | Intellectual development |
| --- | --- |
| ■ is more reliable at using a potty and staying dry<br><br>■ starts to climb well<br><br>■ kicks a ball, tries to jump, stand on one leg and walk along low balancing board<br><br>■ may learn to somersault<br><br>■ learns to come downstairs upright one step at a time<br><br>■ learns to pedal a tricycle with feet on the pedals<br><br>■ tries to manage dressing but needs help, more successful at undressing<br><br>■ uses both hands for a long time yet but preference for one may start to show<br><br>■ learns to use suitable tools, hammer, smaller screw toys, spanner, tries to use scissors<br><br>■ builds well with bricks and learns to make a span bridge<br><br>■ more positive with crayons and paintbrush | ■ knows about and can point to own facial features and other people's. Knows names of head, foot, toes, arm<br><br>■ copies what adults do and gets it wrong because he doesn't know enough<br><br>■ interested in doing rather than making but interested in the result of his efforts<br><br>■ still asks 'What's that?' and uses language to get more information<br><br>■ experiments with colour and texture, learns more about shapes and colours. Sorts and matches but may not know names<br><br>■ has an idea of large and small, fat and thin<br><br>■ some simple pretend play<br><br>■ plays for longer and asks for help. May go back to a game<br><br>■ has some idea of time – before and after, when and tomorrow<br><br>■ remembers songs, stories, rhymes<br><br>■ can carry very simple messages<br><br>■ very single-minded and can forget everything except what he is doing |

**HE NEEDS**

■ patience, tolerance and understanding

■ plus a good deal of ingenuity in providing space, materials, opportunity for play

■ opportunity to play alongside other children

■ tact and care with a new-baby situation

| Social development | Emotional development |
|---|---|
| ■ wants to do things himself<br>■ may say 'No' and be defiant<br>■ very keen to have approval and asks for it<br>■ plays well within the family but can be disruptive in a group<br>■ enjoys being with other children and may play alongside rather than with<br>■ not ready to share and may take things from other children<br>■ learns more about protecting himself and his possessions<br>■ may involve mother in pretend games – other children are usually not able enough to cooperate<br>■ may have baby brother or sister about now – or older child goes to school so his experience may change<br>■ when approaching 3 the parent and toddler group may not be able to offer enough sessions or the necessary activities<br>■ he is not ready to stay alone in a new group but accepts somewhere new if mother goes too<br>■ there are big differences between children which become apparent when they are in a group | ■ may go through a period of tantrums<br>■ there is tension as he tries to become independent but still needs love and approval<br>■ begins to understand other people have needs and rights but still sees his own needs as more important than anyone else's<br>■ likes to laugh and enjoys silly songs and games<br>■ can get very cross and frustrated when he can't do things and equally cross with inanimate objects<br>■ may use play situations to 'play out' bad feelings so can appear to be wilfully destructive<br>■ may become quiet, shy and wary with strangers<br>■ may become jealous of the new baby, lonely when an older child goes to school<br>■ stays close by his mother in a new situation. May leave her for a little while but looks back to her and becomes distressed if she has moved or gone |

## HE NEEDS

- more safety precautions to take account of increasing mobility, ability and strength
- more books, songs, stories
- consistency – If the answer is NO today it ought to be NO tomorrow too
- an appreciation by parents that he may be 'different', 'forward', or 'backward' – but so are other children

**Figure 6** *Age-group characteristics at 3–4 years*

| Physical development | Intellectual development |
| --- | --- |
| ▪ usually reliable at being clean and dry | ▪ may have as many as 900 words |
| ▪ can run – and stop | ▪ persistent in asking questions, asks for help |
| ▪ very good at using a tricycle, climbing, jumping. Uses a swing | ▪ 'chatters' to people he knows well in a way that demands an answer – 'We like cakes, don't we?' |
| ▪ throws a ball further and harder but the aim may not be too accurate | ▪ remembers a sequence of actions |
| ▪ catches a ball with his whole body | ▪ follows instructions provided not too many given at once |
| ▪ learns to cut with scissors and use tools | ▪ gives very simple accounts of what he has done |
| ▪ learns to handle raw materials, tear paper | ▪ learns a good deal of information through practical play which helps develop concepts, basic skills and knowledge of materials |
| ▪ gradually learns to use just the right amount of energy with hands, feet and body to achieve what he wants to do | ▪ experiments deliberately |
| | ▪ starts to use construction kits so has some idea of 'parts of things' and fitting together |
| | ▪ learns names of colours – still has difficulty with shapes – matches pictures |
| | ▪ knows about large, medium, small |
| | ▪ learns how to play with other children |
| | ▪ learns to modify what he does, and his language, to conform to a group |
| | ▪ learns to accept and add to other children's ideas |
| | ▪ has strong opinions on what he wants to eat, wear, and do |

**HE NEEDS**
- other children to play with
- encouragement to do things for himself, work things out for himself
- time with other members of the family
- time for activities like dressing, putting toys away
- more books, stories
- materials to make things with, tools

| Social development | Emotional development |
|---|---|
| ■ tries hard to dress himself and manage in the lavatory | ■ finds it easier to accept a change of position in the family as he becomes more competent and confident |
| ■ may be helpful with a new baby | |
| ■ may deliberately be naughty | ■ may still show some jealousy of a new baby |
| ■ wants to please. Responds well to praise and acknowledgement | ■ may be very upset if not allowed to do what older brothers and sisters do |
| ■ watches and copies other children | ■ may see mother's insistence that he does things for himself as rejection – but will try to do them quite happily in a group where other children do |
| ■ may have difficulty in a group if he is at a different level of language development | |
| ■ may be confused if a group has different 'rules' than the ones he is used to | |
| ■ learns to play with age mates | ■ becomes ready to stay without his mother in a group but there may be a 'set-back' when he starts really joining in |
| ■ learns how to be accepted by older children – but will go and play on his own when he gets tired of this | |
| | ■ may get cross with other children |
| ■ learns to stay without his mother in a nursery group | ■ may appeal to adult for help: 'He won't let me have . . .' |
| ■ may be quiet and watchful at first. May get into difficulties when he 'branches out' | ■ quarrels tend to be forgotten and ignored quite quickly |
| ■ looks to adults for help if he has problems with other children | ■ may be apprehensive of bigger children and boisterous play and watches from a safe distance or near an adult |
| ■ in a group plays for short periods with many activities. Spends a lot of time watching | |

■ **HE NEEDS**
- more opportunity to develop body skills
- more adults to get to know
- to be taught 'good' behaviour and rewarded for 'good' behaviour – not Smarties, but praise and acknowledgement
- to be given small responsibilities and acceptance of the standard he can reach with these

**Figure 7** *Age-group characteristics at 4–5 years*

| Physical development | Intellectual development |
| --- | --- |
| ■ becomes competent in attending to his own needs (but can't manage shoelaces and complicated fastenings on clothes) | ■ may use about 1,500 words |
| ■ very competent physically; climbs, runs, jumps, balances | ■ asks what, how, when, who and also why |
| ■ better at ball games but not yet able to use a bat well | ■ can concentrate for longer |
| ■ tries to hop and skip but has difficulty | ■ learns more about spatial relationships (three-dimensional thinking) which allows for more complicated building and construction |
| ■ hand skills improve, can use smaller tools and gets better at making things and handling materials | ■ thinks first about what to do then does it – then elaborates |
| ■ may enjoy outings to a swimming bath | ■ will go back to an unfinished game |
| ■ may learn to ride a bicycle | ■ shows interest in more complicated books. Can follow a story and thinks about it |
| | ■ usually good at suitable jigsaws |
| | ■ knows colours and can pick out a coloured object when asked, sort into colours and give names of primary colours and some others |
| | ■ recognizes and matches shapes but may have difficulty in naming them, has difficulty copying them |
| | ■ becomes able at 'pre-learning' skills – some children interested in reading |
| | ■ may develop a special interest |
| | ■ interested in what adults do and watches carefully, asks questions and wants to help |

**HE NEEDS**
- help with rivalry which goes too far
- acknowledgement of effort as well as achievement
- tactful help for a non or slow achiever

| Social development | Emotional development |
|---|---|
| ■ starts to use language to negotiate, manipulate and lead | ■ can be selfish but will respond to the distress of others |
| ■ watches what other children do, comments on it, tries to do the same – or better | ■ may become an attention seeker if he does not get attention naturally |
| ■ confident, may boast, brag, and 'boss' others | ■ may become aggressive in words or deeds – or both |
| ■ pretend play can become elaborate and sustained for longer with a larger group | ■ doesn't forget quarrels so easily |
| | ■ reacts badly to 'You can't play' but does it to other children |
| ■ may have special friends | ■ may get cross if younger children spoil his game |
| ■ learns to take turns and becomes fierce about other children observing rules | ■ pretend and fantasy play may reflect direct experience or something which has worried him or which he has not understood |
| ■ may tattle-tale, blame other children for his own misdemeanours | ■ imaginary playmate may become evident |
| ■ may copy swearing and other undesirable behaviour | ■ gets better at deferring immediate wishes in order to have something better later |
| ■ can cooperate in groups which form and re-form | ■ can lose confidence if he 'fails' too often |
| ■ may suffer rejection temporarily, reject others in the same way | |
| ■ may be deliberately disobedient | |
| ■ can be expected to observe reasonable social rules when with adults | |
| ■ non-English-speaking children usually make good progress in an English-speaking group | |
| ■ in a group plays for longer periods. Spends less time watching than 3-year-olds | |

## HE NEEDS

- more complicated play activities and space and freedom from interruption to pursue them
- part-time attendance at a nursery group. Will make more progress if daily sessions follow each other rather than being spaced out over the week, because he can remember what he was doing yesterday

**Figure 8** *Age-group characteristics at 5–7 years*

| Physical development | Intellectual development |
|---|---|
| ■ very competent in many skills and improves on these | ■ has extensive vocabulary – perhaps 3,000 words |
| ■ develops more skill in hands and until this happens finds writing difficult | ■ needs short-term goals and to have progress noted in long-term projects |
| ■ grows thinner, taller and more graceful in movement | ■ usually starts to learn to read, may be slower learning to write |
| ■ starts using a bat to hit a ball. Enjoys practice so long as he actually gets the practice and is not out first go | ■ usually enjoys number work |
| | ■ learns more about cause and effect and enjoys experimenting |
| ■ starts 'showing off' his skills and does dare-devil tricks | ■ starts to draw with more detail |
| ■ may learn (if properly taught) to swim well | ■ enjoys colour and pattern work |
| | ■ may start to measure his progress against others |
| ■ may pick up childhood diseases | ■ may get less information, when he wants it, than he did at home |
| ■ speed of movement coupled with lack of knowledge of speed and distance of vehicles, and being single-minded, can lead him into traffic danger | ■ may find having to stop what he is doing to start something else irritating |
| | ■ enjoys stories – can remember what happened last if it is read in serial form |
| ■ mostly independent of adults in routine body needs | ■ very interested in toys and uses them as focus of play |
| ■ starts losing baby teeth | ■ improves at board games |
| | ■ may have trouble knowing right from left |

**HE NEEDS**

■ support with school activities
■ praise and encouragement along the way
■ new experiences and activities
■ smaller paintbrushes and other tools
■ time and opportunity to go back to an activity

## Social development

- uses language well
- may use language to be unkind – others may react badly to this
- shows rivalry
- may modify his behaviour to become part of a group
- may exaggerate and tell tall stories, enjoys verbal jokes
- may quarrel with other children but learns to 'make-up' by ignoring rather than forgetting there has been an argument
- may see home and school as quite different and keep them separate
- may use 'Well, my teacher says . . .'
- wants to be part of the 'in' thing or craze. Can make himself and his family very miserable over this
- can play happily alone with toys
- may adopt TV character as role model for games but not prepared to improvise, wants all the 'props'

## Emotional development

- can become despondent over 'failure' and not too willing to ask for help
- starts to compare his achievement with that of others
- may have a particular friend
- is interested in groups and wants to be a member
- rivalry may be good-natured but sometimes causes difficulties and aggression
- wants intensely what other people have
- wants his 'very own' toys
- responds with pleasure to what is around him and notices small details, living things, natural phenomena
- by 7 is usually confident and capable, understands other people have needs

## HE NEEDS

- help to practise games
- help to accept losing a game
- help with reading and lots of stories
- patience, sympathy and help with the 'I want' situation

# Part 2
## Providing for Play

Children play very well for themselves – and in the early years provide for themselves too by using what is around them.

There comes a time when they need to do more than explore – they want to 'do'. This is the point at which specific activities become important, and adults have to make special provision for these.

# Chapter 14

# Tidy Thinking about Play Activities and Materials

### Play activities

If we watch a child making an intricate building with a set of large blocks, how do we define his activity?

- Is he being creative? The raw material is being used to create something which is a whole rather than a set of units. What he is making looks attractive, and a photograph of what he has done would look just as decorative as one of his paintings.

- Or is this imaginative play? He is stopping to think and work out exactly how he wants it to be, and makes adjustments from time to time so he has some idea in his mind.

- Or is he developing pre-learning skills? He is selecting each block very carefully and making sure it is the right size and shape to fit into his design. Even then he may reject or change it if he suddenly realizes he will not have enough of one kind to complete his building unless he is careful about how he uses what he has.

- Or is he developing manipulative skill and improving his hand–eye coordination as he places the blocks carefully to make a ramp or a bridge – then has another look and makes minute adjustments without knocking everything down?

- Or is it group play if he lets another child or children help by telling them what to do, or listens to and considers suggestions from them (he may simply say 'Go away, I'm doing this'), so that there is an element of social play and development there?

Categorizing and separating out different types of play is something adults think about rather than something children do. The terms physical activity, creative play, imaginative play, construction play, manipulative play, adventure play, group play, help when adults are learning about and planning for play. As far as children are concerned, all kinds of play interweave and interlock.

So long as categorizing and making sense of play activities does not lead to 'not seeing the wood for the trees', it can be helpful in the same way that a passing knowledge of nutrition is useful in planning meals and buying food and making sure essential items are not missing from the diet. By looking at the materials and activities appropriate to the various stages of development we can choose the most useful birthday or Christmas present, or plan how nursery group funds can best be used, or organize such space as we have at our disposal so that children can use it to the best advantage, or decide that we have to look outside the home for opportunities for activities that are not possible within it. It can also be helpful when considering the stage children are at – perhaps giving a lead as to why they have difficulty with a particular activity or don't seem interested in it or use the material destructively.

At home, hopefully, children have opportunities for all kinds of play over a period of time. In nursery groups one would positively expect some representative activities from each kind of play to be provided for each and every session.

## Play materials

Adults also tend to think of play materials in categories. The child who was building with bricks could have been using cardboard cartons sealed up with Sellotape and fixing them together with sticky paper tape, staples or glue. We might, at a casual glance, have decided he was just playing with junk. It might have been junk to us, and when he finished his game it might have been junk to throw away to the child too, but while he was playing with it it was very useful play material. The building made of boxes would have demanded more skill and imagination than the one made with blocks. He would have to adjust his ideas to suit the materials, and think about what he still needed and where to get it from.

It can be helpful to think of play materials in categories so long as we bear in mind that there are many categories:

■ Basic, natural materials (sand, water, clay, wood and dough).

■ Basic materials to be bought (bricks and blocks, construction sets, matching and grading materials, fit together materials).

■ Very useful items of machinery (tricycles and wheeled toys).

■ Equipment for climbing, sliding and other forms of physical activity.

■ Tools (which may be toy tools or real tools of a suitable size).

■ Materials which can be improvised.

■ Materials which can be made by skilful adults.

■ Materials children can borrow from adults.

■ And there are toys. These are specific items designed by adults to be sold to adults to give to children. Toy libraries are becoming more common. They were originally started for use by parents of handicapped children, but like a good many more excellent ideas which started in this way they are useful for all children. These could be a very good way of providing children with toys without spending a lot of money or making expensive mistakes.

Sorting out and categorizing play material can be useful in the same way as thinking clearly about play activities. It helps adults to organize what they need to do. Children don't think about play material in the same way and our categories won't necessarily mean anything to them. They don't worry about how much something cost or whether it was intended to be used in that way or whether the one piece they are using is part of a set.

## Buying play materials

Providing bought play materials for children can be a complicated as well as a costly business these days. Adults like to see their children happy and busy, they like their children to have what other children have, and they desperately want their children to 'get on' and do well. This means that adults buying toys are very vulnerable to advertising which uses words like 'educational', 'teach', 'learn', and 'develop'.

Toy catalogues have a slightly dated sameness about them as far as basic play materials are concerned. Modern materials and fashionable colours may have been introduced, but the old well-tried materials are there in every range.

Some of the newer toys and playthings do have a distinctive style which immediately identifies a particular firm or manufacturer. In order to keep their image lively and 'fresh' in a very competitive business, designers have to keep introducing new ideas and gimmicks. They may deliberately create a product which is clever or cute or complicated and is intended to appeal to the adult who does the buying. They bring out 'new' versions. The results have more to do with the world of marketing than the world of play.

## Making and improvising play materials

Even with a cupboard full of smart expensive toys, children can miss out on opportunities for satisfying play which allows them to develop and learn rather than simply owning playthings which limit their own contribution to a game. The joys of playing with sand and water or an old cardboard carton can be lost unless we bear in mind a basic list of activities and materials and look carefully at what children are actually doing.

Not buying toys is not mean. It makes sense for children to improvise and become inventive. They do it naturally, given the chance. It makes sense for children to realize that not everything has to be manufactured, and it makes sense for them to learn that we can't go out and buy everything we want.

Obviously some playthings cannot be improvised – for example a tricycle. Some playthings which parents might have made some years ago, such as a climbing frame, perhaps, now involve large quantities of materials which have become too expensive to risk a failure or mistake. Even so, it makes sense for parents to improvise and provide home-made material where possible in order to save for those things which do have to be bought.

There are some positive advantages in using improvised

and home-made playthings which may not be so obvious. Improvised materials are less durable than bought items, but they can be replaced. This ensures a change and allows for modification. A petrol pump for a pedal car (or tricycle if that is what a toddler decides needs petrol) may start off as a cardboard tube from a kitchen roll which he found for himself. This soon gets squashed, so we find him a piece of plastic tubing or garden hose and nail it to the wall outside or tie it to a hook indoors. Then he decides this is not good enough so we fit an empty, clean squeezy bottle with a pump action top to the end of the hose. He enjoys this for a while then forgets all about the game. The bits may fall off the wall or we decide it has looked unsightly long enough and take it down – but the most likely thing to happen is that the child decides he wants the tube for something else, and it ends up in the sand-pit or water play or as a tow bar to tow a cardboard box with his tricycle.

The term 'home-made' may conjure up ideas which, except in relation to food, give the impression of make do and mend and a flavour of second-best. If we start to use the term 'hand-made' this gives quite a different feeling. In many cases hand-made play materials are better finished, last longer and are made from better-quality materials than those which can be bought. This applies particularly to dressing-up clothes, dolls' clothes and bedding, dolls' houses, garages and playboards.

Hand-made toys can be provided at just the right time when a child's interest shows he needs them. They can be made or provided to suit a particular child, and his own ideas can be incorporated, which makes them really special.

## Play material in nursery groups

Nursery groups do not have the resources of a kitchen cupboard to be raided for borrowing, and they have many children to provide for. They will have to buy virtually all the equipment they need, and because it gets long and hard wear it has to be strong and durable.

A good supportive group of parents is essential as regards providing material from home, saving useful junk, making new items and keeping everything clean and in good repair – plus raising money to buy equipment. Those nursery groups or classes which do not have the support of an active, interested parent group may be less well equipped than a home unless they have adequate financial resources. This is something a parent should check when choosing or accepting a place for their child in a group.

Some nursery groups have close links with others in the area, and may share expensive items such as jigsaw puzzles and books so that children can have a change without extra money being needed. Groups may also have a group borrowing scheme for the larger items such as trampolines, so that they can be tried out to see if they would be a sensible purchase for a particular group of children.

## The quantity and quality of play experience

Along with the tidy thinking we do about play activities and play materials we also have to consider the situation in which a child is playing. Much of the early learning and playing children do is influenced by the adults or other children who are there, by whether or not a particular situation gives opportunity for progression, and by how often this play opportunity actually arises.

We can take a simple example of children and cooking:

- It should be a common experience, since cooking is associated with eating and everybody eats frequently.

- It does not require extra or special expenditure, so it ought to be within the range of every child's experience, whatever his circumstances.

- All children are interested in food.

This is one activity we could reasonably expect all children to have equal opportunity to play at and learn from. Yet their experience can be very different, as the accounts below show. (Both children are real children living within six miles of each other, and both are boys.)

John didn't see much cooking at home. His mother used as many convenience foods as possible and, to fit in with the adult's needs, the main meal was prepared in the evening after John had been put to bed.

At 2 he went to full-time nursery group with an age range

of 2–4. There were no facilities for cooking and the staff, although the right number in ratio to children as recommended, were very stretched because of the high proportion of young children who needed mothering care.

They did make a big effort to include some food preparation in their programme of activities, and had a sandwich-making or biscuit-icing session for all the children once every half-term. John was ill on one of these occasions, so during his 2-year nursery group stay he cooked eleven times.

At the age of 4 he started full-time infant school and went into the reception class. The reception class teacher was very keen to do some cooking activities, but all the children were as inexperienced as John and needed a good deal of help. The rare cooking sessions that could be fitted into the timetable had to be tightly organized to fit in all the children and became more of an adult-directed exercise than a true learning experience.

By the age of 7 John knew something about cooking and enjoyed it, but lacked confidence, needed and expected a great deal of help and was anxious about whether or not what he cooked had 'come out right'.

Andrew lived in a home where a great deal of cooking was done. The pattern of the family meals meant that he saw most of the food preparation. Because of the way the kitchen was arranged, his mother did most of the food preparation on a kitchen table where he could see what she was doing from his high chair (as opposed to what happens in modern kitchens where mothers work on a higher surface facing a wall and all children can see is her back). As he grew older he could also reach what she was doing and gradually started to join in when he felt like it.

At $2\frac{3}{4}$ years he was settled in to a nursery group of 3–5-year-old children. The average age of the children was higher than in John's group. The staff did not have to spend so much time on mothering and were able to provide some kind of food preparation every day with a small group of children.

At 3 years, Andrew started attending three sessions each week without his mother. Although his turn to cook came only twice every three weeks, he could watch someone cooking every day if he felt inclined. Some of the children he watched were nearly 5 and very competent. He also continued to watch and help his mother at home, particularly when she was doing anything new or especially interesting, and he was allowed to help more as his ability increased.

By the age of 5 Andrew was knowledgeable about cooking and competent at simple processes. He was also philosophic about anything that did not turn out as expected, since he could have another go quite soon. He usually had some idea of what had caused the problem – the butter was too hard to spread and 'broke' the slice of bread, the icing was too runny because it had too much water in it, the cakes had burned because they had been in the oven for too long or it had been too hot, the pastry stuck to the rolling pin because it was too sticky and needed more flour.

At 5 he went to an infant school where the infant teacher had no more resources than John's teacher had – but all the children starting in the class were as competent as Andrew. They didn't need so much help with their cooking and if any child got into difficulties one of the others helped with the problem.

Cooking was a regular and frequent feature on the timetable and was linked to reading, writing and maths work. By the time he was 7 Andrew could read a simple recipe with a little adult help, weigh dry ingredients, measure fluid ones, knew what stir, mix, rub-in, cream and whisk meant, knew about temperatures and oven settings.

These accounts show two extremes, but they are by no means rare. There are plenty of children who will have exactly the same experiences as John and Andrew. The reason for the difference in their levels of skill lay in their experience rather than their personal ability. This is just one instance of looking at one activity (John was much more able at building with bricks than Andrew, in case anyone is feeling sorry for him), but the point remains – when we are doing our tidy thinking about play activities we have to bear in mind both the quantity and quality of the child's experience.

The following chapters have been given names and follow themes which are intended to introduce the whole range of play activities rather than to suggest that a child has to be organized into doing them. If we provide the opportunities he will organize himself perfectly well.

# Chapter 15

## Physical Activity – Growing Larger, Stronger and More Skilful

Babies start life as floppy beings with very little control over what they do. The 7-year-old has grown to half his adult size, and along the way has developed rapidly: he can walk, run, jump, balance, pick things up and put them down and use tools and machines, he can throw, catch, kick and hit objects. Provision had to be made at each stage to give opportunity, encouragement and enjoyment, or these skills would not have developed.

### Getting around

Once children learn to walk they practise until they can do it well and then start on variations, doing tricks and showing off. Walking straight lines, bendy lines, on stepping stones or up and down slopes is quite difficult – they have to keep their eyes on where they are stepping and concentrate much harder than just walking head up in a straight line.

Crawling is something we associate with babies but older children enjoy this too, as part of an assault course which they make for themselves or which can be laid out for them.

Once children are able to run well they do it for a specific purpose rather than just for the sake of doing it. They need a clear space or path which is safe enough not to trip over and soft enough to fall on if they do. It seems to encourage them if they have something to run to – perhaps a climbing frame, a sandpit, a swing or just a special tree or maybe a rabbit hutch. If the special feature is something where they need supervision, then it needs to be within sight of a window or somewhere where an adult can comfortably keep an eye on them.

## Jumping and bouncing

Once babies are past the stage of using adults as something to jump and bounce on, the adult role is usually stopping them jumping and bouncing on stairs, furniture and beds, particularly bunk beds. Providing something which is suitable to bounce on is usually more effective than just saying 'No'. Restricting the height and providing something soft to land on is most important.

Some parents and nursery groups say trampolines are invaluable, but nasty accidents can occur on these. Even if the trampoline has a bar to hold, the bar can never be the right height as the height of the child's body changes as he jumps. This equipment should never be left unattended, and if adults can't be there it should be put away.

## Balancing and rocking

Learning to balance well takes time and practice, and some children find it very difficult. Rocking toys involve not so much balance as a shift of balance to make the toy or equipment rock.

## Climbing

This starts when children want to get from one level to another and it carries on because they enjoy it. As they usually find it easier to climb up than down (their arms and hands are stronger and more skilful than legs and feet), it is often associated with jumping off, or falling off, so anything which is meant to be climbed should have a soft surface underneath. Climbing frames with a slide to come down on are great favourites, but removing the slide occasionally does offer climbing down practice.

## Riding

Some very painful sessions are spent learning to ride a machine just for fun, yet these are the first stages towards achieving speeds and distances that the human body alone cannot reach. A strong 5-year-old on a good tricycle can out-run any parent trying to keep up with him, and go on doing so long after the adult has run out of puff.

The child's first task is to learn to balance his trunk firmly enough to be able to use feet and legs to move the machine and hands and arms to steer it. Then there is a long progression to different and finer movements at the same time. There is no point in giving small children wheeled vehicles which they cannot control. To begin with they need to use their feet as both propelling power and braking power, which means their feet should touch the ground. Something which is too big can hinder confident progress.

Bicycles with stabilizers are a half-way measure and do the balancing for the child until he has mastered the movement of pedalling and steering and braking with his hands. Once he is fully confident and feels comfortable with the bicycle the stabilizers can come off, and he learns to balance just on two wheels.

Roller skates and skateboards may come at the end of the seventh year, but they are difficult to manage because no part of the child is in contact with the ground. The wheels move fast and freely and there is no way of stopping except by swaying the body. Children do a lot of falling off before they can use this equipment safely and well. They need a large, flat surface where they will not bump into other children, where traffic will not bump into them, which is soft enough to fall on, and this is not an easy combination to find.

Whether trundle toys, tricycles and bicycles have a useful place in nursery groups is debatable. They are one-child toys, they are expensive, they need a lot of storage space as well as riding space, and they can be the cause of a lot of quarrels. On the other hand, in an area where children don't have an opportunity to use them at home, perhaps because they live in a crowded environment or have no garden, or it is a country area which is very hilly, they can be seen as a useful experience to offer. Even so, some thought has to be given as to how tricycles can be safely used in a group. Letting children loose on them when there really isn't enough space is asking for trouble.

## Pushing and pulling

The first useful pushing toy is a baby walker truck, mainly because it provides good support for the new toddler rather than because it can be used as a carrier for toys. They usually have good strong wheels and a low centre of gravity. It is not a very fast vehicle but that is its advantage. Something which moves too freely would run away with the child. As they become more skilful in their movements children learn to manoeuvre dolls' prams, pushchairs and wheelbarrows.

Toys for pulling are quite a different matter, as they do need to run freely. Just pulling something soon loses its appeal for little children once they have managed the rather lop-sided balance necessary, so the most useful are toys which make a noise. If they can hear it they know it is still there. Older children really use their pull-along trucks and wagons and become adept at using a simple steering system. A 5-year-old parking his tricycle and attached trailer can usually do a very good three-point turn. Larger trucks can be two-person equipment which is useful for nursery groups.

## Throwing, catching, kicking and hitting

These activities are associated mainly with sport. Many of us realize early on in our growing up that our lack of expertise and prowess in these directions means we will never be top-notch games players. It is the exception rather than the rule to reach the dizzy heights of Wembley or Wimbledon. Sports, however, can be played at many levels, and are enjoyable leisure pursuits which quite simply give point to fresh air and exercise apart from being a socially acceptable outlet for competitiveness and a means of channelling aggression. They can bring a self-confidence which may not be achieved in other ways, and they can widen social and geographical horizons. Games are useful as well as fun, and everyone can benefit even if they are not very good at them.

Games skills have to be learned and practised, and the 0–7-year period is a time when children make a start rather than achieve any great ability. If we can make this start successful and enjoyable then it will be a good start. Under-7s are going to need adult help with this learning. A group of young children doesn't usually include any individuals who are able enough to keep a ball moving in the right way to give opportunities for as many goes at catching and throwing, kicking and hitting as the children need to keep their interest. This is one time when adult help, even adult leadership, is going to be needed.

We associate sports most often with a ball, but a proper

ball is not necessarily the best object to learn with during early stages. It can be too hard and can move too fast and too far. A 2-year-old will find a plastic ice-cream box easier to kick than a ball. A 3-year-old might catch a soft ball or bean bag more easily than a hard ball.

## Building and making

Children learn a lot about building in the first seven years. First they place things together. It takes them some time to work out how to create strength in a construction by interlocking and counter-balancing the bricks. Once they want to make rather than just build, they need simple self-locking pieces which fit firmly together.

The next stage is using a separate agent to join two pieces, which could be nuts and bolts, screws, pegs or glue; staples, paper clips and even rubber bands may serve.

There is a bewildering variety of construction sets on the market. If a child can have enough opportunity to try the different types, to make sure the pieces are the right size for his hands and the joining method is appropriate for his degree of skill and manipulative ability, then this should help in making a choice. It may be possible to borrow some to try out before actually buying a set.

Many nursery groups say they are disappointed by the quality of the brick and block play which goes on there. This could be due to lack of sufficient material and/or lack of space in which to use it. The other drawback could be time. A good building game takes time to develop. If the bricks and blocks have to be put away too quickly and the work taken to pieces each time, the children can never progress. It is interesting to see what happens if an adult makes a quick sketch of what has been done and remakes it quickly before the children arrive the next morning.

In groups which have a low average age, the young children can't learn by watching older ones and a bit of tactful adult interest may make a difference.

## Using machines and tools

Baby toys such as hammer pegs and screw toys are an excellent start to using tools. There has to be a reasonable progression in what we provide, to suit the size of their hands and the difficulty of the action needed to use them. Some toy tools are not as efficient as they should be. Screwdrivers should fit the slot in the screws they are meant to be used with, the slots should be deep enough to get a good purchase, spanners should be a good fit, and screws and bolts should have threads which are strong enough not to strip when inexperienced hands apply more than necessary pressure.

At the beginning, just using the tool itself is enough to satisfy small children. When they progress to wanting to make things, they need enough in quantity as well as quality of well chosen materials. Later they will prefer real tools in a suitable size rather than a toy set.

## Hand–eye coordination

This is a very limited term. By the time they are 7 most children are good at using hands and eyes together, using eyes and feet together – in fact they are good at using their whole bodies skilfully and gracefully.

We take this for granted, yet when we come across a 7-year-old who is not so skilful we hear him being called clumsy, butterfingers and other derogatory terms. Unfortunately, by the time the need for help has become so obvious that it cannot be ignored this child also thinks of himself as clumsy – which makes things worse.

If we think back to an occasion when we have had a bandaged thumb or fingers, this will have given us some idea of the clumsy child's experience. We felt harried and defensive as we fumbled with coins at the shop till with other people waiting impatiently behind – then we felt stupid as we dropped the change the check-out girl thrust at us in exasperation – and we felt even more desperate when we had difficulty in picking up coins from the floor as the queue of people had to move their feet for us to find them. We probably took twice as long to do anything, and put off doing it at all for as long as possible. We were not being stupid or careless or lazy but we got cross with ourselves – and with other people if they commented on our slowness.

Giving all children the opportunity to reinforce skills might help these less skilful children earlier. Just about everything children do comes into this category, but some activities are particularly helpful – all the putting in/taking out, fitting together and taking apart toys, all the tools, all the physical activities, plus anything which encourages control and following a pattern.

## Cooperating and combining strength

Two-person playthings such as double rockers, seesaws, very large trucks and cardboard cartons of the size that washing machines come in are more often to be found in the nursery group than in the home for obvious reasons.

Actually working with someone else means more than adding our strength to theirs. We have to adapt our movements, work out when to lift, pull, push, go forward or backward or turn sideways, when to raise or lower our end of whatever is being carried, when to stand still as the other person moves and vice versa. Think back to DIY sessions of wallpapering, putting up shelves, moving furniture through doorways or doing emergency repairs on a car when two not very experienced people are working together, and we begin to appreciate the learning that starts with a seesaw or manoeuvring a heavy wooden truck full of sand.

The same skills of working together apply to more than just shifting things around and using physical strength. They relate to any situation where people cooperate – perhaps by thinking together, planning together, designing and creating together. These cooperating skills are the essence of good team work, and they start to be learned at the age of 3 with a 3-year-old friend.

## Specific physical skills

There is a tendency for activities like swimming, gymnastics and dancing to be started earlier than used to be the case some years ago – not so much to teach the children, as they are usually not ready for proper teaching and coaching until well after the age of 7, but to introduce them to the idea and provide them with another experience.

### SWIMMING

Some swimming groups encourage introducing very tiny babies to a swimming bath to get them confident in preparation for later learning. Parents who are confident water people are often enthusiastic about this. This is a specialist field, and information will be available at your local swimming pool if there is a swimming club there. Warm water, space, a secure confident parent and short enjoyable sessions are essential if this early experience is to be successful.

### GYMNASTICS

In some areas there are opportunities for special gym sessions for very young children. They start by working with their mothers, using specially designed equipment, and then progress to working in a small group with a special instructor while mothers sit and watch (see Appendix 1, page 297). The sessions are short and geared to the age of the children. Most children who attend enjoy them enormously, and the mothers who bring them are enthusiastic about how much confidence their children gain. This makes sense, since if children did not enjoy it and mothers were not enthusiastic they would not be there.

The sessions are relatively expensive compared with play-group fees, since the cost of expensive equipment and trained instructors plus insurance inevitably has to be recovered. The fees may mean that the children who would benefit most, those from homes with restricted circumstances and finances, are not going to be able to go.

### DANCING LESSONS

Some teachers hold movement sessions rather than dancing lessons for young children from the age of 3. It should be possible to find out more about these from local advertisements and word of mouth, and it would be sensible to ask about the teacher's qualifications.

### 'SOFT' ROOMS

By this rather inadequate description is meant the furnishing of a suitable area in a leisure centre or sports centre with the new types of soft equipment made of covered foam plastic. Children can climb, roll, bounce or somersault on these large shapes and mats without coming to any harm. Some of this material was originally designed for use by handicapped children and, like a good deal of other equipment which comes from this source of ideas, is very much enjoyed by the non-handicapped.

Soft rooms, which may be known by other names, are suitable for under-7s, and sometimes a nursery group regularly books a session when they can take all their children. Unfortunately they seem to exist only in large urban areas, but it is a relatively new idea and hopefully will become more popular. It could become a facility which schools might share, or which local district councils might bear in mind when considering allocation of funds for leisure provision in their area.

### ADVENTURE PLAYGROUNDS

These are areas where children can run about, climb, swing, jump and play Tarzan games on equipment specially provided or natural materials specially adapted and, most important of all, under strict adult supervision. They are usually intended for children over 7, and on the whole are found only in large urban areas or within holiday or leisure situations, where they make a welcome alternative to adult-designed thrills like the Big Dipper and other fairground attractions.

Younger children may enjoy outings to the conventional children's areas in local parks, which may or may not be imaginatively laid out and equipped. The equipment and the situation may not be as safe as one might expect (see page 229). Parents can play a very useful role in monitoring what goes on and reporting any repairs which ought to be carried out.

### MUSIC AND MOVEMENT SESSIONS

A relatively recent opportunity available in some areas is music and movement sessions for young children with their mothers. Activities are simple – doing action songs, singing songs together, very simple movement games, listening to different instruments and short pieces of music – not unlike what happens in some nursery groups during part of their session. The difference is that the children's mothers are there. There can be a spin-off from this, because mothers who know the songs and games will carry on with these activities at home.

With careful planning the songs can become more difficult and cover a wide range of music, and the movement can progress from a child sitting on his mother's lap at the age of 1 to 'dancing' by himself at the age of 3. Local libraries will probably have details of these groups.

# Chapter 16

# Learning and Playing about Homes and People

This is the most inevitable and natural kind of play. Learning about his environment and the people in it is both the keystone and the stepping stone for any individual to become an independent adult. Since home is where a young child spends his time, his learning will start there. How the children do this learning is often labelled imaginative play – but it is much more than that, as we can see if we watch what the children do. They learn to cooperate, communicate, practise physical skills, pre-learning skills and learn about groups.

## Family play

AT HOME

Babies at home look and listen, then copy and imitate what adults do. They progress to pretend and imaginative games based on what they see and hear. Family play for under-3s means having scaled-down equipment which is similar to that which adults use.

As they grow older children want to do more than just copy. They create situations in which they are the boss figure. They need a private little space near the rest of the household where they can pretend to do all the things they see going on in the home which mean anything to them – looking after children (dolls) comes high on the list, plus cooking and eating, cleaning and shopping, washing and ironing. Both boys and girls enjoy this play because it is what they know best.

Usually they provide for themselves by borrowing what they need for play, but material can be improvised or made.

Within reason, the simpler it is the better. As they grow older they like extra detail, but not necessarily the detail a toy designer provides. They are not wanting to do real cooking, or washing or ironing. They just want to pretend at their own level. Equipment which is too complicated can be intimidating, and they have to spend time learning to master it rather than using it.

### IN THE NURSERY GROUP

Family play changes and takes a leap forward in the nursery group. There are more children to take part and they can take on different roles from the 'boss' role played by the child at home who has only himself to please.

The new young children watch what the older ones do and may be allowed to play if they are willing to be a baby or a visiting friend. Boys who played happily at home pretending to cook meals, pour tea and ironing find themselves pushed out to be the Daddy who goes out to work (and this happens whether or not this reflects the children's actual experience). This can be difficult for them, because children are not usually very knowledgeable about what Daddies do when they go out of the door each day unless it is a job with which the children can identify. Nevertheless boys do enjoy family play, and sometimes push the bossy girls out or find themselves an acceptable role – 'Well I'll be the milkman, then, and come in for a cup of tea.' Sometimes one child opts out of the larger group and plays happily alone in the home corner quite oblivious to what is going on around him.

The success of the play does not depend on how much has been spent on the equipment any more than it does at home, but with a larger group and more use the materials need to be strong and durable and generous in quantity. The space used needs to provide privacy, carefully balanced with the need for young children to be able to see some of what goes on without committing themselves to joining the group and running the risk of rejection. It should contain all the basic activities which go on in a real home. A toddler-sized doll is a great asset. It can be given treatment even the most tractable 3-year-old would complain about bitterly.

It is important that equipment is kept in good condition and tidy enough to be attractive, but there has to be a balance between the adults rushing in every time there is no one in the

home corner and having a good tidy up, which prevents children going back to finish or extend their game, and the situation where everything is such a mess that no one wants to play there.

Family play at home inevitably reflects the family. Within a nursery there can be different ethnic groups and it is important that these groups are represented in the play equipment. This makes each individual child feel comfortable – and different cooking pots, clothes, dishes, dolls of different colour and feature, and observing different ways of doing simple everyday routines is not a bad way to start a culture exchange at the age of 3.

If family play is disappointing or underused in a nursery group, it may be that the group consists of very young children with no older ones to lead. Adults could adapt what is offered to include real cooking, polishing and cleaning under supervision, and in effect play the same role as a mother does at home when the children join in with what she is doing. It may simply be that what is offered is not sufficient and that there are not enough basic items to gain the interest of the children. Introducing something new from time to time always creates interest.

If one group of children (usually older and usually boys) keep rushing into the home corner, wrecking it, and rushing out again they need a telling off – but they also need a den.

### Doll play

For successful doll play, the dolls we provide have to 'grow' with the children. Babies like soft simple dollies or teddies to hug and drag around by one leg. As the children grow older and more capable, dolls which can be treated as babies and dressed, bathed, put to bed or sat up to a pretend table are more appropriate.

There needs to be a similar progression with doll's clothes and equipment such as cots, beds, prams, pushchairs and dolly bathing bowls. If we match the doll to the child this is a good yardstick.

Eventually boys move on to Action Man type manikins and girls to dolls which resemble themselves or even teenagers. The interest lies more in the wardrobe and equipment which comes with the doll. The doll itself simply becomes a focus for a miniature situation where the child can be in charge and uses organizational skill rather than free imagination. Dolls' houses lead to the same kind of play. The simpler they are the better, as this leaves the child free to have enough elbow room and scope to play freely.

### Dens and hidey-holes

Small toddlers who graduate from a playpen often find a space which is their favourite place to play, and hopefully this will be respected by other family members as far as possible. This question of space is more than just elbow room to play. There are invisible barriers in the way a home is used – the little area children use, the shared areas everyone uses, and the 'adult only' areas from which children are banned such as near the cooker, the top of the stairs or a best piece of furniture they are not allowed to play on. This ruling and regulating is very valuable. When we live in any group or community, 'what is mine', 'what I must share', 'what I must respect because it belongs to someone else' applies not only to space but to property, human relationships and privacy in any culture.

Dens are simply private spaces in which a small group of children are able to carry out their own private activities. We usually discover they need a den when they find one for themselves – or start wrecking other areas of a nursery group. This often happens at the rising-5 stage and is one of the problems adults complain about. The answer is to give them a space, or to let them keep what they have found for themselves. It doesn't need to be elaborate. We don't have to worry about giving them something to do in it, as they will work that out for themselves. Boys seem to be happy just to be in there and nearly-5-year-old girls are quite capable of organizing what they want to have – but we may have to provide alternatives if equipment which is needed elsewhere keeps disappearing into the private place.

### Hospital play

At home this game may be sparked off by some direct experience – or adults may feel it is a good idea to suggest this by providing some simple props because they know some kind of medical experience is coming up soon, such as a visit to the dentist or an injection.

In nursery groups it may be provided as part of dressing up or occasionally the home corner is given over to this activity. The play usually becomes more intense when one of the children has just had a spell in hospital.

As with all pretend play, the most useful props are the simplest. A tabard with a red cross can be acceptable for either doctors or nurses, a cap made from stiff paper or a collar cut from an old shirt, a few bandages, the fingers cut from rubber gloves for finger stalls, and a toy stethoscope (although a real one would be better) would be a good start. Don't forget the smell. Most adults only have to sniff a trace of antiseptic to be reminded of hospitals and surgeries. A tiny dab of Dettol on an old handbag provided to keep all the kit in can do more to create an atmosphere than the most elaborate equipment sold in toy sets.

## Playing shops

There is not much to be said about shopping play these days. For most children the shopping games played two decades ago – asking for things, weighing out, wrapping and paying, the 'may I have, have you got, please and thank you' exchanges are quite lost, as they rarely see this any more. The nearest we can get to it is a shopping trolley and lots of empty, re-sealed cartons. Some children like using a cash register but it is the pop-out, crash-bang element enjoyed by younger children rather than the adding up and organization of coins that 4–5s used to do which we see.

Children still can and do enjoy weighing things on a proper old-fashioned set of scales with weights. They can use sand, conkers, potatoes or anything else which comes to hand and, of course, weighing can be part of a cooking session.

Wrapping things is a useful occasional activity, with old boxes, pretty wrapping paper salvaged from Christmas and birthdays, and rather extravagant use of Sellotape.

There are other 'services' children may be aware of and enjoy playing:

- An office game with an old typewriter, rubber stamps and ink pads, staplers and paper clips, envelopes, cards and paper, a few trading stamps to lick and stick on envelopes. The need for a postman's cap and bag and a pillar-box follow on from this.

- A hairdressing game with dolls, wigs, rollers and brushes, and this time a dab of perfume on overalls and smocks. Note that no mention is made of hair-spray, which would not be a good idea even if the can was an empty one. As to scissors – this is definitely one time to produce inadequate ones. It is possible to make crude simple wigs for dolls which children can be allowed to cut, and this might be a good idea for children who are terrified of having their hair cut.

■ Other games develop by setting out the dressing-up clothes like a clothes shop or borrowing shoes for a shoe shop once in a while. Apart from shoes, a low stool for the 'fitter' to sit on and a measuring device are about all that is needed – plus the mirror which is usually near the dressing-up clothes.

## Puppets

Puppets come in all shapes, sizes and styles, from a simple finger or hand puppet to complicated marionettes with strings and the beautiful shadow puppets used in eastern regions of the world.

Hand and finger puppets are best for under-7s, and they can become a companion, a mouthpiece, a 'naughty' screen to hide behind as the puppet says or does things its manipulator doesn't feel able to do directly. They can be a good medium for conversation, and a shy child who avoids eye contact may respond to a puppet figure much more comfortably than he would to an adult.

A puppet theatre is not really useful for young children. There are two definite aspects to a puppet show – either the mechanics of working the puppet and props (look behind any Punch and Judy booth – what the puppeteer sees is the face of the audience and the rather bleak wrong side of the stage) – or the magic of the performance. It is not possible to be on both sides of the curtain at the same time for even the simplest puppet act. One very useful piece of equipment, however, is a mirror placed safely where children can see what their puppet is doing. There are some simple props which can be attached to puppets so that children can do just a little more than waggle the heads and arms – the cone of the pop-up puppet or the nest of a family of finger puppet birds or the dog kennel which is part of a dog glove puppet.

Adults can use puppets for children to watch, perhaps at home for peep-bo games or at story and song time in the nursery group. One puppet can be used to focus the attention of a younger group of children or to go round the group asking questions – names, for example. A set of hand puppets can be given to different children in turn (a farmer, wife, child, dog and a bone) for a change from a ring game where there may not be enough space or the children are not yet able to move around as a group. It could just as easily be a set of finger puppets which the adult uses either for the farmer in the den or the little ducks who swam away or the five mice pussy pounced on (see *This Little Puffin*, a collection of action songs and finger plays).

## Dressing up

Dressing up is something we all like to do now and then – we feel different, aware of ourselves, we behave in a different manner and expect other people's attitudes towards us to be different (and they usually are). We also have favourites in our wardrobe – a painting shirt, gardening trousers, the dress which always seems to bring luck. Very small children like dressing up too. Sometimes they enjoy just putting on special things for fun – a tea-cosy on their heads, adults' boots on their feet.

Three- and 4-year-olds like to dress up to be someone, and it is part of their pretend games of trying on for size someone else's role. The most useful items for this are the token garments which are recognizable as a uniform – the postman's cap, the nurse's apron, the cowboy's hat.

They also like the cowboy's gun and there is a whole minefield of attitudes which need careful thought and adult discussion in a nursery group situation. If, hopefully, guns are not provided either at home or at nursery then, sadly, children will make them. They make daggers with two pieces of wood and a nail, they make swords from cardboard, and in one group a visiting adult was shot dead with a plastic banana. There is a long way to go towards eradicating would-be violence in play even if we do confiscate the weapons.

There are some garments children seem to like although they are not anything particularly special. The child who did the shooting with the plastic banana was wearing one of the three garments known as 'super capes' in his playgroup dressing-up collection. They were little more than a rectangle of material gathered at the neck and fastened with Velcro, but had been favourites to be squabbled over, queued up for and 'bagged' for first thing the next day for months. None of the adults really knew why, any more than they knew why they were called super-capes.

Dressing-up clothes need to be safe (no strings at the neck, not long enough to trip over, no shoes with high heels), easy to put on, easy to fasten and easy to wash and dry. They can be bought, but manufactured garments are not well made, not very good quality fabric and the detail which may make them attractive soon falls off, washes off or is picked off. They also cost, inch for inch, as much as a good adult garment.

A useful start for a collection is to find somewhere to keep it all. The jumble sale approach of having a collection of plastic bags through which children rummage does not add to the game at all. Having found a drawer, suitcase or box or cupboard, this can be filled with raw materials such as old lace curtains, pieces of beautiful fabric, handbags, safe shoes, a box of jewellery and a useful box of safety pins, elastic, pretty trimming salvaged from old lingerie, as many old work caps as can be collected, a few basic hand-made garments, handbags and accessories and then adding to it as the mood takes the children. The problem will have become obvious – there is never enough space just to keep adding to the collection and some will have to be moved on to make room for more.

The other necessity is a mirror – preferably full-length in relation to the height of the children. It will need to be firmly fastened to a wall or some stable surface.

Some nurseries have reservations about shared hats and make-up, but at home hats can be heavy, hard, soft, light, furry, frilly, lacy, floppy, and they will all feel different to the wearer. After all, a hat we are not aware of is not much fun for a dress-up occasion. Make-up can be an extra for a special treat at home, but it needs to be supervised. Cosmetics appear in the list of poisoning of young children, and *surma*, which is used by some Asian communities, is to be avoided as some may contain a high level of lead.

Young children don't like wearing masks, and very often other young children don't like seeing them being used. This is a good reason not to have them in a nursery group. Old spectacle frames with lenses removed are enough for under-5s and even for some 5–7s.

If we take the opportunity to use beautiful fabrics and colours, interesting textures and patterns, and different fibres for the simple garments we make as our contribution to the dressing-up box, then this imaginative game spills over into other kinds of learning experience.

## Scale models

One way of increasing a child's knowledge of the world around him is to provide small scale models of animals, vehicles and buildings. He uses them to create his own little world and situations where he is in charge.

There is a distinction to be made between actual scale models and those which are very simply represented. These are usually baby toys which come as all kinds of objects in all kinds of materials and sizes, and they appeal to babies for what they are rather than what they are supposed to represent.

When children are older and know a little more they want more realistic toys – farm and zoo animals, vehicles, buildings that look like the real thing. It takes some time for them to sort out relative sizes, even when they are quite knowledgeable about realistic detail. The 2- and 3-year-old will quite happily tow a large Tonka lorry with a small Matchbox crane or pull a Matchbox caravan with an outsize jeep, just as in doll play a pipe cleaner granny doll becomes the mother to a 20-inch baby doll.

The 4-year-old is more fussy about what goes with what, and he likes realistic detail. The 7-year-old knows all about sets of things, and will look at catalogues and leaflets from shops and work out what he needs to complete a set.

Under-7s want to be in charge of things, and although they may ask for friction-drive vehicles, remote control boats and aeroplanes, or dolls which walk and talk, these are usually only seven-day wonders. Once a toy is wound up or otherwise activated and let go, the toy itself is in charge of the action. The children soon go back to the toys they can manipulate at their own pace and in the direction they decide.

USEFUL ADDITIONS TO MODEL PLAY

Play layouts are a useful addition to playing with scale models. One quite simple practical advantage is that they limit the field of operation, which is safer for everyone than games which spread all over every room in the house plus the stairs.

## Vehicle play

A useful layout is a collection of sections of roadway to be placed or linked together. Straight strips, curves and intersections are a good start. They can be bought or made quite simply from hardboard. To make the traffic lines and roadway signs one of the new paint pens would be a great improvement on the matchstick dipped in paint we used to use.

An alternative is a play board – simply a traffic layout painted on a sheet of hardboard or even the top of a chest of drawers if it is the right height for a child to play at. It needs to be large enough to include a good deal of road, parking places and intersections, but narrow enough for a child to reach the far side. Some manufacturers have picked up this idea and produce boards, cloths and even mats and rugs, but they have still not taken the point (or perhaps not done adequate consumer-testing) that if the road or track simply runs off at the edge the whole purpose is lost. Just one access road point is sufficient.

GARAGES

Most bought garages are made from moulded plastic which will take a lot of detail – and in many cases this has been overdone. A competent handyman/woman/older brother needs only the simplest tools and ideas to make a garage of hardboard and soft wood. The same rules apply as for dolls' houses – plenty of elbow room, but nothing too elaborate apart from one feature that allows for more than just parking cars (perhaps a ramp or a lift). Garages are cheaper to make than dolls' houses as they don't have to be any special shape. It is possible to buy likely looking offcuts and make a garage to fit them rather than vice versa.

One tip might help to persuade parents and children to have a go at making their own layouts – ordinary powder paint mixed with PVA glue and a little water makes a manageable, quick-drying paint for either wood or cardboard, and if it gets spilt it will wash off if dealt with quickly.

One last point might clinch the idea – bought layouts and garages are incredibly expensive. It is sensible to save the money to spend on a generous collection of models. Models are not cheap either, and it is not possible to make or improvise them.

## Animal play

Farm boards, zoo boards (and even harbours and airports) can be made in exactly the same way as road layouts if that is what children are interested in. They can spread out into a collage activity if suitable materials can be provided to create different surfaces.

Games for a one-off session can be happily improvised with a large sheet of brown paper and a felt pen, although under-5s may need some adult help. A reasonably surfaced back yard or porch and coloured chalks is also a possibility, and leads to another enjoyable half-hour scrubbing it all off again.

If a sandpit is large enough, if the sand is the right degree of dampness and if other children can be persuaded to play somewhere else, some very involved layout games can take place there.

Model houses, buildings and trees can be bought; alternatively they can be made or improvised by adults, by adults and children together, or by children alone if they are provided with suitable material, so no layout should need to be bare and unfurnished. A well-stocked junk box, some self-hardening clay or dough made with plain flour hardened off in the oven after it has been moulded, offcuts of wood from the wood yard, can all be used to make the extra items to go with layouts.

# Chapter 17

# Learning about the World around Us

Obviously 'the world' around a child means everything in it – materials, people, groups, procedures – but for the purpose of tidy thinking we take it to mean the natural materials and the living, growing elements of the child's environment.

### Natural materials

Natural play material is a rather formal term which simply means the everyday substances which are the basis of our existence – water, earth and clay, sand and wood. Natural substances have a living individual quality. Children respond to them from an early age and seem to find them soothing and satisfying to handle. The same holds good for older children, and many adults also derive a great deal of pleasure from gardening, working with wood, cooking and water activities. Have a close look at the seaside, and see just who is building the sand castles or digging the channels for the incoming tide to fill.

Handling natural materials gives experience of their properties, their textures, the different states they can change to. Clay can be a powder, a heavy hard substance or a heavy soft substance which can be moulded, or a liquid which can be trickled and will stay in the trickle shape as it dries out. Water can be cold or warm – sometimes it just disappears, and when other things are mixed with it they change and look different. We don't have to point this out to children. They learn for themselves as they play. A good deal of vocabulary is associated with natural materials – size, weight, texture and volume words which need some practical experience to be associated with them before they can be learned.

### Water play

This is probably the favourite activity for many children. It is cheap, easy to provide, doesn't have to be stored and is very satisfying – it can also be very messy and it can be dangerous, so it needs organization and care.

At about 2–3 weeks, babies start to relax and enjoy their bath and this is where water play starts. They kick and splash with hands and feet, and watch as someone trickles or pours water from a sponge or cup on to their body. Once they can sit up firmly in the big bath they can play with bath toys themselves and they need a collection of things that float, sink, pour and spray.

Toddlers will spend a long time playing happily with water as a plaything. They can use it violently without doing any real damage or spoiling it, and they don't feel they have to make anything with it. However little skill a child has he can use water in some way, so it is a very undemanding material. At the same time it has a life of its own and responds in different ways which are sometimes a surprise. Children learn about the properties of this liquid – that it is heavy, can get cold, will soak away into anything soft which it touches, that unless they are careful the amount they have gets less and less as they splash it, that it can be quite deep in a bowl but if it goes on the floor it spreads thinly over a large area. They learn about capacity – half full, nearly empty, overflowing – long before they can put words to this experience.

The container and playthings they use can be very simple, and they will organize their own activities.

At home 3–5s will play happily with what they already have, with the addition of any interesting bits and pieces we or they can find – plus being allowed to stand up to the sink on a solid chair or stool to wash up anything unbreakable or perhaps just wash the sink. The sink needs to be clean, the hot water not too hot, the washing-up liquid needs to be hidden, the floor needs some protection – as does the child – and it needs an adult eye kept on both child and water level.

#### NURSERY GROUP WATER ACTIVITIES

Water play is one of the most useful basic activities for nursery age children, and is usually provided in sufficient quantities for

a small group all the time every day. It is often the first activity new young children are attracted to. Because two or three children will play together, a container larger and deeper than a bowl or baby bath is a justifiable expense. There are many different types at different prices, but the most useful one, which incorporates a shelf to put things on, a drain hole for easy emptying and has a stand which makes it the right height, is fortunately one of the cheapest.

New 3-year-olds just coming into a group will want to play in a different way from experienced, experimenting nearly 5-year-olds. Extra water activities such as washing dolls' clothes and bedding, spring cleaning everything from the home corner, scrubbing tables and chairs, can be offered as an alternative to those children who can't find elbow room at the water trough.

### KEEPING SAFE AND STAYING DRY

Water play needs to be under an adult's eye all the time, so it should be carefully sited – where it can be seen but not in the way of other activities where it will be knocked over. The water should be pleasantly warm and the same rule applies as for filling babies' baths – cold water first. Some non-slippery surface plus frequent squeegee mopping, which the children love doing but need help with, should help protect floors. Sheet plastic is not a good idea for placing under the water trough as it is very slippery when wet. Some tarpaulin sheets are useful, but if the container is the right height, not too full, and the playthings are a sensible size, children get quite clever at not splashing.

If a caretaker is complaining about the floor, perhaps less water in the trough, fewer playthings in there at any one time, smaller playthings, more work with the squeegee and inviting him in for cups of coffee will help.

The most effective protection for children's clothing is taking it off, but this is not always practical in cool weather nor is it always favourably received by parents and children. Rolled up (not pushed up) sleeves and a good water apron help. Limiting the number of aprons can be a good way of limiting the number of children at the water trough, provided they accept and observe the rule that they can't play there unless they have an apron on. For very young splashy children a change of clothing may be the answer if parents are complaining about wet jumpers and soggy shoes.

If water play in a nursery group is not well used or is being misused then something is wrong with what is being provided, or how it is being presented, or there is a large proportion of younger children who still want to splash. Some watching and thinking about what changes can be made needs to be done.

## Sand

There are many different kinds of sand which all make a difference to how children can play with it. Fine dry silver sand pours almost like water without the wetness and can be used with the same equipment. It is very expensive, so may have to be provided in a shallow seed tray with tiny playthings rather than in full sandpit-size quantity. Washed plasterers' sand or builders' sand of a suitable grit size (ask for a balanced mixture of particles from coarse 1.5mm to fine) is much cheaper than silver sand and packs well for building and moulding depending on how wet it is.

At about 18 months, children enjoy sitting in a sandpit patting and pummelling the sand, digging with a small spade or spoon and emptying and filling containers. They need supervision, as sand thrown up into hair is unpleasant and sand in eyes is dangerous. It is also painful, so the next thing they do is rub their eyes with sand-encrusted hands.

Once they can use trucks and wheelbarrows sand is a natural load to use, and they wheel it from one place to another which accounts for most of the mess associated with it. Two sand places with a defined path between the two is a good idea.

### SAND IN NURSERY GROUPS

Sand is another basic material to be provided every day. It is not always possible to go outside, so this means having a sand tray inside as well as a pit outside. The container can be exactly the same as for water play, with pots, fillers, rakes and sand combs or anything else which will make a pattern in damp sand. The sand also gets used for filling cups at tea parties, for loading lorries, and can even be sprinkled on a glued card for collage, so sand gets lost rather than worn out. A regular sweep-up routine is good for regaining some of the loss, and is also safer since sandy surfaces can be slippery. An old bedspread under an indoor sand tray will catch most of the spills. (Caretakers don't like sand any more than they like water.)

Children sometimes mix the sand and water play so that the water tray contains a thin solution of sand and the sand tray contains a thick solution of sand. If this comes from genuine experimenting that seems reasonable. If it happens every day because the children can't think of anything more constructive to do with either, then some re-thinking, a change of equipment and new ideas are needed – try coloured or bubbly water or a new set of sand rakes, or a story about the seaside.

An outside sandpit can get dirty and unpleasant and needs to be kept fresh. Forking and digging to turn it over will let air get to it. Raking will remove leaves – and the spades, model cars and bits of Lego which get buried in it. If there is a possibility of fouling by dogs and cats some sort of cover is needed, preferably a mesh, as a solid lid does not allow the sand to dry off. If regular disinfecting is necessary, a solution of Milton or one of the thin bleaches (used as recommended on the bottle) sprayed on and forked in should deal with any germs. It needs to be allowed to dry out before the children can use it again, so this has to be done over a weekend or when the children are not there. If there are two sand places they can be cleaned alternately so that one is always available. At home the sand has usually disappeared by the time it would have needed this treatment. Most of it comes indoors, so it is a good idea to have a rule about taking off shoes and socks and having a jump about before children come in the house.

### ALTERNATIVE TO SAND (OR JUST A CHANGE FROM SAND)

If there is a really good reason for not using sand (as opposed to adult excuses because they think it will make an uncontrollable mess), there are one or two alternatives which are better than nothing or simply make a pleasant change:

- Sawdust or wood shavings (check on the type of wood, as some hardwoods are quite unpleasant).

- Processed bark or peat (combined with planting bulbs or potting plants).

- Dead leaves or conkers in a large shallow box or plastic tray.

These materials can be used for emptying and filling games, and they behave quite differently from sand. We used to use rice, lentils, pasta, barley and dried peas, but these are now too expensive for groups to use in quantity. At home it is possible to use them for the half-hour children want to play this game and then, if no one is looking, wash them thoroughly and use them for their proper purpose.

'Proper purpose' is an adult concept. When we look at these things in the store cupboard we think of them as food. Children don't think of anything as food until it is on the plate ready to be eaten.

### Earth

Most toddlers who get the opportunity will happily potter alongside an adult working in the garden, using whatever comes to hand to dig little holes, or pulling up vegetation. If they can find some source of water this usually progresses from watering plants to puddles, floods and mud. It is adults who put a stop to this game because of the mess. Children find it very satisfying. If they can be given a space of their own to dig in, a small watering can or mist-sprayer, something to dig with and something to fill, plus wellingtons and old, washable clothes, they will spend a long time on this activity and need only one cleaning up session. In terms of adult effort this might be less time-consuming than providing some of the more 'acceptable' activities every ten minutes.

### Clay

Clay is another (more manageable) form of earth. Children enjoy handling it from about 2 years onwards. In the nursery group it is another basic activity for every day. There will always be some child wanting to use it.

Clay and small children get on best if nothing comes between them except an apron. They simply roll, punch and twist it with great satisfaction. It is indestructible, they can't do it any damage, nothing they can do with it is either right or wrong. It is the non-demanding nature of clay which makes it such a useful play material. Even if a child does make something with it he may well simply squash it up and use it again, because under-5s rarely want to keep what they make.

The quantities in which to buy clay sound huge because it is so heavy. Each child needs a lump at least as big as a grapefruit and preferably as big as a cabbage. It can be bought ready mixed or in powder form. For younger children it needs to be soft enough to be pliable and easy to handle. Each time it is put away it needs a small amount of water in the middle of the ball, like jam in a doughnut.

Older children usually start to experiment with clay because the consistency is changed by accident – it is left out and gets dry, or too much water is added and it goes very soft or even liquid. It can still be retrieved whatever happens to it. If clay really dries out and is too hard to mould or even cut up with a blunt knife or lolly stick, another good game can be found in smashing up the pieces with a mallet (inside a plastic bag if it has to be done inside the house or nursery group), then covering the lumpy powder with water in a bucket, stirring vigorously and letting it settle. The clear liquid at the top is gradually poured or siphoned off day by day until the thick mass can be spread out on a tray to dry off enough to be handled.

The 4–7-year-olds may decide they want to do more than squash and bash clay. A roller made from a piece of broom handle, a board made from hardboard used wrong side up, a blunt knife or a lolly stick or a wire cutter as used for cheese and, if they are getting frustrated, a quick demonstration of how to roll evenly between two slats of wood is usually enough.

If they get cross because their two pieces of clay won't stick together, we can show them how to apply water to make a slip join. This leads on to slip trailing. Slip clay (clay made into a creamy liquid with water) can be dribbled from a squirty bottle to make patterns which dry out to clay 'lace' or to make a raised design on a clay tile or slab. Other patterns can be made by pressing in objects which give an interesting texture.

The clay table is often a good place for conversation between children or, if an adult can spare the time, between an adult and a group of children or a single child. This is the point at which adults may be inveigled into the 'show me' or 'make me' situation. Once this happens children try to copy our model, or worse, get dissatisfied with their own efforts. On the other hand, if a child has a clear view of what he wants to do and asks for help to achieve it, then this is no more and no less help than we would give in any other situation.

Caretakers don't like clay either. It tends to leave streaky marks. A large plastic sheet on the table will help. If surfaces are rubbed with a dry soft cloth after thorough washing and rinsing there will be less in the way of white streaks. Clay should be kept on the clay table and any little bits that fall on the floor should be brought to the notice of the children so that they can pick them up. When they are using really sticky clay, a bucket of warm water near the clay table for sluicing hands before proper washing is a good idea.

## Play dough

Play dough is another substance which makes a change from clay. It can't be modelled with the same precision as clay, but young children are not really wanting precision.

Because it is made of flour and water, tidy thinking on the part of adults sometimes creates confusion between dough used in the same way as clay and the dough used for pastry play. The same substance will do for both unless we want to eat it. If adults forget that this modelling substance is made of an edible material, they become less concerned about how children use it and more adventurous about how they make it. There is no right or wrong consistency, and different textures lead to different play and activities, although for very young children a non-sticky mass is obviously better.

There are many dough recipes around that are given the same respect as an *haute cuisine* dish. It really doesn't matter, and one superb recipe day after day is just as boring for play dough as it would be to eat the same thing every day. It is noticeable that the more finicky and expensive the recipe the less the quantities quoted are. Under-7s like generous quantities, and it takes at least a 1.5kg bag of flour to provide for four children. Basic materials are:

> *Flour*: plain gives a 'short' dough, self-raising (or plain with a good shake of baking powder) gives a puffy dough, bread flour (or strong flour) makes a tough elastic dough. Granary flour gives a gritty-looking dough.

*Cream of tartar*: helps to make a smoother dough which keeps well. It is usually referred to in recipes that start with 8oz of flour.

*Salt*: draws moisture from the atmosphere, which helps to keep the dough moist and malleable. It is also a mild antiseptic. On a hot dry day 12oz of salt to a large bag of flour is about right. Use the same amount on a wet muggy day and the dough will flow off the table, so some caution is needed.

*Fluid*: basically water, but adding a good dash of cooking oil makes the dough smoother and more pliable.

The method is just as simple. Using a large bowl, add about 12oz of fluid to a 3lb bag of flour and the salt, and work it in. If it makes a sticky dough (flour varies in how much fluid it will take), then this is the day for sticky dough and lots of flour to sprinkle on it. If the mixture is too dry, more fluid can be added a splash at a time. There is no reason why children should not help with making the dough, and this is where the activity spills over into a pre-cooking activity.

One type of dough is made by cooking it in a pan and stirring vigorously. This is hard going, and it is only possible to produce a one-child quantity. A less exhausting variation is to put all the dry ingredients in an electric mixer bowl, stir in the boiling fluid, cover everything with a tea towel in case it splashes, and switch the mixer on to low speed. Leave it going until the resulting dough is cool enough to handle. This does need to be made out of range of children.

Food colourings or powder paints can be mixed dry with the flour – or worked into the mixed dough which will make it go a bit streaky. Some colours stain hands and some powder paints, particularly blues, have a peculiar smell, so this needs some small-scale experimenting first. Perhaps we should experiment occasionally with nice smells too, such as peppermint or vanilla, unless this might tempt the children to eat the dough.

Provided the dough is not maltreated by adding sand or nails, or being wiped round the floor or used to fill all the toy lorries, or quietly eaten, it can be stored in a plastic bag in the refrigerator overnight and used again several times.

## Other modelling materials

Plasticine, Play Doh and other commercial modelling materials or the self-hardening clays make a change from everyday cabbage-sized lumps of flour dough. They are expensive and have to be supplied in small quantities, which means they are appreciated by 5–7s who want to make something specific rather than by younger children. They could equally well be used for model-making.

## Wood

Wood is a natural material which may fast be disappearing from children's experience as more and more plastic toys and play-things are produced. Natural wood gives great pleasure to most people – even if we have to have plastic surfaces in our home we tend to choose those made to simulate wood.

Each kind of wood has its different characteristics – the colour, the grain, the smell. Some woods are soft, some hard, some heavy, some close-grained and smooth. It makes quite a different noise from metal or plastic when hit or dropped. It is also expensive, because those same natural characteristics we enjoy mean it is wasteful in use and difficult to work.

Wooden toys cost a great deal, but the right wood used for the right toy is practically indestructible. They could be considered as a good long-term purchase for things like bricks and blocks, which are used up to and beyond the age of 7 years and can be used by several children or even several generations of children. Small children (but not babies who still suck and chew everything) will enjoy a box full of offcuts of different woods sanded smooth and sealed with a clear finish. The shapes don't have to be regular or part of a modular set and are useful for imaginative play.

Learning to use wood is quite a different matter from learning to use clay. It is difficult to work and needs skill with tools. The woodwork done by under-7s is going to fall far short of cabinet-making, and the most they will achieve is some rudimentary skill with the appropriate tools and joining agents (glue, nails, screws) to join one or two pieces of wood together. This object will then be given a name, and since it is usually two pieces of wood and one nail it will be called a sword or dagger or gun, because that is what it looks like.

Adults can make learning to use tools and materials easier by providing graded opportunities:

- Very soft wood or fibreboard, even half a potato, to hammer large headed nails into.

- Strong cardboard boxes on which to practise sawing.

- The right size of proper tool. Baby hammers and screw toys have served a useful purpose, but children now need something better to work with.

- A firm surface at the right height to work on.

- A vice and bench hook to hold pieces of wood firmly, a clamp to hold pieces of wood while non-impact adhesive dries (PVA glue will stick wood quite well enough for this purpose).

- A progression in sizes of nails from metal studs, upholstery tacks, carpet tacks to large nails, then smaller nails plus a pair of pincers to get them out again.

Once children have exhausted the possibilities and the fun to be had in just handling tools and materials, they will do the deciding about what they want to make – a box full of offcuts of wood, sandpaper and a powder paint/PVA glue/water paint mix can be added to their woodwork sessions.

The other thing adults need to do is to make sure watching children don't come close enough to get hurt.

### Things we eat

These are natural materials too, and children don't always see them properly before we eat them. We can cut vegetables and fruit different ways, allow children to compare the skin of an orange with the papery skin of an onion, look closely at an egg before it goes into the frying pan, finger the rind of cheese, let them smell food before it is cooked, talk about what has happened to food during cooking.

### Things which live and grow

Young children are interested in all living things. They can share our plants, gardens and animals and just occasionally have some special project of their own.

Houseplants can be slow to show change, but children can help us tend plants and we can explain what we are doing and why. We can also give them their own plants to grow. Mustard and cress and mung beans are the quickest-growing seeds. Within a week or so children can not only see how the plants have grown but they can eat them too. For slower-growing materials there is not much to see for a long time above the soil surface. If we can arrange for children to see the root growth, there is more to see more quickly. Try bulbs grown on a narrow-necked jar of water, peas and beans grown on blotting paper, acorns and fruit stones grown in a plastic bag of peat in the airing cupboard.

Competent 4-year-olds can make themselves a dish garden which doesn't take much looking after. Looking for little cushions of moss, a piece of twig, pretty stones to start off their creation can add point to any walk.

## Planning for children in the garden

Interest in proper gardening comes from actually having a nearby garden tended by an adult who is not only keen on gardening but is willing to let a child join in the activities. Even the best-laid-out parks tend to fail on this last point. Providing children with a little plot they can call theirs and within reason use as they wish, some areas and plants which are shared and some areas and plants they must not touch, seems to work out best. Even in a back yard a trough or shallow bowl can be used for a child to grow small plants – or large ones, provided they will grow upwards against a wall rather than outwards.

If a nursery group garden can be planned with children in mind – adequate fencing and gating (but not so high and solid as to seem prison-like), some hard areas which dry off quickly for play in wet weather, shrubs and bushes to provide interest and shelter, trees to provide a windbreak, some space for equipment such as a sandpit and a climbing frame or a slide with a suitable surface beneath (see Appendix 4, page 305), this is a good start. Unfortunately it is a very rare start. Most nursery groups don't have this kind of outside space, and if they do they are not free to plan it as they would wish. Exactly the same points can be borne in mind when planning a garden at home.

Some shrubs are not desirable, such as those which have

very nasty thorns. Others are positively dangerous, as some or all parts of them are poisonous or cause rashes. On the other hand, some plants not only look good but smell good too and/or attract butterflies, so any adult planning to buy new plants might bear this in mind.

Some garden chemicals are very dangerous, but no garden chemicals are going to do children any good. The safest course of action is to think of all of them as dangerous and treat them accordingly (or better still, avoid them altogether).

## Pets and animals

If there is no family pet already, it is not usually till around the age of 7 that children ask for a dog or a cat as a present. Under-7s get on best with something small, not too fragile or demanding, good-natured as regards being handled and interesting to watch.

Rabbits are usually kept outside and need a hutch and run (although in one nursery school the rabbit lived in the piano), so a certain amount of outside space is needed. Guinea-pigs are gentle, small enough to be held in small hands, and they don't mind their very respectable-looking new babies being handled. Other small furry animals are not so accommodating on this last point, and their new babies may look rather unattractive till they grow fur and open their eyes. Hamsters, gerbils and mice are small enough to be kept indoors but don't play much during the day. They can be left unattended during a weekend if enough food and water is left for them, which is the reason many nursery groups have them in preference to other pets.

Not everyone likes the idea of caged birds but young children enjoy them. Fish are better than nothing and are relaxing to watch but can't be handled. Tortoises, which are not as slow, docile and uninteresting as one might think, make good pets if there is a small area of garden they can use.

Very young children who are shy or withdrawn often respond to a small, warm, furry, live animal. For children settling in at nursery groups, rushing over to give the hamster a lettuce leaf brought from home is a good start to the session. A distressed child can often be comforted by having the guinea-pig on their lap while he sits on an adult's lap. Children who are not very talkative will often talk to an animal or be willing to tell an adult about an animal.

There can be a two-way traffic, with pets from home being brought into the nursery group or nursery group pets being borrowed for a weekend or holiday. It all helps.

## Making do without a pet

If pets are not possible, then we just have to make the most of what the outside world can provide. Children have to be warned about stray dogs and cats, but we can provide food for birds, bird-boxes and tables.

We tend to think of wildlife as something which happens elsewhere. Children are taken to the zoo and shown pictures of large exotic animals from other countries. There is wildlife all around us which children can enjoy if we take each opportunity to point it out to them – worms in the garden, ants on the path, spiders and spiders' webs on walls, caterpillars and moths on plants, butterflies on bushes, beetles under stones, daddy-long-legs on windows. Many adults don't like insects but children usually do until we pass on our inhibitions.

One group of children in a playgroup spent a fascinating half-hour watching a ladybird crawling round a wall and following its path with a chalk mark. This involved standing on chairs, moving furniture, lying on the floor, a lot of searching when it took wing and flew off to another spot, and when it finally disappeared a piece of string was used to measure how far it had walked and its path was traced by chubby little fingers – all highly enjoyable. There are many opportunities like this if we take the time to make the most of them.

## Books and television

No one would imply that looking at books and watching television programmes about the living world could be a substitute for direct experience – actually seeing, touching, smelling, hearing, walking round, going back to have another look. But nor would anyone imply that any individual could explore every area of the world and have direct experience of everything there is to see. Because of books and television we can know much more than any other generation – more even than the most intrepid explorers ever did. They only explored in their own particular field, not every field.

On the whole, people who produce nature books and TV programmes are experts in their field and they have some very sophisticated equipment to help them. They can record far more detail and information than we could see with the naked eye even if we were there. Children can benefit greatly from this source of information – it not only fills in gaps in their present experience, but leaves them better prepared in knowing what to look for, knowing how what they may finally experience fits into the scheme of things.

## Natural phenomena

The world we live in goes through many changes: the weather changes, the seasons change, night and day alternate, sunlight makes things look different, rain deepens and brightens colours, we see rainbows in the sky and something similar in puddles, or when light passes through a prism. Water can be a cloud or a liquid or a solid.

Under-7s are not going to understand what happens and how and why – but we can help them to notice and appreciate what goes on around them. If that is all they ever do it is a very great deal. If they do develop a deeper curiosity at a later stage, it will be because we set them on the first step of this path.

# Chapter 18

# Making and Creating

Creative play is the category which suffers from the limitations of adults' tidy thinking more than any other activity . . .

## What is creativity?

A child in a nursery group works hard outside in the sandpit for a whole morning, making an elaborate road system with tunnels, overpasses, hills and hairpin bends. He dampens and mixes the sand to get the right consistency and comes in several times to find something to use as a tool for a particular operation. The work goes through several phases as more ideas occur to him. He doesn't want to come in for his milk, so someone takes it out for him. He chatters to himself as he works, and explains carefully to the adult who brings his milk exactly what he is doing and why. At the end of the morning he is called to 'Finish off now and clean up ready for story time', so he gets the rake and flattens the sand to leave it tidy for the afternoon group because this is what the children have been taught to do.

On the way in he passes by the painting easels, one of which has a clean piece of paper pegged on it – so he picks up a brush from the nearest paint pot, makes a couple of quick strokes and then goes on his way to the cloakroom to wash his hands. When his mother comes to collect him she asks, 'Did you do anything this morning?' and an adult helper gives her the 'painting'. 'That's lovely darling, lovely colour, you could do one with more colours tomorrow!' No one mentions what went on in the sandpit.

Adults tend to think of creativity as being defined and measured in something which is permanent, something to keep and look at. If we think about it, the 'painting' only went home because there was an element of destruction there – the paper and paint couldn't be used again, in practical terms they became a record because they were destroyed. Yet it was this which was produced to be taken home as evidence of the child's creative effort for the morning (after all, who would be stupid enough to suggest the mother took the pile of sand home?).

These permanent pieces of evidence of creativity can be misleading. We may think that a child's painting reveals something of his feelings, but we have to know a lot more about him than simply looking at finished 'pictures'. They tell us nothing of how or why a child worked or what they meant to him.

Creative play for children is a process, not an end product. It involves various stages of learning and experience:

- Finding out about many different materials and becoming familiar with their properties.

- Achieving skill with hands and tools.

- Learning about colours, shapes, sizes, textures and patterns.

- Learning and developing techniques.

- Learning to consider what is being done as a whole, rather than as a collection of pieces placed together.

- Gaining confidence as competence grows.

And having done all this, they start to add their ideas to create something original and specific to them – if they have these sort of ideas.

Not all of us have artistic gifts, any more than we have the physical gifts which allow us to be excellent at sports, but even the gifted individual is not going to be able to use his gift until he has developed competence and familiarity with the materials he uses. On the other hand, those of us who are not 'artistic' can enjoy many situations where a skill with materials and a feeling for shape, colour, texture and design is useful.

## Who is creative?

How far children are going to get in their first seven years depends . . .

- On the individual.
- On the opportunities he is given.
- On how much 'reward' he receives at each stage in the shape of personal pleasure and satisfaction.

Actually these conditions apply to the first seventy years rather than the first seven years, because this learning is an on-going process.

The following account of a mixed group of adults taking part in a creative session where a whole range of materials and tools were supplied illustrates the normal spread of interest and ability:

- About 20 per cent (three out of a group of fifteen) can't wait to get started. They make a beeline for the materials and tools they want and get on with it. They know exactly what they want to do. At the end of the session they have produced something which pleases them and impresses everyone else, so they are also 'rewarded' by everyone else's approval.

- About 60 per cent (nine people) have a good look at what the first three are doing, have little consultations with each other, pick out pieces because they like the look of them. They move the materials around and try out various combinations and ideas before they commit themselves to anything irrevocable such as painting or gluing or stapling their work together. At the end of the session they compare what they have done with everyone else's work, are very kind to each other in their praise (they are adults after all – children are not so kind) and are self-critical about their own work . . . 'Perhaps it would have looked better if I had done this – or that'. Some are pleased with what they did. Some say they enjoyed doing it but don't want to keep it.

- The other 20 per cent (three people) wander around looking at what everyone else is doing, finger the materials that remain and have difficulty making a choice. They find all the tools are gone and they will have to 'borrow'. They ask the group leader exactly what is it that they are supposed to do and get very frustrated when she says, 'Whatever you like'. They have another wander round looking at what everyone else is doing and then suggest it is tea-time and disappear to make tea for everybody. In the last half-hour or so of the session, after having a much longer tea break than anyone else, plus washing all the cups, plus tidying up the kitchen which is now sparkling clean, they work out a simple design and complete it – but they don't want anyone to look at it because they 'couldn't find the colours they wanted' or 'ran out of time', and the work itself is scrunched up and taken out to the dustbin.

There is a good deal in this true and familiar story which relates to any age group, including children. This instance was a practical session on a training course carried out with a group of students. The tutor was not quite so insensitive as she may have seemed. One object of the exercise was to let students experiment with the materials children use – but there was a 'set up' element the students didn't know about. The other, and perhaps more important, part of the exercise was for students to discuss afterwards how they had felt about the afternoon. The quantity of really nice materials was deliberately limited, some scissors had been removed and two of the pairs were decidedly substandard. The tutor's refusal to be drawn on what the students should do was very hard to keep up as the three people got more and more desperate and finally retreated to the kitchen.

From these types of experiences, some strong conclusions and suggestions arise which have proved helpful with young children:

- Choosing from a whole mass of materials is difficult. Some structuring of the presentation of materials could help the less experienced child. The competent, able child will find anything extra that he needs.

- Insufficient materials and inadequate tools are very frustrating and off-putting for anyone, but are even more so for the less competent and confident individual.

- The feeling of being pressured into doing something which is beyond one's capacity (whether the pressure is directly applied or comes from within) is very painful and leads to feelings of inadequacy and failure before even trying to do whatever it is. This can lead to opting out. (The three ladies cleaned the kitchen. Small children retreat to the sandpit or water tray or to a situation where they can't fail.) Children need these options, which is why they need a choice of activities.

■ Less confident individuals need some 'fail-safe' activities which will inevitably produce a pleasing result at the same time as developing skill. Pattern-making and printing, provision of beautiful colours and materials and just a small piece of paper or card to fill are useful possibilities.

■ Adult-planned and adult-directed projects for children to carry out are not likely to encourage creativity or confidence. Children are anxious, or may even be encouraged, to 'get it right'. Once there is a 'right way' then there is a wrong way too, and the children may feel they have failed if they do not achieve the adult standard or equally they may feel this is the only 'right' way to use some materials.

■ On the other hand, if children who are carrying out ideas of their own ask for help then there is no reason not to provide it.

■ Equally there is no reason why an adult should not carry out a project of his or her own which children can watch and join in with if they wish. This is how most of their early learning is done, and in a young age group of only 3–4s it can be seen as replacing the influence older children would have had, had they been there. Adult confidence and enthusiasm are infectious, and young children can 'catch' this attitude.

For under-7s we can take a wide view of creativity and creative materials, and provide a situation where they have the opportunity to start collecting information about colour, size, shape and textures from the materials we present, and to develop skill with tools and adhesives.

If they then progress to add their own creative ideas, we can give support rather than direction. If they do not add their own creative ideas we can structure some of the materials (rather than organize the children) to ensure enough success to give them the 'reward' of pleasure. We can break down the difficulty of learning techniques so that they can learn gradually one stage at a time. (See 'Cutting Out and Pasting', page 195.)

## Painting

'Painting' often starts at the stage of spreading around fruit juice on the tray of a high chair. Children under 4 are usually still at the experimenting stages and may do five 'paintings' in as many minutes. They will progress through using lines, patches, squiggles and later perhaps dots and circles.

Young groups which lose their 4-year-olds may not get much further than this. They need:

- Generous provision of materials – this means lots of paper (which could be sugar paper or computer paper), at least six colours of paint, to include the primary colours plus green, black and white, in a smooth spreading consistency which is thick enough not to drip everywhere.

- Brushes (of all kinds and including artists' brushes of a suitable length for a child's arm, i.e. not adult size artists' brushes).

- Somewhere comfortable to work.

- Protection for themselves and everything else.

- A change now and then in how materials are presented.

- Somewhere to dry off wet paintings if they want to keep them (and somewhere to dry off paintings even if they say they don't want to keep them, because they change their minds).

Having become confident with paint, children may start painting 'something'. The materials are exactly the same – it is the children who add the new element themselves, and it is a question of stage rather than age.

Quite often they paint then give their painting a name. They may progress to saying 'I am going to paint a . . ' They may use just one or two colours, or ask for a specific colour to be mixed, or mix it for themselves, but it is not always the colour we would expect them to ask for.

Some children paint cars or houses, sometimes something which is in their mind because of a recent event, and sometimes they paint what their best friend is painting. Some children paint figures, which often start off with 'big head' figures, but this is a more likely subject when using drawing materials such as felt pens. Tact is needed:

- Children who are experimenting can be confused if they are asked 'What is it?' It wasn't meant to be anything. They may give it any name that comes into their head, or say 'Nuffing' or 'Blue' or 'Painting' or just walk away. They have been given the idea that you have to 'do' something with paint, and this puzzles them.

- If we say 'Tell me about your painting' they are again put under pressure. They will tell us about it if they want to. On the other hand, if all the adults are so busy they have no time to listen, then they can't tell us about it even if they do want to do so.

- If we start making suggestions as to how to improve their painting it is not 'their' painting any more and we are implying that what they have done is not good enough or not quite right. They will ask us for help if they want it – provided someone is there to be asked.

### Finger-painting

Finger-painting is a much more direct form of painting and involves applying fingers to a surface coated with a paint of suitable consistency. It could be thought of as a progression from spreading cereal around the tray of a high chair.

Fingers and hands (or a cardboard 'comb' for a child who is a bit doubtful about the process) are used to make free designs and patterns, so that the paint is the background and the part where the paint has been removed is the picture or pattern. Using both hands, or two forefingers, or two thumbs together lead to beautiful symmetrical designs.

There is no need or compulsion to 'make' or 'do' anything in particular except enjoy the movement and the kaleidoscopic effect. Occasionally children will appreciate taking a print of what they have done, and they may notice that it is a mirror image and that succeeding prints all look different because the paint is flattened and diminished in quantity each time.

Finger-painting is one of the foolproof, fail-safe 'creative activities' which make no demands on children. It does, of course, make demands on the adults who provide and supervise, but the more often children do it the better they become at managing not to spread the effect all the way to the cloakroom and back when they have finished.

What is required is a non-porous surface on which to dollop paint mixed to a coating-sauce consistency. Formica-topped or plastic-covered tables, or very large plastic trays, make suitable surfaces. Children usually stand up to do finger-painting and can make larger body movements this way, so a table or surface of a suitable height is necessary.

Paint can be bought ready mixed, but this is expensive. There are some recipes which involve soap flakes and gum arabic, but these are also expensive, and since finger-painting only stops when the paint runs out there is no need to add any ingredient to make it 'keep better'. Wallpaper paste used to be an excellent medium, but it is rare to find a brand that does not contain fungicide nowadays and these should be avoided. Cold water starch or a cold cooked cornflour and water sauce can be mixed with powder paint, or a bowl of paste plus several pots of dry powder colour (each with its own spoon) can be provided so that the colours are actually mixed by the children on the table. Not so many colours are needed as for brush-painting. One colour plus white will make exciting patterns, as the two colours mix and create many different shades however inexperienced the painter may be.

## Pattern- and print-making

The other ways of using paint which give an interesting and pleasing result for very little skill and even less 'creative ability' involve using it with pattern-makers or letting the paint itself do the designing by applying it in different ways.

Pattern-makers can be large or small (large is more fun but takes more paper and space and a lot more supervision). They can be direct, like potato printing or interesting surfaces stuck on to cotton reels to make stamps, or the application can be reversed and paper can be applied to a textured surface coated with paint to take a print.

Print-making can lead on to making 'rubbings' of anything textured, with a layer of paper between the texture and the wax crayon, chalk or brass-rubbing wax.

Making the paint do the work can mean using really drippy paint being blown with a straw or allowed to run down the paper, or a blob of paint squidged in folded paper, or string dipped in paint being pulled through folded paper.

These activities have to be carefully suited to the age and skill of the children. Very young children will enjoy helping an adult do 'her' painting if they are not able to do it for themselves. Since most adults enjoy these activities too – the three ladies who cleaned the kitchen (see pages 188, 189) were in their element during this training session and had a go at everything in sight plus using a few wilder ideas of their own – our own genuine and spontaneous enjoyment and enthusiasm rub off on children.

## Drawing

Small children will scribble almost as soon as they can hold a pencil to paper, and this will progress eventually to drawing. There is probably more variation in how well individuals learn to draw than in any other art medium or technique.

For under-7s we can simply provide the materials without either them or us worrying too much about whether or not they are going to be 'good at drawing'.

Felt pens, pencils, crayons and chalks are the most likely art materials to be found at home. They can be supplied in a nursery group, and often are, but it is to be hoped that this would be as something for children to help themselves to if they felt like it rather than as a staple activity; after all, nursery groups should be able to provide activities which are not so easy to provide at home simply because they have the time and the space.

Occasionally an extra element can be added to drawing, such as shaped paper, wet paper or chalk damped in milk.

## Collage

The art world may have a specific definition of 'collage', but as far as under-7s are concerned 'if you stick it on it's called collage'.

Young children (3–4s) enjoy the glue most, and are quite likely to finish up with a paste sandwich. They get on best with a small base of card rather than paper – and a polystyrene tray or cardboard box lid is useful, since the raised edge helps to contain the generous quantity of adhesive.

However many interesting materials are supplied (preferably in a sectioned box), most children eventually use only four or five – but selecting what to use means they are looking at different shapes, colours, materials, sizes and making a choice, so there is more to collage than eventually meets the eye.

The 4–5-year-old group who have had a good deal of experience with glue begin to realize that too much is not necessarily a good thing, and start to glue the object to be stuck rather than the whole of the base. They may also be more fussy about which side up they want their decorative pieces to be – it takes some time and tactful help from adults to learn that if you want 'this side' to show you 'paste the other side'.

## Junk play

Junk play is rather like three-dimensional collage, involving tubes, boxes and anything else which can be diverted to the 'useful box' between leaving the kitchen and entering the dust-bin. What children do with it will depend on their degree of skill but they can also be influenced by how interesting the material is, since there is a limit to what anyone can do with one bagful of kitchen roll tubes and egg boxes.

Apart from the useful box, this activity will need a 'joining box' containing glue, stapler, paper-clips, brass paper-clips, Sellotape, brown sticky paper tape, wire twisters, a coil of wire and wire cutters, good kitchen scissors and Blu-tak. If children want to paint their creations, a paint made from PVA glue, powder paint and a little water dries quickly and covers well.

## Cutting and pasting

This is a very common activity to be provided both at home and nursery group. The results are not necessarily very exciting, nor do many children seem to enjoy doing it. This may be because it is more difficult to do than adults realize, especially when it is not presented with care. A common experience for children is:

- Find a picture (from perhaps the 1,000 or so in a mail order catalogue).
- Cut it out (with the weight of the whole catalogue pulling against the one page they want to use).
- With dreadful scissors (or at least they often are).
- Cut the picture neatly (yet it is often small and fiddly).
- Paste one side (which may or may not be the reverse side).
- Stick it on a painting-sized piece of paper or in a large scrapbook (where it looks quite lost).

It can be very little reward for a lot of frustrating effort. Adults could help by breaking down the skills to make each stage easier and by presenting the activity so that small children only have to do one part of it – for example, by providing pictures which are ready to stick on so that the children are left with just the two operations of choosing and pasting, or providing sheets of coloured sticky paper to cut shapes from, or cuttting shapes from Christmas cards which are stiffer than paper and therefore easier to cut.

## Cooking

Cooking is a creative process in which everyone has some interest, even if it is only eating what has been created. This is one activity which is easier to provide at home than in the nursery group.

Like any other learning/doing we can make it easier for children by breaking down some of the steps, the degree of skill and the number of skills, so that they progress confidently from stage to stage.

When they want to cook for themselves instead of sharing what the adult is doing, they could start with a cake mix which needs only water, then progress to one which needs an egg, and gradually work up to rubbing in fat (scones) and creaming fat (small cakes), by which time they will need scales to measure proper ingredients. Handling dough comes with scones, pastry and bread dough, which they can help the adult to mix.

They can help with some vegetable and fruit preparation – cutting up bananas or squashing them, scrubbing a potato ready for baking, peeling mushrooms, shelling peas, breaking florets from a cauliflower. If the children get tired of this they can always nibble the last carrot, or clean out the bowl as someone else finishes off the cooking.

Some processes need special tools – a mouli-grater for cheese, a pepper grinder, a tiny nutmeg grater, a balloon whisk for beating eggs, a rotary whisk to make egg white frothy and stiff.

In the nursery group small numbers and frequent cooking sessions are easier on the adults and need less equipment than having all the children do it at the same time. Trying to produce twenty mixing bowls and spoons cannot be done on a frequent regular basis, and weighing twenty lots of 2 oz of flour on one pair of scales is a good morning's work in itself by the time each child has gone through the 'not enough, little bit more, oh dear, too much' routine.

Not having an available oven doesn't really matter, as children think preparing anything which can be eaten is 'cooking'. Making sandwiches may seem dull to us, but if we provide different kinds of bread, rolls, batons, crispbread and crackers, and all kinds of fillings from jam to mashed boiled egg with snipped chives, they can, with some help, make closed, open, double-decker, square, rectangular, triangular and round (cut with a pastry cutter) sandwiches. They could then start on different garnishes.

Add to these activities icing biscuits, making fondant for peppermint creams, rolling little marzipan sausages to stuff dates, mixing a 'dip' for raw vegetable sticks, and making butter by shaking top of the milk in a screw-top jar, and a nursery group could provide cooking sessions for a whole year without even feeling the need for an oven.

(NOTE: *Recent concern about possible contamination in eggs and other foodstuffs has to be borne in mind. There can be no doubt that children like to lick fingers and spoons and scrape out bowls and this may involve raw mixtures containing as yet uncooked egg. Every parent will have to make up her own mind about this — and nursery leaders will need to consult parents to find out what their views are.*)

There are many more activities which could be included in this chapter, but they belong equally to other categories of play. Creativity comes into every kind of play once the early exploratory stages and the learning of basic skills and techniques have been mastered.

Children may or may not develop a high degree of 'artistic ability', even if they do have all this early practical experience. Hopefully, however, the 7-year-old will at least go on to his next stage with undamaged confidence, without preconceived ideas picked up from adults, with the enthusiasm to have a go at anything and the ability to take 'failure' and disappointment in his stride.

# Chapter 19

# Learning to Communicate and Cooperate

The first task of the baby is to get someone to look after him, as he can't do this on his own. As he grows bigger and develops, he learns to do more for himself. By the time he is 7 he can do a good deal, but he still can't exist without the support of a group.

Apart from sheer physical survival, he needs to be part of a group for social contact, to learn the skills of his culture, to share and combine ideas and strength so that he can achieve more than the limits of just his own personal ability.

### The process of adjustment

In order to reach this point of being part of a group, each child has to learn to communicate and cooperate with each group he belongs to at each stage of his development. There is a natural, obvious progression:

- At first everyone adjusts to the baby and modifies what they do to suit him.

- The amount of modification of others' behaviour gradually decreases as the baby's level of activity and competence increases.

- He learns about other people and children by having other people and children to watch.

- He learns to adjust and modify his behaviour towards members of his family.

- He learns to coexist with other children with family support.

- He learns to coexist with other children outside the family with non-family adult supervision.

- He learns to coexist with a peer group of children, and only resorts to asking for adult help when he cannot solve the communication/cooperation problems by himself.

- He learns what the rules are and how to fit into groups as a follower.

- He learns (given the opportunity) how to be a leader and to make and change rules.

- He learns how to survive by being flexible about changing his role within a group situation depending on the circumstances – sometimes being a leader, sometimes being led, sometimes being on the outskirts of the group, sometimes being a powerful member within it.

All these stages will have to be reached within the security of an adult supervised situation – whether it is home, parent and toddler group, nursery group or infant school. Even at the age of 7 a child cannot be let loose or pushed out into the world to learn the skills of communication and cooperation alone, because he would not survive.

Each child has to learn to be independent while still being dependent . . . so he learns through the process we call play.

## Learning to cooperate and communicate within the family

Each child has a good start within the family simply because he is a member of it – he will be my son, my brother, my grandson, my nephew or something specific and special to each member. They are interested in him and disposed to help him to learn to communicate and cooperate with the family group simply because he was born into it.

There will be family habits and customs and a family pattern of language for him to absorb. They will allow him to communicate at his own level and help him to move up through the levels of competence because it is in the interests of the family to do so.

If the family provides a good language environment – where there is conversation and a good vocabulary, where someone will actually listen to a child and give him the word he needs, where there are stimulating experiences to encourage a

child to talk, where there is not so much background noise that he can't hear properly what is being said, where there are stories and books and pictures to share and talk about, songs and rhymes to sing, games to be played – then this is an excellent start.

Some children may be at a disadvantage if they have a hearing difficulty. They are at an even greater disadvantage if their hearing difficulty makes others assume that there is no point in trying to communicate with them. One observer in a nursery group spent a very happy half-hour playing with a little boy pushing toy cars along a roadway layout and into a toy garage. The child did not say anything, but responded by looking and smiling as the observer talked about what they were doing – 'Round the corner, up the ramp, whoosh into the garage, brrm brrm out again and off we go down the road – now your turn Paul.' He would have his turn, then look up to the observer to indicate that she should have another go. The lady who had been watching some of this turned out to be waiting to take him home – and as she put his coat on she said to the observer, 'You're wasting your time with him, love, he's deaf.'

Some children are at a disadvantage if they have a non-hearing or non-speaking mother, or if there are a large number of children in the family and everyone does a lot of talking but no one does any listening. Sometimes twins communicate with each other so well that they are slow to learn to talk, sometimes a child belongs to a naturally quiet family, sometimes he lives with one parent and that parent is too depressed to talk much to her child. Some children come from a bilingual family and learn both languages but not as well as the other children learn one language. There are families which do not speak the language of the community in which they live.

For these children, as for all children, mother and baby groups and parent and toddler groups can extend their experience.

## Learning to cooperate in the nursery group

There are obviously very big differences between how a child fits in at home and how he has to fit in at a nursery group. He is not special in the same way – he is not automatically accepted because of who he is. He has to make his own way as an individual in a group of individuals, using the basis of what he is.

Fortunately he has the urge to do this because by nursery group age he wants to play, and playing is the common, shared interest of the group. He also wants to play with other children, so he is disposed to learn to modify and adapt his behaviour to be accepted by them.

The well-equipped, well-organized, well-staffed nursery group will, like the home, provide him with the opportunity to operate at his own level and to work up through the levels of competence. There will be plenty of adult support as and when he needs it. A full range of varied activities will provide him with the opportunity to play alone, to play with one other child or two or three children. He can retire to the sandpit or the water tray for a quiet period, or he can watch, or he can join in. He can use two-person toys which may not have been much use at home, and he can learn to take his turn on larger equipment. He may have had a climbing frame all to himself for most of his playing time up till now, but now he learns to share.

Many activities in nursery groups are provided in quantities for four children to play at a time quite simply because a table has four sides – but this happy accident could not have worked out better if it had been planned. Since they are free to choose what they want to do, there may be one, two, three or four children there at any one time. A child on one side of the table with his own share of the equipment can play alone, or alongside one of the people next to him, or with the person opposite, or with all three, or two pairs of children can join forces to vie against the other two to see who can build highest, or who can make the longest snake out of dough.

If an adult joins the children, then four children is just about right for them to have a group conversation. A shy child can keep quiet if he wants to, as there are enough other people to keep the conversation going without him. He can still feel he is part of the group without being intimidated by feeling he has to say something.

In the well-staffed group there will be enough adults to spend time listening to individual children, to read a book to a little group in the book corner, and there will also be times when a larger group comes together for a music or story session.

The other advantage of being well-staffed is sometimes

having an adult to spare. If one person can sit quietly, perhaps cutting paper or writing a notice, or making a poster or mending dressing-up clothes or some other little chore, children will come up to see what she is doing and may stay for a conversation. This can range from Granny is coming next week, the new baby is not very well or what happened last week at the dentist's. We tend to forget the value of these casual opportunities for child-directed, relaxed conversations.

The normal social exchanges in nursery groups tend to be very much on a here and now basis of giving information, and can miss out on what happened a long time ago or what will happen in the future. All the words and tenses associated with language relating to the past, the future, the 'what if', 'if only' situations can be missed out unless the group of children have enough language experience between them or the adults offer the opportunity for them to arise.

## Opportunities for conversation

It is worth briefly considering how 'conversation' works. Even for adults who have learned the art, there are certain conditions to be met before it can take place:

- There have to be at least two people if there is to be an exchange (some of us talk very satisfactorily with animals but we get back something other than words. If two people do not share the same language the same situation exists in their exchange).

- If it is someone we don't know well we say, 'Good morning, nice day again', and pass on.

- If we are in a hurry we say, 'Hi there, can't stop', and although we may know them well there is no exchange.

- If we do not share a common interest with a person then we have to stick to a general topic – in which case we may have the same conversation over and over again.

- If we show an interest in the other person's particular subject but they don't let us have our turn when they do the listening then there has to be some special reason for us to go on listening to them. It is no longer an exchange situation.

■ If we do share a common interest with someone else we may talk about this but do not necessarily share our thoughts on any other topic unless and until the common interest is exhausted.

■ If we do have an interesting thought we would like to pursue with someone else then (a) they have to be available, (b) they have to have the time to listen, (c) they have to be receptive.

■ The widest-ranging conversations we have are often at a time when we are relaxed or maybe when we are doing something which leaves our head free to listen and think – doing some repetitive job which our hands can do quite well by themselves without our conscious attention, while we are travelling, at meal times provided we are not under pressure with the mechanics of the meal, on a walk provided we are not in a hurry or too concerned about the purpose of the walk, on holiday when we are relieved from normal pressures or when our normal jobs are finished and there is some time before we have to do the next thing on our list.

All this relates to adults – but many of the points are relevant to children too. They need to be with adults regularly and to have time to get to know them well, to have common interests, to be with adults who will listen when they talk about their special interest and who will accept a one-sided exchange for the special reason that they are a child. Children need adults to share the times when they are relaxed or have an interesting thought to share this minute – otherwise they forget what it was they wanted to say or talk about.

There are some activities both at home and in the nursery group which provide good opportunities to meet these conditions.

## Activities which allow for conversation

*Natural materials:* sand, water, dough and clay can be non-demanding materials which leave children free to talk and listen if they are not trying to make or do something special.

*Drink times:* if small groups of children come together with an adult for milk there can be a relaxed easy conversation group. If the whole nursery group is brought together the children may talk to their neighbour in the ring or at the table, but this is only reproducing the same situation they have been in for the rest of the session.

*Reading books in a small group:* this is a useful way to have a brief common interest which might be outside the experience of all the children. It often leads them to say what they think about it or to talk about their own experience and share it with the others. The adults can make sure that all the children get their turn because the group is only small. In a large group everyone would have lost concentration by the time the twentieth child had had his chance – and the twentieth child would, in any case, have forgotten what he wanted to say.

*Stories in a large group:* these are only possible if all the children are old enough and mature enough to concentrate on a storyteller who is not physically near to them without being distracted by the bodies which are near to them. They have to be able to listen to the words and follow them, which means that a certain amount of language skill is needed.

If these conditions are met, and suitable length and type of stories are given, this can be a most enjoyable and useful experience. There is a case for repeating stories often enough for the children to get to know them well, so that they know what is coming and can join in. Equally there is a case for introducing new material, so there has to be a balance between the old and the new.

In a settled group the children become more experienced at listening, so by the end of what we think of as a school year (most nursery groups are affected downwards by the way the older children are taken into school) the stories could be quite different from those at the start of the period. If children do not have long in a group or if it is not a settled group and there is a lot of coming and going, then this progression cannot happen. If the children move to groups which contain children with different levels of experience, then all the children have to start at the lowest level again (see page 144 on the quality and quantity of experience).

*Activity stories, songs, rhymes and games:* these are all useful. Children follow actions, become aware of their bodies (for example the 'Heads and shoulders, knees and toes' rhyme ... see *This Little Puffin*), and do what everybody else is doing, so they are learning to follow instructions, joining in, remembering and developing a sense of rhythm.

The games where older children sort out instructions, for example, 'I want the girl in the red dress to stand/or kneel/or jump /or hop-behind/or in front of/or at the side of/the boy in the blue shoes' can be great fun. Although only one child at a time is actually doing the actions, the others watch like hawks just to make sure the right person does the right thing so they are all involved at every stage. Most of the other games like 'O'Grady Says' have a 'You have failed therefore you must leave the group' element. Groups of children of this age need games where the activity is goal-orientated rather than winning-and-losing-orientated.

*Special interest situations:* at home there are times when things are rearranged or different from usual (the best china and tablecloth when visitors come, looking at seed catalogues ready for planting the garden, preparing for someone's birthday or for Christmas), and these provide new thought and give a different slant on everyday life. The same situation can be created within the nursery group with special interest projects.

A corner may be set aside now and then for a table on which everything is blue (or round, or made of wood, etc.). Children love to contribute to these themes and bring in things from home to show at group time. It is wise to say, 'Bring just one thing tomorrow and you can bring something else the next day', otherwise twenty children arrive with a full carrier bag each.

A blue week could start with a blue table. The best and most useful part of an interest table is the adult who sits quietly nearby, ready to talk with the children about the objects there if that is what they want to do. There can be different shades of blue paint one day, different shades of blue paper to paint on another day, then blue dough, blue water in the water trough, a story about a blue balloon.

*Animals and pets:* these are useful because even shy and inarticulate children respond to them. They are a source of interest, something to talk to, something to be talked about and something to be cared for. Even the smallest child can feel powerful as he feeds a dandelion through the wire of the rabbit hutch or refills the hamster's food bowl. If the animals obligingly have babies that is another great source of excitement and conversation everyone can share.

*Puppets, teddies and dolls:* these are rather like pets. Children can talk to them without having to wait for a reply or being inconveniently diverted from their stream of thought. Even better, they can make this 'conversation partner' say what they would like them to say.

All this may sound as if speech and language are the only key to cooperation and communication. This is not the case, but it is an important key. It is also helpful to focus on language because it demonstrates the give and take, the progression, the rhythm of taking turns, the variation there is between roles at different times, the need to be able to attend to what others want to say or do while remembering the contribution one wishes to make when the opportunity arises.

Hopefully all children will have at least adequate experience to help them develop socially to being confident, capable, articulate and well-adjusted. The observer who played with the little boy who was deaf was not wasting her time. She was cooperating and communicating with him at the level of competence he had reached and just maybe was enabling him to take one little step forward. Apart from that, they were enjoying each other's company. Hopefully that little boy has grown to be a man who has learned to cooperate and communicate with his fellows and take pleasure in their company in spite of being deaf.

The child who comes from a home which provides a good environment for this development needs to move on to an outside group which also provides a good social learning environment, otherwise he is wasting what has already been learned.

The child who does not come from a home which encourages social development and communication also needs to move on to a group which provides a good social learning environment – otherwise he is losing the only chance he will have.

# Chapter 20

# Learning to Do, Think and Find Out

The amount of growing a child will do between birth and his seventh birthday is impressive. The amount of learning he does between birth and 7 years is astounding.

He learns how to do things by watching and imitating, developing and practising skills, learning techniques and combining these with thinking about cause and effect.

He learns to find out by experimenting and making mistakes, by observing, thinking and then adjusting his experiment, so he is using some logical process to work out what to do to get him to where he wants to be.

He learns to know, to think, to reason, to make judgements and choices and to solve problems. By seven he will have learned how to speed up his learning by taking short cuts and finding out what he wants to know from other people and from the various sources of information to which he has access. This means that the results of other people's learning can be added to, and blended in with, his own knowledge and ability.

### How they do it

Perhaps the most surprising and most comforting thing of all is that the vast majority of children will do this by themselves without our interference or effort. We can inhibit their learning by starving them of the opportunity to learn, or by creating a situation where their learning is painful or unrewarding. We can encourage their learning by enabling them to learn efficiently and with enjoyment. But we can't *make* them learn. We can, however, learn more about how children learn simply by watching them do it.

If we observe carefully and unobtrusively and watch exactly what they do and how they do it, we can not only see how they move from one minute stage to the next but we can see the points at which they get stuck. If we know enough about the particular child we can, at this point, decide whether or not he will work it out for himself, whether he has no hope of working it out for himself, or whether a small piece of information or a little tactful assistance could be useful in getting him over this particular hump in his learning and achieving progress.

## How much help do children need?

Our help may be something as small and simple as gently turning round one piece of jigsaw puzzle so that he sees it in the right way to make the connection between the space which needs filling and the pieces available to fill it. To do this for one child might be unnecessary interference. To do it for another child might be useful intervention.

In some cases the adult might do a lot more for the child. The jigsaw puzzle he has chosen may be too difficult for him – but since he does desperately want to do it we do most of the work while letting him find the easy obvious pieces. At the end, as he puts in the last piece, we share the triumph – 'We did that well, didn't we?' Next time, that same satisfying triumph might see him through the frustration of doing a much simpler puzzle by himself. (We have intervened this time by putting the difficult one away and finding an easier one for him to do.)

## Sensible provision

If we think of a situation where a 6-foot weightlifter is sweeping a yard with a 3-foot wide broom, we realize that most women would find it very tiring to do the same work with the same broom. They would get on better with a smaller broom – not because it makes the job different but because it simply makes it easier to do.

The same thing applies to small children. If we give them materials and tools which are appropriate for their hands and strength, their effort can go into learning to use them instead of into getting frustrated and exhausted simply managing the size

or weight or length of something inappropriate. Obviously we can't do this all the time because exactly what children need is not always available and, of course, their hands and strength are going to grow – but, just to encourage children over those first stages of wanting to learn skills, it is worth making some effort to meet their needs. An artist, for instance, uses a long-handled brush to give the balance he needs. If the same brush is given to a 2-year-old there is over-balance because his arm is much shorter. All the 'painting' he is learning to do at this stage is to transfer paint from one place to another, so he could even start with a shaving brush since that would be easy for him to handle.

It may not necessarily be something smaller that he needs – it could be something larger than an adult would use. The size of bodkin we would choose to thread beads would be too small and too thin for a child to use – so we give him a very much longer, thicker one, or we stiffen the end of the threading cord with sticky tape so that he can get the beads on to it more easily.

## One step at a time

We can also help children with their learning by breaking down the task to be done. When they want to do something new or difficult – or both – we give them easy practice. When a 2-year-old wants to set the table we give him one or two unbreakable items to put on the table and we do the rest. By the time he is 7 he can do the whole lot, because through the years we have added more and more items to what we ask him or simply expect him to do.

## Making sense of the world

We help children make sense of the world by helping them sort out information. The key to a child's sorting out and classifying his world is language. Language helps us to think instead of having to 'do', it helps us to remember, to get information and to give information, it can communicate meaning far more delicately than gestures. The child who learns to use language well has a head start in his learning in addition to the head start it gives him in his social development.

Most parents start helping a child's language ability to develop quite naturally and automatically by telling him the names of things – 'Look, there's a dog', 'There's a big dog', 'There's a brown dog', 'That's granny's dog', 'Isn't he a nice dog?', 'He's a naughty dog', so along with the message of 'dog' the baby gets the idea that there are dogs but there are different dogs. Gradually he learns that there are 'big' dogs, 'big' apples, 'big' boys, 'big' cars, and he starts on his sorting out of ideas.

As his ability increases we give him more words, but also as his ability increases he can ask us for more information. The 1-year-old who had just learned to use a few words looked at his cross mother and said, 'Are you nice?' He knew perfectly well she wasn't feeling 'nice', but since he did not know the word for 'cross' he was trying to get the information he needed with the only word he did know. When he had eventually learned the word 'cross' he asked, 'Are you cross, what I do den?' The more words children have, the more information they can get.

The babies who try to fit a large shape into a small hole work by trial and error. If someone gives them the words 'wide and narrow' or 'fat and thin' or 'too large and too small' they can transfer this to other situations where it saves a lot of time – especially when children are working and playing together.

From a purely practical point of view this means that the adult has to be there at the time children need a word otherwise (a) they are not aware that he needs it or (b) they can't give it to him. In the first three years children spend most of their time near and with an adult who probably has, at most, two young children to look after, so giving and getting words as they are relevant to what a child is doing happens quite naturally.

## Adults as a language resource

In a group situation it is hoped that there would be enough adults with enough time to carry on this process of giving words as they are relevant. A group of young children will share the words they have but will not, at any one stage, have all the words they need. Older children may help the younger ones because the younger ones watch and listen. If they are allowed to join in the play of the big children then they will certainly learn new words, because they are told quite clearly what to do and how to do it, since this is how they are fitted into the game.

In a situation where only young children are in a group, there are many times when they need and could absorb new words. If the adults are very stretched just doing the practical jobs that need to be done there is not always time for them to be aware of these opportunities, so although the children certainly benefit from the stimulus of varied opportunities for play, they do not receive as much help with language as they may have done at home.

When the role of the adult in a nursery group is being considered to decide the ratio of adults needed, the element of sitting down quietly near the children or with the children to be available as a language resource, or just having time to stop and answer questions, or simply talking with a child if that is what he wants to do, is often forgotten.

## All play materials and activities help with thinking

Absolutely everything a child does is part of the doing, finding out, learning to think process, so every play material and activity could be in this chapter, but most have been included already in other chapters because they fit into other categories of play.

There are some types of materials and situations where adults can see what children are doing and learning because they are sitting still or 'staying in one place' activities, often called table toys.

There is, of course, no guarantee that children will use these materials in the way this name would suggest. A child may use a set of picture lotto cards as a load for his lorry because, as he will tell us, they just happen to be the right size. Most adults would stop him doing this on the grounds that there are other things he can load in his lorry and if the cards are spoiled then they will not be available for matching games – but we can still give him some credit for having learned about 'just the right size', because that is a very useful concept to have grasped.

These types of play material can be grouped to make sense to adults when they are thinking of what they are providing, for example:

- Matching, fitting, grading.
- Shapes, sizes and families.
- Making and following patterns.

- Recognizing and recalling.
- Three-dimensional shapes.
- Finding out about parts of things.
- Learning to copy.
- Developing ideas of body image.
- Putting 'time' in order.
- Developing rhythm.
- Language games.

The toy catalogues are full of examples of materials for these activities, but virtually all the everyday activities provide practice.

## Pre-learning skills

Pre-learning skills is a phrase we start to hear about when children are coming up to school age. It is a rather clumsy term, as it encompasses a whole range of abilities children will need before being successful at school activities.

It is also an inaccurate term. Children do not 'pre-learn', because every stage of learning is part of the learning process. What is really meant is 'pre-being-teachable' skills. These are the skills and knowledge a child will need to have before he is ready to be 'taught' in a structured situation rather than learning for himself at his own pace in a 'free learning' situation. This is the difference between 'learning on command' and 'learning on demand'.

To quote an experienced teacher of children with severe learning difficulties: 'Experience with severely backward children, particularly older children, reveals that one of the principal causes of failure is teaching which has failed to take into account the importance of not introducing children to learning situations before they are ready.' All children have been in learning situations from the minute they were born, but this teacher was referring to the school-teaching situation rather than to natural learning.

Clearly these 'pre-being-teachable' skills are important, so if we look at them and find out what they are we can think about what we should or could do about giving our children the opportunity to acquire them. They would include . . .

- Form perception and discrimination (recognizing shapes and knowing the difference between them – from any angle).

- Sound perception (recognizing sounds and knowing what they mean).

- Hand–eye coordination (being able to translate a message to and from the brain into appropriate and effective physical action).

- Spatial relationships (how things fit together, relate to each other, how to make a shape, how a shape will look if it is turned round, or sideways or upside down).

- Visual memory and discrimination (remembering what things look like and being able to pick out a shape, being able to pick out things which look the same and things that are different).

- Visual copying (looking at something and being able to copy it or reproduce it).

- Visual rhythms and sequencing (being able to follow a pattern and copy it).

- Auditory sequencing (remembering a pattern of sounds and knowing what comes next).

- Temporal sequencing (putting things in order of what comes first, second, third and knowing what the next thing is likely to be after knowing what has happened already).

- Language and communication skills (understanding and being able to make oneself understood, having an adequate vocabulary, being able to talk about a picture, being able to tell a sequence of events, being able to carry out instructions).

- Good body image and knowing how parts fit together to make a 'whole' (recognizing separate parts and knowing how they relate to a complete object or body).

- Knowing colours and shapes (children have more difficulty with shapes than they do with colours, and are usually nearly 5 or 6 or even 7 before they can confidently name and copy shapes – although they can pick out a shape we name before this).

- Being ready for number work by having some knowledge of:

(a) *Conservation* (how a specific quantity is still a specific quantity however the shape or appearance is changed).
(b) *Cardination* (knowing that three is three whether it is three apples, three buttons, three children, three bricks).
(c) *Ordination* (knowing about comparative sizes – Father Bear, Mother Bear, Baby Bear, or large, larger, largest or small, smaller, smallest), and
(d) *Classification* (putting things into groups according to common factors, which could be size or shape or colour or taste or use – or any other grouping which is appropriate).

■ Being able to use a pencil or crayon (and make it do what they are asked to do).

■ Being able to concentrate.

■ Being confident.

If we think back to what has been said at each stage of development and each type of play activity, it becomes clear that the child who has been given rich opportunities for play (with all the implications of adequate space, adequate material, adequate encouragement, adequate information, adequate success) has done all this learning quite naturally. We don't have to single out these activities if children have a 'play rich diet'. They are already there and the normal child is developing these skills all by himself at his own pace – and furthermore he is enjoying doing so.

The problems start when we try to rush him too quickly to the next step. If a child goes too early to a formal teaching situation, (a) he is going to 'fail' because he is not ready for this, and (b) probably even more important, by actually being in this teaching situation he is being deprived of the time and opportunity to continue learning in his own way – so he is losing out twice.

This 'common sense – obvious when you think about it' conclusion is amply borne out by the research findings and recommendations in the CHES study *The Effects Of Early Education* (see page 271).

There are some children who are deprived of a rich play diet by the circumstances in which they have to live. Their need is to have their play diet supplemented – not to have it cut out altogether by moving them into a teaching situation.

There are some children who cannot take full advantage of a rich play diet because they have a personal problem or difficulty. They need a specially adapted one, but they do not need the play element removed altogether.

# Chapter 21
# Playing Safe

All children hurt themselves – absolutely everyone who lives or works with young children will, at some time, have to deal with the cuts, grazes, bumps and bruises that happen to every child. Most of us are very good at dealing with everyday first aid and 'kissing better' routines.

Some children really damage themselves. There can be few people, whether or not they live and work with young children, who do not know of some child having an accident that was more than a mother could deal with and which resulted in calling in a doctor and/or a trip to the accident and emergency department of a local hospital. It may have been one of our own children, a child we were looking after, the child of a neighbour or friend or relative.

We see statistics about what has happened, and news items which should warn us about what could happen, but this does not seem to reduce the tremendous number of accidents that occur.

Statistics don't mean much to most of us. They are estimates and figures – not real people. We don't really know what large figures mean. (How many *is* a million? Have there been a million days since the first Christmas? How old would we be if we lived a million hours? How far would we get if we walked a million yards?) We tend to interpret risks optimistically. With odds of ten to one we think of having a one in ten chance *for* winning a raffle and buy a whole book of tickets – but with exactly the same odds in a danger situation we decide we have a nine in ten chance *against* being a victim.

The human body heals itself very effectively, and the evidence which would remind us of accidents tends to fade away. If every dent, cut, bruise, fracture remained as visible on our children as it does on our furniture, we might remember each incident more. We forget, just as our children do. To live in a constant fear situation would create unbearable stress, and the natural tendency of the human is to adjust to fear. If we were constantly fearful we would never let our children do anything.

### Facts and figures

The estimated number of home accidents to children aged 0–14 years is 1,300,000 per year (i.e. for every thirty seconds of every hour, of every week, of every month of the year, a child has an accident in his home). The estimated cost of medical attention and treatment is £538,650,000.

It is worth having a closer look at the information available, to work out what is happening, to whom, and why, where and when.

### Who has the accidents?

A glance at Fig. 9 shows that children aged 0–14 years have nearly four times their 'fair share' of home accidents – and if the age range is considered more closely, it is the toddler age group which is at most risk. Boys have more accidents than girls in every age range – most mothers will not be surprised by this, but it is strange that this finding is so consistent.

Some of the large figures for younger children can be accounted for if we look at what happens after an incident occurs.

Not every child who is taken to a doctor or a casualty department needs treatment, and some, after being examined, are sent home. This is not to say that the child is not very distressed, however, and certainly his mother will feel she needs some treatment – her legs will still feel very wobbly the next day. This happens particularly with very young children and accounts for some of the very large figures. They can't tell us what is wrong or exactly what happened. Coping with the distress of a baby or toddler is as much as one person can do, and someone else is needed to make a proper examination of the damage. It takes a skilled eye and a lot of experience to decide,

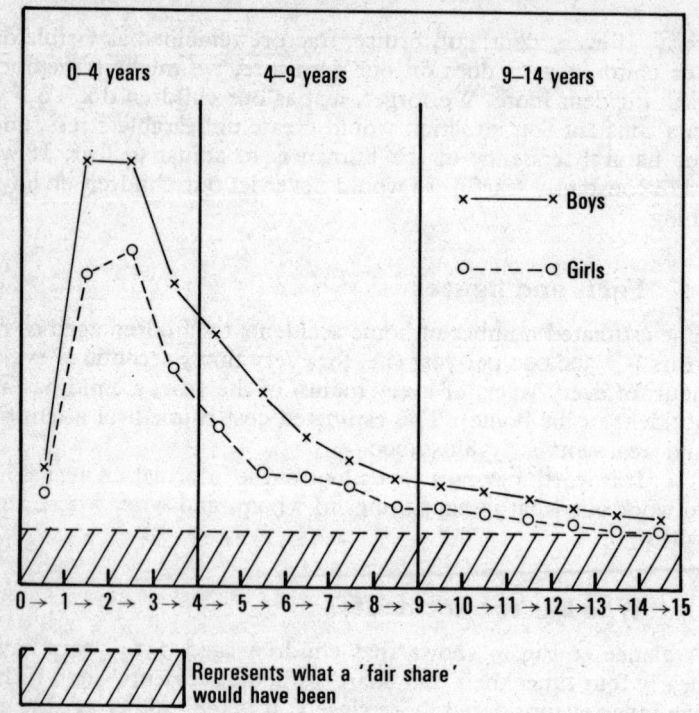

**x——x Boys**

**o----o Girls**

0→ 1→ 2→ 3→ 4→ 5→ 6→ 7→ 8→ 9→ 10→11→12→13→14→15

Represents what a 'fair share' would have been

*Figure 9 Home accidents: Relative percentage of accidents 0–14 years*

'Nothing is wrong – no damage – therefore no treatment necessary.' We leave this decision to an expert in the same way that we feel we must leave it to an expert to decide something *is* wrong and how it should be treated.

Some children are not so lucky, and do need treatment before they are sent home. Some children are less lucky still and will have to stay in hospital for observation and treatment. One out of every eleven children who are taken to a casualty department will be admitted to a hospital ward, and the length of stay varies. The majority of children will be kept there for between one and four days – but for a few it will be longer than that – for a very few it will be a very long stay indeed.

For some children luck has run out altogether, and they die either before they get to the hospital or soon after they get there. The numbers of children who die are relatively few compared with the number of accidents, but this fact will be of no comfort to anyone.

In 1985 nearly three times as many children aged 0–4 died than in the 5–14 age group – which contains twice as many children. Not only are 0–4s more likely to have accidents, they are more likely to die as a result of an accident in the home.

## Who has which accidents?

There are big differences in the types of accident which happen to children and those which happen to adults:

■ On the whole adults do not push foreign bodies into their noses and ears, or climb up to a level three times their own height to find a bottle or jar or tin, struggle to get the lid off and then eat the nasty-tasting things inside. Usually adults know what they can and cannot do and have the sense to draw back or give up long before a child would. They know about over-balancing, about heat, about how near or how far objects are. They know enough about potential danger to remove themselves from it – or remove it from themselves.

■ Adults in the age range who look after young children are in the group which has least home accidents – far less than their 'fair' share. Yet adults don't stop to think every time they do something and work out the safest way or calculate the hazards. If they did they would never get through the day. Adults are safety sub-conscious rather than safety conscious. It is largely strong safety habits which are automatic which keep them safe.

■ Small children have a dangerous period in front of them while they learn and practise good safety habits which are appropriate for the stage they are at (what is safe for a baby of 3 months is not necessarily safe for a toddler of 2 years). Children have to learn sensible habits – but the adults who look after children also have to learn new habits, in some cases unlearn old ones and adjust their ideas of safety. A house which was safe for adults can be very unsafe for small children.

There are also big differences in the types of accident children have at different ages and stages.

## Accidents to babies from 0–9 months

One might think that the tiny baby who cannot move by himself would be safe enough, and to a great extent this is true. The accidents which happen to them are usually due to someone else having an accident.

Towards the end of the 0–9 month period, most babies are becoming very active, if not mobile. In addition to keeping danger away from them, we have to start keeping them away from danger. This is where our old safety habits may fail – they are no longer good enough. We not only have to learn new habits, we have to change these new ones regularly to account for the increasing ability of the baby. Just because he did something slightly dangerous today and got away with it doesn't mean he will get away with it tomorrow. By tomorrow he will be slightly more able and is more likely rather than less likely to have an accident. A good basic start would be:

- Straps and harness with everything, or one harness on the baby which will attach to all the equipment he sits in.

- Removing anything which he may pull over.

- Pan guards on cookers, short flexes on kettles, electric socket guards, fire guards.

- Door pads on door handles to stop doors slamming.

- Safe floors at all times. Towards the end of this period babies get very good at picking up small articles and they put them in their mouths. If they are mobile they can cover a lot of ground on their scavenging trips, and they have eyes like hawks. It is not just a case of picking up something we know has been dropped. We have to check to see if something we don't know about has been dropped.

Non-metallic items such as peanuts, small pieces of plastic toys or little pieces of polystyrene are particularly dangerous, as they cannot be detected by X-ray if there is an incident.

# Home accidents to babies and toddlers from 9 months–4 years

Children in this age range show the worst accident figures of all, and it is the 1-, 2- and 3-year-olds who account for the bulk of the high figures. It is not really surprising when we consider what this age group are doing:

■ They spend most of their time at home, so this is where any accidents will occur.

■ They are learning to walk and move and use their body. The most dangerous time for anyone learning a new skill is during the earliest stages.

■ They are naturally curious. This is part of their learning equipment.

■ They are quick to seize an opportunity, and they have all the time they are awake to do their finding out.

■ They have very little idea of cause and effect, so even when they are hurt they do not always know why.

■ They have even less idea about what is dangerous.

■ They forget between incidents and do the same thing again.

The accidents they have now and the damage they do to themselves show a different pattern from when they were babies. Records and statistics show a picture more like that for older children:

■ They get cuts as well as bruises.

■ They have most of the poisoning/suspected poisoning incidents which occur.

■ They have more than their share of burns and scalds, and in the main will cause these by their own actions.

■ Over half the injuries are associated with a fall, but now the fall is likely to be due to falling downstairs or tripping over on the level or falling over some equipment on the ground.

■ Sometimes nursery equipment is involved – they fall out of prams, high chairs and cots. Baby frame walkers seem to be a particular hazard (an estimated 7,000 accidents occur each year), particularly for children under 1 year. These walkers give children who are not able to cope with it a degree of mobility they cannot control. They also tip over when the very small wheels come up against the edge of a carpet, and they tip down unguarded stairs. Very careful supervision is necessary, and the figures suggest that very young children do not have the necessary strength and control to use these walkers safely.

- They put things in their mouths like babies do, but they also put things in their ears and noses.

- They get some splinter injuries, which were not a common feature of baby accidents.

- There are more fractures and dislocations.

- Heads are still the most damaged part of the body, followed by arms and hands, but the digestive system shows more injury than feet and legs.

Lessons to be learned by adults will have to be an ongoing process because children change so fast. What was safe yesterday will not necessarily be safe today:

- **DON'T ASSUME** young children know what is dangerous.

- **DON'T EXPECT** them to remember what they have been told – but go on telling them anyway. Just saying 'No' may work, but we need to give a simple reason too, for example, it's hot, it's sharp, it's heavy, so that these words come to be associated with 'leave it alone'.

- **DO GET USED TO** safety gates, play pens, straps and harnesses and putting up the side of the big cot well before such precautions are needed rather than after they have painfully proved necessary.

- **DO CONSIDER** what has to be kept away from children and put it away – preferably well out of reach and locked. Equally important is putting things back in their safe place after use, because it is often during the time between something being used and when it is put back that children get hold of it.

- **DO DEAL WITH** the fixed hazards children have to be kept away from – kettles, pans, fires, stairs, windows, electricity sockets – which means providing and unfailingly using guards, gates and restraints, boarding up or protecting low glass, fitting safety bars to windows.

■ DO CHECK toys and playthings meant for small children, but also make sure they are used properly. Toys and playthings meant for older children are not suitable. More often than not it is the child himself who is the dangerous element – not the toy.

■ DO INSIST that toys and playthings are kept off stairs and away from where they will be tripped over (fathers are often the victims in this situation).

■ DO KEEP children's play equipment where they can reach it (not too high up, and in a box rather than a drawer as the latter might pull right out).

### Fatal home accidents to under-5s

More children in the 0–4 age range die as a result of home accidents than in the 5–14 age group.

The largest number of deaths occur as the result of fires in the home. Another cause of home accident death to this age group which we do not hear so much about is drowning.

Approximately twenty 0–14-year-old children die each year from drowning in the home – not larking about at the seaside or near a river or a lake or a swimming bath, but in a place where one might think the risk was negligible. Children can drown in a very shallow depth of water. They should not be left alone in the bath, fish ponds should be guarded (RoSPA suggests filling them with sand to make a sandpit), and home swimming-pools might be considered as a hazard rather than a financial luxury. RoSPA point out that water-confident children need more supervision rather than less.

There are simple things like water-butts or buckets of soaking washing. We might think that the most likely accident would be a child knocking over the bucket, washing and all, and it undoubtedly is – but children can also fall into them head first, and can't get out.

Some children die as a result of inhaling and swallowing objects and also as a result of suffocation – the warning on plastic bags is there for a very good reason. Others fall from buildings, out of windows, off balconies. Some children die from poisoning.

## Home accidents to children of 5–9 years

This age group, who regularly spend six to seven hours a day for five days of each week for approximately forty weeks of each year away from home, still have nearly twice their fair share of home accidents resulting in a visit to the hospital.

Of the 5–9-year-old children who attend hospital as casualties following an accident at home, about half are treated and sent home, and about half will have to attend again as outpatients or receive follow-up treatment from their own doctor, which is a higher proportion of children actually needing treatment than for very young children. This adds weight to the thought that parents feel more confident in deciding for themselves that no treatment is necessary when dealing with this age group than they do with very young children. Relatively few 5–9-year-olds have to stay in hospital (about 4 per cent), and the majority will be home in four days or less.

This all sounds as though these children are learning to cope with themselves and their environment much better – but these figures relate only to home accidents. They have accidents outside the home too.

Lessons to be learned must include the fact that there are indeed lessons still to be learned. This age group still have more than their fair share of accidents:

- We have to make the garden and garden equipment safe. No one actually comes to any harm while they are falling – it is the landing that does the damage. Shock-absorbing surfaces under swings, slides and climbing frames can take some of the sting out of landing (see Appendix 4, page 304). Balcony and window protection is still as necessary as it was for the younger age group.

- We have to teach them to use tools safely and let them practise under our eye.

- We have to teach them to be wary of broken glass.

- We have to teach them to be aware of what other people are doing. Very often it is the child standing too close to a swing (especially if it does not have a recommended type of seat) who gets hurt, rather than the child who is on it. If a child watching his friend use a hammer comes too close it is just as likely to be his face which gets damaged as the other child's thumb.

■ We have to teach them not to stand too close to doors, not to rush through doors and not to let doors slam. If we sensibly have a patent door stop on outside doors, they need to be shown how to use it.

■ We need to look in our homes for frayed carpet edges, loose floor coverings, stair carpets coming unfastened – and deal with them straight away.

■ If play in the bedroom sounds as if it is getting too rumbustious we have to go and see what is going on, especially if there are bunk beds there – shouting threateningly from the bottom of the stairs just means they stop the noise, not the leaping about.

## Home accidents involving toys

Nearly half the home accidents to children are associated with playing, which implies that the children are playing with toys, playthings or equipment specially meant for this purpose.

■ Virtually every available toy is mentioned in the list of incidents relating to toys.

■ The greatest number of accidents occur to 2-year-olds, and boys account for more than half of them (as in every other category).

■ Half the accidents involve falls, and nearly half result in cuts and lacerations.

■ Most accidents take place in the garden.

■ 20 per cent of the accidents are the result of being struck by an object or a person – that is, it was someone else's play which did the damage.

All this leads to the conclusion that in the main the toy itself is not at fault – it is what the children do with it which causes the damage.

If we buy toys made in this country to British Standards specifications (BS 5665 or EN 71), if we make sure they are suitable for the age of the children we give them to and keep them away from younger children – and if we make sure that children have the right amount of space for using them and that other children are not going to be damaged by coming too close, then that is a good start.

The toys and playthings most often involved in accidents give a clue to where the real hazards lie:

- Bicycles are associated with 17 per cent of play accidents, and the biggest age group is the 3-year-olds. Frame baby walker accidents are estimated at 7,000 per year, and the biggest group is the 0–1-year-olds. Trundle toys (which children sit on and propel with their feet) are for young children, so it is to be expected that the children who have accidents on them will be young – but there is a very high number of 1-year-olds involved. Perhaps children are given these toys too early.

- Garden toy accidents show only just fewer figures than bicycle accidents, and the largest grouping is 3–4 years for boys and 4–5 years for girls. They need supervision and they need shock absorbing surfaces underneath.

- Playing with a ball causes accidents, and it is the movement associated with this that leads children to fall over and/or bump into other children. They need space for this activity.

- Roller skates, scooters, skateboards, go-carts and toboggans are associated with accidents, and the most likely part of the body to be damaged is the wrist. Perhaps the only surprise in this category is that boys have most of these accidents at 12–13 years, whereas the peak age for girls is 5–6 years. Perhaps the boys are 'showing off' at 12–13 and the girls have grown out of these activities by then.

Fairly 'passive' items/activities are also linked to home accidents:

- Marbles are swallowed mainly by 4–8-year-olds, when we might think they ought to know better.

- Construction kit pieces are swallowed and pushed into noses and ears mainly by 2-year-olds (perhaps marbles are too big for them to swallow as many as the 4–8-year-olds do).

- Balloons are involved because children are struck by an object or person, presumably while they are chasing their balloon. The peak age for this is 4 years – which fits with the vigorous action but lack of fine control of the 4-year-old.

Instead of wondering what is safe for children in the home, perhaps we ought to consider what children are safe for. The accidents in the main are caused by their own behaviour. The one safeguard is constant vigilance and training by the adults who care for them.

## In fairness to parents

Few people who care for children do so as their only responsibility. There are other family members and homes to look after, meals to prepare, dishes to be washed, laundry to be done. Young children are very tiring to care for and keep safe. This is a good reason for providing some respite for mothers on a regular basis, such as mother and baby clubs, and particularly parent and toddler groups.

There is some indication that young children whose mothers are depressed or are under stress, or who live in families where there is stress, are more likely to have accidents. The only surprising thing about this is that the evidence is not stronger. Anyone who has had to carry on caring for young children while feeling unwell would recognize this as being inevitable without the need for figures to prove it. Perhaps it is significant that sleeping pills, tranquillisers and anti-depressants feature in the list of medicines involved with child poisonings.

From the point of view of accident prevention, in addition to all the other reasons, these are the families who need support and help within the home most of all.

## Accidents outside the home

Public parks and playgrounds are not without their hazards. It is estimated that there may be as many as 150,000 playground accidents every year which need medical treatment – and this is only the tip of the iceberg.

Parents may feel they cannot influence what is provided and what happens in public places, but that is not so. If these places are public places, then public money is being used to provide them. Parents have every right to make their voice heard, and the following information may be helpful in persuading them to do this:

■ Public authorities *and* private owners have a legal duty to inspect and properly maintain playground equipment. Parents can help by reporting any equipment which needs attention.

■ Some playgrounds still have the very large, old-fashioned equipment which is known to cause terrible accidents – pendulum seesaws (capable of decapitating a child), plank or plane swings, ocean wave roundabouts, the heavy long horse rocker, seesaws which bump hard on the ground and damage spines. Parents could campaign to have these removed.

■ Playground surfaces, particularly under items of equipment, should be suitably shock-absorbent (see Appendix 4, page 304). 85 per cent of serious injuries involve falls, and hard surfaces such as packed earth, tarmac and concrete. Claims for damages and injuries caused by falls on to unsuitable surfaces are likely to become common, so local authorities ought to be receptive to pressure from parents to install approved surfaces.

■ There is a clear relationship between the seriousness of an injury and the height from which a child has fallen. The current B S allows for a fall height of 2.5 metres on play equipment (compared with a situation where building site workers can only work 2 metres above the ground before guard rails have to be provided). The European standard for the fall height for playground equipment is 2 metres. Perhaps parents could point this out to local authorities.

■ There are fewer accidents where there are playground supervisors. If suitable seats were provided, parents might be more willing to stay and supervise their children. If there is no paid supervision, parents could at least ask for seats so that they can supervise comfortably. If there is a paid supervisor they could ask for seats as well – the more pairs of eyes the better.

## Safety in the nursery group

On the whole there are relatively few accidents in nursery groups, since there should be an adequate number of adults to supervise and they can plan the group layout to make supervision more efficient.

The most likely time for any incident to occur is during

setting out equipment or putting it away. This preparation and clearing away should be done when the children are not there. Parents can help by not arriving with children until the proper time – and also by picking up children at the proper time.

Where parents help to build and install special equipment this is fine – but they do need to find out what is recommended as safe and acceptable before they start (see Appendix 4, page 304). It is also important that there is continuity of maintenance. Parents who provide and install equipment are committing succeeding generations of parents to undertake the responsibility when they themselves have moved on. This needs to be noted in records and minutes of meetings, and succeeding committees or working parties should be reminded of this obligation.

## Accidents in school

Children also have accidents at school. Compared with most other accidents, they tend to be much fewer and less severe. The fact that in general the 'school' accidents which end up at the accident and emergency departments of hospitals are less severe may reflect teachers' recognition of their statutory responsibilities for children in their care and that they err on the side of being extra careful. There is also the point that while they were attending to one injured child the other thirty-five or more children in their class would be unsupervised.

- Boys have more accidents than girls (three boys to every two girls).

- They occur mostly in the 10–14-year age range.

- Most occur in the playground. In addition to bumps, scrapes, and falls (and the occasional fight, even organized bullying), children have accidents with school playground equipment just as they do in parks and public playgrounds. Perhaps a healthy parent/teacher association could help provide safer equipment.

## Accidents on the roads

Child pedestrians and child cyclists show in the figures for road accidents and road deaths.

One in four of all road accidents occur at the times children are going to and coming home from school. Within the 0–7-year age range we are considering, all parents would make sure their children are escorted to school either by themselves or a responsible adult – they would also make sure official school crossings were used. Nevertheless, there will come a time when these young children are old enough to go out alone, either to school or elsewhere. The daily trek with the under-7s to the school gate should be regarded as a positive opportunity for training.

If children are eventually going to use bicycles, then the National Cycling Proficiency training scheme is often provided for in junior schools (see Appendix 4, page 304). Where this is not the case, the parent teacher group could offer help with a training course.

## The dangerous age, and who deals with it

Obviously our 0–7 age range is the most dangerous period of any individual's life. The particularly hazardous toddler stage between 1 and 3 is going to be mainly a home responsibility, and it is mainly mothers who have to deal with this – with very little respite or help. The hazards vary from stage to stage, and it can be confusing to realize that what was safe yesterday will not be safe today. A safety code which simply says 'Do this/ Don't do that' can't ever be enough, but there are some general suggestions which should be helpful:

1   Keep ahead of what children are likely to do today.

2   Keep an eye open for signs of what they may well do tomorrow.

3   Keep an adequate first aid box.

4   Take a first aid course – it doesn't have to be a full-blown one (although that would be a good idea). Ask at the local health centre if there are courses especially in first aid for children.

5   If there is a nasty incident:
  (a) Keep calm – there will be plenty of time to be sick and feel ill afterwards.
  (b) Remember that a very little blood goes a very long way

(see how far just two tablespoons of red paint can be smeared over a table top).

(c) Always take a second look at any obvious damage. It may not be as bad as it seemed at first glance.

(d) Kissing better does help – and is very efficient. A terrified child has a very fast heartbeat. If he is bleeding he will lose even more blood because of this. Anything we can do to reassure him is good treatment.

(e) If a child is bawling loudly it is probably good news – there is probably less serious damage there than if he is terribly quiet or unconscious.

This has been a long chapter – and it has to be admitted that the general tone has been nag, nag, nag, do this, don't do that . . . but perhaps that is the very essence of safety training. Proving the efficiency of safety habits is very difficult. We are aiming at NO accidents, so the more success we have the less we have to show for it.

The only way to demonstrate that our safety precautions do work is not to take them and to count up the accidents which occur as a result – and none of us could stand by and let that happen to our children.

# Chapter 22

# Why Can't You Play Nicely?

If every adult who lived or worked with young children put a ten pence piece in a piggy bank every time they said, 'Why can't you play nicely' – or something like it – they would need a very large piggy bank and would have a sizeable nest-egg by the time the children were old enough to leave their care.

### Normal bad behaviour

This chapter concerns the behaviour of normal children – what children do and how they react in ordinary everyday situations and the effect this has on the adults who are with them virtually all day and every day.

The information comes from lively, open-ended, frank discussions, over a period of twenty years, with and between at least 1,000 students on various in-service training courses concerning child development and child care.

Each discussion started with the students being asked to write down twenty things children did which annoyed them. Collating the resulting lists led to an inevitable grouping of various aspects of behaviour, and very often a particularly outrageous piece of behaviour as related by an adult would cause great amusement. For example: 'Throwing stones is the thing that gets to me most' led to someone else chipping in with: 'I've got that on my list as well – but I can't say it bothers me as much as it seems to bother you' and this brought the rejoinder: 'Yes, but he's throwing them at ME ...' On this particular occasion the laughter led to the lecturer in the next room coming in to complain about the noise, ending with the pointed remark: 'I thought you were here to learn about children, not behave like children' – which was just about the most useful and valuable thing he could have said. He had highlighted the fact that quite often the behaviour we describe as childish is not 'childish' at all – everybody does it. The more mature we become, the more we learn to sublimate and express our reactions in a socially acceptable manner (or be more careful about being found out or observed), but occasionally we slip backwards a decade or two.

The main categories of behaviour each group found they had to deal with fell under general headings which could have been applied to society at large.

*Dangerous Behaviour*: this included, for example, throwing sand, tipping chairs backwards, leaning out of windows, leaving toys on stairs, damaging other children, etc. which were often linked to

. . . *Disobedient Behaviour*: there is obviously a stage at which adults expect young children to know that what they are doing is dangerous because they have been told what they are doing is dangerous – and yet they go on doing it. This leads to the category of defiance, which links it in with aggression. If we stay with the idea of actual, tangible damage, this links in with

. . . *Destructive Behaviour*: with small children this includes tearing books, spoiling other children's work or wrecking whatever the group is trying to do. There are also cases of damage caused by children having accidents simply because they are young; they know very little about cause and effect, and their efforts sometimes lead to an unforeseen incident. The factor of disobedience arises again, because there is an age at which adults expect children not to do these things.

*Aggressive Behaviour*: this sometimes leads to tangible damage to property or to other individuals:

■ The occasion when two friends were painting side by side and one picked up a full brush load of paint and scrubbed it over the other's painting saying: 'It's not fair, yours is better than mine.'

■ The little boy in the toy shop who came up to a very prim and proper little girl with long blonde hair in a pony tail, quietly enjoying a 10p ride in a large mechanical toy at the doorway of a toy shop. He grabbed hold of her hair and had very nearly hauled her out of the toy by the time the little girl's mother got to him. Some of the pony tail was still in his hand when she separated the two.

- The children who bite, pinch and scratch and leave marks on other children and adults.

- Throwing stones and hitting with some kind of weapon.

Sometimes there is no tangible result to aggression – it can be *Verbal Aggression*. Its effects can last long after the words have died into silence – the rudeness, name-calling, teasing, telling tales to get someone into trouble, swearing at (as opposed to just swearing), sneering, mimicking, taunting, deliberately being silly and shouting during a story session which ruins it for everyone.

Then there is the non-tangible, non-verbal aggression of *Offensive Body Language* – the face-pulling, silent insolence, rude gesture, simply walking away and deliberately ignoring what is said to them, which leave the aggressee in the position of not being able quite to explain, either to themselves or anyone else who did not see the incident, just what it was that made them feel so aggressive in return.

*Anti-social Behaviour*: was defined by most groups who did this exercise as behaviour which is unacceptable by any age group to any age group (but there were some very interesting cultural differences in how strongly adults felt about them) – spitting, swearing, picking noses and worse (the 'worse' was rarely defined, so everyone was left to draw their own conclusion), selfishness, making a dreadful mess, deliberate lying (as opposed to fantasizing or exaggerating), lack of cooperation beyond reason, 'switching off' to the point of completely ignoring other individuals or the rest of the group.

A number of items did not fit into the main categories, so these were looked at carefully to see if there was a common factor. They included sniffing, dribbling, sucking thumbs; eating with mouths open, noisy eating, messy eating; fidgeting and twitching, whining, clinging, screeching, complaining; not putting toys away, mis-using things, misplacing things, losing things; turning away when asked to do something, giggling with another child and running away when asked to do things, disappearing when they thought they might be asked to do things, saying they would do things and then not doing them; waiting for someone else's toy instead of finding something else to play with or do . . . and the main and immediate common factor was that they were *Irritating to Adults* and would be so whether it was children, teenagers, husbands, mothers-in-law or anyone else who did them.

All of this gives a horrendous picture of young children, but it is a composite list collected over a long period of time. Each student list represented a lot of children and they had been given an open invitation to be as critical as they could possibly be.

Some very interesting and useful discussion arose from these lists of day-to-day problems of living and working with young children.

## Solving the problems

Some conclusions emerged very quickly. Some problems were easier to deal with than others – not because they were less severe but because:

- It was easy to see what to do about them because the adult could avoid the situation in which the problem occurred.

- Students had a very strong personal reaction to them and were in no doubt as to how they would, rightly or wrongly, deal with them. One area of aggression, for instance, was universally seen as unacceptable – each and every adult said they would not tolerate biting and scratching by a child of any age under any circumstances. Perhaps there is a message there for any mother who has a child who does this.

- Some of the problems would hopefully resolve themselves as children learned to deal with their feelings in a more acceptable way and developed more social skills.

- It was obvious some of these children needed outside help (page 244).

Some of the problems needed more thought, and had to be considered in the light of what the adult could do about them either by helping a child change his behaviour or by altering the outcome of his behaviour.

### Evidence helps

Destructiveness and damage, whether deliberate or not, has a concrete aspect which can be pointed out to children. At least the child can see what we are talking about and can relate this to what he did.

### The no-evidence situation

It is not easy to deal with the results of aggression if there is no evidence and if the adult did not see or hear what happened. It is difficult to explain to a child how his behaviour has led to an incident, because he can't see his own facial expressions and body stance and he can't relate to the 'how would you feel if' approach if he hasn't got to that stage yet.

It was generally agreed that both verbal and non-verbal aggression were catching, since children imitate and reflect what they see and hear going on around them. In some groups children pulled faces at each other, in others they said nasty things to each other, in yet others they were more likely to hit out. Both environmental and social factors seemed to play a part in this, so some care has to be taken in a multi-cultural or mixed social group as there are differences about what is acceptable and what is not. Group leaders may have to modify their own attitudes and reaction and also be very tactful about parents' reaction to each other's children.

### Childish behaviour

Some anti-social behaviour which can just about be tolerated in a child for whom everyone makes allowances, will not be tolerated as he grows older.

Behaviour which is labelled childish is not necessarily related to children – it is simply inappropriate. The lecturer who was so cross about the noise could have said we were being inconsiderate – which we were. We were laughing in the wrong place at the wrong time – and of course children do this too. We all have times when we are 'childish'. In fact the person who scrubbed paint on her friend's work was nearer forty than four (it was during one of the art sessions described on page 188). The follow-up was that her friend turned round and said: 'That was a very childish thing to do,' and they both burst out laughing. Later the 'aggressor' said: 'I know it didn't make my painting any better, and I didn't really want to spoil yours, but I did mean it and I felt better when I had done it.' The 'aggressee' said: 'I know I laughed, but I was in two minds about whether to give you a good thump and I might have done if I hadn't noticed Mrs M. watching us. I'd worked very hard on that painting!'

## Dangerous behaviour

Dangerous behaviour is particularly difficult to deal with, because adults are responsible for the consequences of a child's irresponsible actions. The only time when we are in a position to point out concrete evidence to a child as to what danger actually means is when we have failed, and are therefore in a position to say 'I told you so.' There was general agreement that tension and mutual irritation between adults and children concerning dangerous behaviour was inevitable and that both parties would simply have to accept this.

## Defiant behaviour

Defiant behaviour, the direct challenge to an adult, is difficult for adults to accept – perhaps because the child is rejecting us personally along with our values. It starts with NO and non-cooperation (see Chapter 7). However, there are some positive advantages to a child learning to say NO (the mother talking about her daughter ... 'The first word she ever said was NO and she has gone on saying it ever since – but I remember thinking that if she is still saying NO at the age of eighteen there could be some situations in which it would be a good and positive thing to say – and I might eventually be grateful that she had done all that maddening practice on me').

Where defiance becomes a habitual part of a child's personality, adults can sometimes take the heat out of situations by avoiding the direct confrontation. For example, the adult says: 'I should think you are just about ready for your drink, John, you've been playing very hard,' to which the child can say, 'I don't want my drink' or 'Not yet' and no one loses anything. If the adult says, 'Will you come in this minute, I told everyone to come in for milk ages ago,' and he replies, 'No', the adult can *either* (a) ignore the defiance by saying 'That's all right, I don't mind' and (if she manages not to say out loud 'It's your milk anyway') she can end the matter at this stage, *or* (b) she can say, 'I shall pour it away, then,' to which he replies, 'Oh no you won't,' to which the adult says 'Oh yes I will,' and there is yet another escalating incident.

If we can save the full-scale confrontation for times when it really does matter – perhaps a situation where what is being done is dangerous, such as a child kicking at other children from the top of a climbing frame even though he has been warned about it – this will at least reduce the number of incidents. In this particular example it might have been better not to give him the benefit of the doubt, and instead of warning him just to have bodily lifted him down from his perch, so that the confrontation was short, sharp and to the point.

As to the child who threw stones at his playgroup leader – her group came up with the suggestion that clearly this had to be stopped, but the child did seem to need some personal means of working out his aggression. Since he appeared to like throwing things, perhaps this could be diverted into a more acceptable channel – such as half a dozen old squash balls to throw at an upturned bucket well away from windows and other children. His aim was clearly quite good, so he should achieve some success in the form of a satisfying noise.

## Tolerance

One thing which became clear from these sessions, especially when discussing those items listed as *Irritating to Adults*, was just how much variation there can be in the degree of tolerance adults have. Apart from the fact that all adults have bad days and good days, which leads to personal variations in how much they will put up with or accept, their basic personalities make a significant difference.

At one end of the scale are some very relaxed, very tolerant, very accepting adults who appear serene and unruffled in any situation – but this can be for very different reasons.

Take, for example, the incident of the little boy who pulled another child out of the pay-and-ride toy by the hair. The mother of the little girl who was just about being scalped was not far away – hearing the yells, she came over and very gently held the boy off with one hand and with the other held her child's long pony tail, so that he was pulling against her hand rather than the child's head, saying quite gently, 'Oh no, you're hurting her, you can have a ride in a minute when Anne is finished.' This is one kind of tolerance.

The mother of the boy appeared from the back of the shop some seconds later, looked at her son's furious scowl, didn't seem to notice the little girl's tear-stained face, said, 'Won't she let you have a go darling? Just wait there and I'll be back in a minute,' and went off again. The boy moved over to some stands of books and started throwing them to the floor, and the girl at the till picked them all up muttering loudly and giving the child nasty looks he didn't seem to notice.

Later the same child was seen leaving the shop and scattering a trail of promotion leaflets from the fistful he was carrying, with his still unruffled mother saying, 'You don't really want all those leaflets, darling' while he was shouting 'I do, I do.'

This was a very different kind of tolerance – it came from not noticing what this child was doing, not being sensitive enough to other people's reactions to realize something was wrong, a total lack of consideration for others, and a total lack of concern that her unsupervised child was within a pavement's width of moving traffic.

This is not normal behaviour for mothers of young children. Her personal serenity was achieved by ignoring the reasonable needs of others, the need for her child to conform to reasonable standards of behaviour, and the potential hazard of the heavy traffic he could have reached in the space of one second.

The question of tolerance level obviously affects mothers and their own children, but it is quite crucial when an adult is working with a group of other people's children:

- There is no place for the intolerant adult.

- There is equally no place for the person who is apparently tolerant but is so because there is a total lack of 'normal' parental concern.

- The very serene, genuinely tolerant person is ideal to work with difficult children if, in this situation, she can keep her serenity. She will need a good deal of support from other adults, because this tolerance often goes with a fairly casual attitude to what other parents see as undesirable (something as simple as children getting smothered in finger paint or as difficult as anti-social habits being picked up).

- Clearly the stress of being responsible for a group of children, plus the stress of a personal bad day, have to be taken into account, along with the stress caused if there is not enough support from helpers or if there is a continuous period of bad weather when the children can't go out to play and get irritable with each other.

Adults have to think carefully about the type of person they are and the sort of group and work they are looking at before committing themselves to working in a particular situation. Some groups are much harder to work in than others.

## How much aggravation should there be?

If adults are asked how many incidents occur in a family or group situation, and how frequent they are, they give different answers because they all interpret 'incident' in a different way. The interesting thing is that no one thinks there are going to be *no* incidents. Clearly everyone accepts that there are going to be arguments and quarrels between children and that there is going to be friction between children and adults.

Every mother will recognize the phrase 'Why do I have to shout before anyone will do anything?' It typifies a situation which arises in so many homes: help has been requested or instructions given perfectly reasonably and calmly, yet no one responds – so the request is repeated several times – and still no one responds. Most mothers learn to live with it, although their resentment can boil over at times. As some say, 'It is more effective to miss out the nice reasonable approach and just get on with the shouting.'

The only helpful suggestion to be made is that 'John, come here,' followed by 'Will you go and bring in your toys because it is starting to rain' is more likely to be effective than calling, 'Will somebody get the toys in please, it's going to rain in a minute.' If we pinpoint exactly who is to do exactly what and have their full attention before giving the instruction, there is not so much opportunity for the whole group to think comfortably that someone else will do it or that someone else will get the blame for not doing it.

## Reducing aggression

When incidents occur frequently in the home and in a group, it is worth watching and thinking to see at what point and why things happen. Sometimes a slight adjustment can make a big difference – everyone, including adults, gets tired and irritable when their blood sugar level gets low. Some children get very thirsty, some are active in short spurts then need a rest, others can go on until they fall asleep standing up against a chair. Recent findings that some food additives affect children's behaviour should be borne in mind.

In the group where things are going very wrong, all the adults need to put their observations together to work out why. This is a situation in which an experienced observer who can come in and watch might be very helpful. Adults who are fully stretched inevitably miss one little incident or one little circumstance that is leading to difficulties.

On the grounds that prevention is easier than cure, there are some helpful suggestions regarding groups in particular:

■ Adequate equipment will not necessarily make a good group, but no group can be a good group without it. Adequate means enough for everybody, but it also means duplicating any particularly popular material and it means a change now and then.

■ If the adults are ready and prepared when the children come in, this gives a good start for everybody. The children have probably been planning what to do first as long as an hour ago, when they first put on their coats to come.

■ The ratio of adults to children is very important. The younger the children the more adult care and supervision they need.

■ Adults have a calming effect even if they don't say anything or do anything. Think of the incident of the painting friends. The second adult refrained from giving her friend a 'good thump' because the tutor was watching, yet the tutor was obviously enjoying the situation. Think of what happens as we drive perfectly legally and safely down a motorway and a police car comes up behind us. There can't be many drivers who don't ease up their foot from the accelerator while they have a quick think about the situation.

This is why supervision is so important in playgrounds. Just the presence of an adult inhibits silly behaviour.

The experienced adult automatically knows where to be to observe children – sitting in a chair facing out of a corner looking over the whole room rather than sitting in a position facing a corner, where she can only see the children immediately in front of her. She also learns to use her ears, and develops a sixth sense about what she can't see and hear yet should be seeing and hearing. If she can't see and hear what is going on she will rearrange the room or rearrange the helpers.

The balance of behaviour tends to move towards the norm for the group. Where there are just a few young children they are more likely to learn quickly from older children and their behaviour improves. A few older children in a group of mainly younger ones will tend to regress to younger behaviour. (This happened again with the painting friends – even under provocation, the second one was influenced by the fact that retaliating by hitting out would be inappropriate. Although she was provoked by a friend who was behaving 'childishly', her own 'childish' instinct to retaliate was suppressed because the norm of behaviour for the group was that of adults.)

## The child who needs outside help

The question of what to do about the child who may need outside help is not new – and in the light of recent concern about child abuse is even more important at the present time. Many of the conclusions reached long ago by experienced but non-expert people looking after their own or other people's children still hold good.

It is sometimes felt from watching a child's behaviour, or noting an apparent change in his behaviour, that something is 'wrong'. It takes a mature, experienced observer, ideally one who knows the child very well, to justify reaching this conclusion. We have to be objective about what we see, because trying to collect evidence to justify a subjective judgement can do a great deal of damage – maybe even more damage than the original 'wrong' (even if there was a 'wrong' in the first place). Clumsy investigation of the bullying situation, for instance, can sometimes lead to even more trouble for the child. All this applies equally to situations where, for instance, we *think that*:

- A child is 'sickening for something'.

- His behaviour has suddenly changed for no obvious reason.

- He may be being bullied.

- He is having some kind of learning difficulty.

- He doesn't seem to be getting on too well with his peers.

- He is not adjusting as we might have expected to a new situation.

After objective consideration, i.e. asking oneself 'Exactly what makes me think this?', parents can make a move to finding out what help is available and from what source.

If the observer is not the parent, then the parents should be discreetly and tactfully sounded out to see if they share the concern. They are the people who have the most knowledge about the child, they are the ones who have the ultimate responsibility and they are the ones who have the 'rights'. Any help a child can be given will only be successful with the support and cooperation of parents, so how parents are approached matters a good deal. A clumsy approach may leave parents feeling too inadequate, too resentful or too unconvinced to help.

There are very few parents who are not concerned about the welfare of their children. Even if they do not share our concern on a particular issue, they are almost always amenable to the approach: 'I feel I am failing your child in my particular capacity as his health visitor/play leader/teacher/doctor, and I could do with some expert advice to help me perform better. Would you mind if I asked . . . for some help?' This is, after all, a pretty fair assessment of the situation.

Most of these points hold good when considering the possibility of sexual and physical abuse. It takes an experienced observer, preferably someone who knows the child well, and it needs objectivity because the damage that can be caused by being wrong and, under the present system, the damage that can be caused simply by the process of being proved right, is not something to be undertaken lightly.

Apart from being observant, we also need to be informed and knowledgeable about what help is available. Preventing one kind of abuse by replacing it with yet another kind of 'abuse' which results in removing a child from everything which, and everyone who, could help, and at the same time adding the pain and misery of investigation to support a subjective judgement, is no help at all. It is rather like chopping off both arms of a child who is having his wrist twisted behind his back by a bully, on the grounds that the bully will not be able to do that to him again.

The present situation is one in which many experienced, concerned observers do not feel safe in passing on their concern unless what they observe is so gross that they have no option. The result is that a number of children who could probably do with some help get none, apart from extra loving care and support from the observer – but that can be a great deal better than nothing. In many cases the same approach as to other problems – saying to parents, 'I am failing your child – do you mind if I ask for some help for myself?' – is still relevant.

Hopefully the current procedure and practice for dealing with alleged physical and sexual abuse of children will be changed radically and quickly.

There are some useful 'rules of thumb' for anyone considering possible problems with any child, whether it is their own child or one with whom they have some kind of regular relationship.

1 Be observant – and be objective about what is observed.

2 Be informed – about what help might be available and the form it will take.

3 Be discreet, tactful and sensitive in approaches to other people about a suspected problem – whether the approach is from parents to outsiders or from outsiders to parents – bearing in mind the natural reactions these can lead to.

4 Continue giving help and support whether or not outside help materializes, because this is a valuable contribution to make whatever the outcome.

# Part 3
# Playing Away from Home

In this country parents are legally obliged to send their children to school at the age of 5 (in most other countries it would be 6 or 7). Apart from this there is no statutory reason why a child should not spend all his time at home. Yet we know from media reports, from statistics, from past and present research and from what we see going on around us, that the majority of our under-5s will have some experience of being in a group that is not their home long before their fifth birthday.

# Chapter 23

# Where are Our Children and Why are They There?

**Reasons vary**

Mothers (and, in a few cases, fathers) give many reasons for their child having non-home care or experience before school age. The majority of parents say one, or maybe more, of the following:

- I need somewhere to leave my child so that I can go back to work. We desperately need the extra money.

- He seems lost at home now his sister has gone to school. He needs other children to play with but there aren't any of his age near us.

- We could do with a break from each other. We see no one else all day and we get on each other's nerves – at least he gets on mine so I suppose he gets fed up with me too.

- Much as I love my children, I would like to have a bit of time to myself. I'd really like to take up (for example, yoga) classes again.

- He's quite clever really and I think they would teach him more at school than I can. It is a pity to waste time when he could be getting on with proper learning.

- He's got to go to school soon and he's nowhere near ready – he can't keep still for two minutes together and he's for ever wanting something different to play with.

- I think I shall go quite mad if I don't get a break from being at home with the children all day. All we do is look at the same four walls day in, day out – and sometimes I hit him really hard and I know when I'm doing it that he's not really all that naughty. He's just fed up like me.

■ I need someone to look after my baby – I have to go back to work soon or they won't keep my job open for me (or: I must go back and finish my training or all that time will be wasted and I couldn't face having to start it all again.)

■ Now he's bigger there isn't room for him to play properly at home. The flat is very small and we don't have a garden. There is a play space in the next but one street but we don't go there very often. There are some very – you know – funny people there.

■ All the other children in the road go and I don't like to think of him missing out.

■ I am under so much pressure at the moment with my mother being ill and needing a lot of help and the new baby to look after as well – I can't give him the amount of time he seems to need.

■ We are homeless – in a bed and breakfast hotel. It's bad for everyone but it's worse for the children. There is nowhere to go in the day round here, and there's no way we could manage bus fares to go anywhere else.

■ We only speak Hindi at home and he needs to learn some English before he goes to school.

■ My child has a handicap and I think it would encourage him to do things more if he saw other children doing them – I try to get him to do things but it always ends up more like nagging than playing.

■ My other two children went to nursery group and we all enjoyed it – me too.

■ He has enjoyed his playgroup but it cost quite a lot even for just three sessions – and I have to help once a fortnight. I think five sessions at nursery class will be better for him and it will be a big help not to have to pay fees.

These parents are looking for something different in each case. The first main difference between them is whether, for the benefit of themselves or of the family as a whole, they need alternative care for their child to free them to do something else, or whether what they are looking for is something in addition to what the home presently provides. They may want this 'extra' provision both for themselves and for their child or just for the child – or they may need this 'extra' provision for themselves and two children of different ages.

Having got to this point the situation becomes very complicated, as a glance at Figs. 10, 11 and 12 shows.

## Finding what is needed

The odds are that no one is going to find exactly what they want – and the more urgent the need, or the more special the need, then the less likely it is that the family will find the ideal solution. Some compromise will be necessary.

Provision for the under-5s varies tremendously from area to area, so similar families with similar children may fare differently depending on where they live. The first step to finding out what is available in any area is the local Social Services Department. They have lists because they are responsible for registering groups where:

- Children attend for two hours or more without their parent.

- A fee is charged.

Very often they have a lot more information than this – in some areas they produce useful leaflets about all the provision in the area, especially if there is a member of staff who concentrates on the under-5 field.

A second source of information will be the local Education Department – they know about nursery schools, nursery classes and infant schools.

A very useful third source will be the local branch of the Pre-school Playgroups Association, who would know about playgroups and about parent and toddler groups connected with playgroups and may well have other information as well.

Finally, the local welfare centre will have information on mother and baby, and parent and toddler groups – and the local library will have information on any special groups.

**Figure 10** *Reasons for children being away from home*

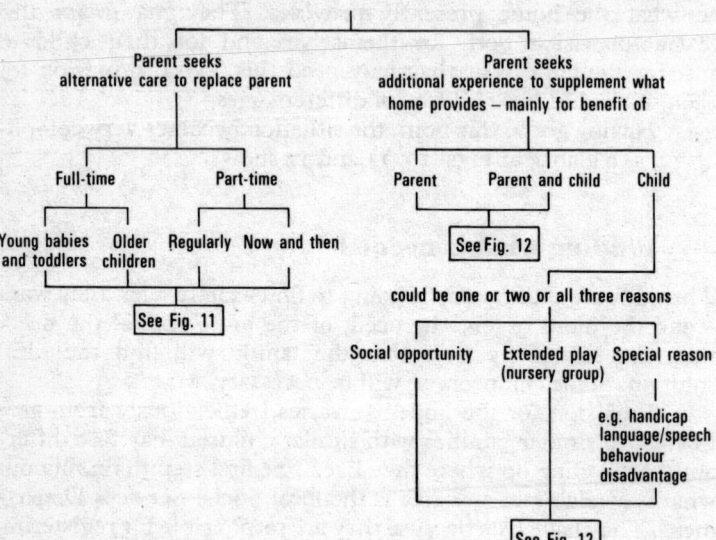

Having found out what groups there are and where they are, another problem arises – the names groups use are not always helpful. Two groups using the same name could be quite different. A private nursery school could be more like a playgroup, a nursery class could be like either a nursery school or an infant class, a playgroup could be more like a parent and toddler group, depending on the age range of children there. A family centre may be a place where a whole family can go for different reasons (which may mean that the nursery group age of nearly 3–5 years is not provided for as a separate group with specific needs) – or it may not.

The only way to find out what a group actually does is to go and have a look at it. Obviously the things to look for will depend on whose needs are to be met – those of the family/parent or those of the child. Even so, the needs of the 'secondary party' have to be considered too.

**Figure 11** *Alternative care for children*

| Type of Provison | Full-time | | Part-time | |
|---|---|---|---|---|
| | *Baby and Toddlers* | *Older Children* | *Regular* | *Now and Then* |
| Childminder | ✓ | ✓ | ? | |
| Nanny | ✓ | ✓ | | |
| Au pair | ? | ? | ? | ? |
| Day nursery, local authority or private | ✓ | ✓ | ? | |
| Work place nursery | ✓ | ✓ | ? | |
| Nursery centre | ? | ? | ? | ? |
| Family centre | ? | ? | ? | ? |
| Relative | ? | ? | ? | ? |
| Friend | ? | ? | ? | ? |
| Crèche | | | ? | ✓ |
| Infant class ⎫ | | ? | ✓ | |
| Nursery class ⎬ term | | ? | ✓ | |
| Nursery school ⎬ time | | ? | ✓ | |
| o–5 group ⎬ only | | | ? | |
| Playgroup ⎭ | | | ? | |
| Rare: Drop-in-centre | | | ? | ? |
| Community nursery | ? | ? | ? | ? |
| Childminding cooperative | ? | ? | ? | ? |
| Neighbourhood centre | ? | ? | ? | ? |
| After school/holiday schemes | | | ? | ? |

**Figure 12** *Experience additional to home*

| Type of group for the benefit of: | Parent | Parent and child | Child – could be all three reasons | | |
|---|---|---|---|---|---|
| | | | Social opportunity | Extended play | Special need |
| Mother and baby club | ✓ | | | | |
| Crèche attached to Mother's activity | ✓ | | | | |
| Drop-in centre | ✓ | ? | | | |
| Parent and toddler group | | ✓ | ? | | |
| Family workshop | ✓ | ? | | | |
| Play centre | | ✓ | ✓ | ? | |
| 0–5 group | | | ✓ | ? | |
| Family centre | | ? | ? | ? | ? |
| Opportunity group | | ✓ | ✓ | ✓ | ✓ |
| Hall playgroup | | | ✓ | ✓ | |
| Home playgroup | | | ✓ | ✓ | |
| Nursery school | | | ✓ | ✓ | ? |
| Nursery class | | | ✓ | ? | |
| Infant school before 5 | | | ✓ | | |
| Special unit | | | | | ✓ |
| Home visiting schemes | | | | | ✓ |
| Toy library Library/dance/music/swimming/gymnastics/skating/Under-5s sessions | | | | | ✓ |

Childminders often take a child to a parent and toddler group just as his mother would. Groups mainly for the benefit of children, such as playgroups, often have a great deal to offer parents in the way of social contact, an opportunity to become involved or even to become an integral part of the organization. (See Parent Involvement Chart, page 276.)

## Benefit to parent/family should not be detrimental to the child

There is a 'threshold' to be aware of: some arrangement might suit the parent but be devastating for her child – for example, there might be a situation where the mother can take part in her activity but the arrangements for the children are in inadequate premises, woefully understaffed, incredibly noisy and where there is nothing for the children to play with.

The adult, after all, can opt out of the activity she is following if it does not bring the benefit she had hoped it would. The small child who becomes distressed doesn't even know why he is so unhappy, and even if he did he would not have the words to tell us – nor is it in his power to say he won't go any more.

He does tell us in other ways, however, and adults have to be sensitive to these indications that all is not well. We may decide he will 'get used to it' or 'it's only for a couple of hours a week'. By the time we decide something is seriously wrong, however, it can be too late. We should err on the side of giving him and his reactions the benefit of the doubt and at least look for ways of improving his situation.

## Making a choice

Careful choice in the first place is one safeguard. Even in the situation of there being only one group available, there is the option to opt out.

No one can make this positive choice on behalf of a parent, because everyone has different priorities. Some things will be more important to one family or child than another:

- The child who lives in a flat needs somewhere with outside space.

- The child who lives in bed and breakfast accommodation would be better off anywhere warm and dry away from his usual dismal restricted surroundings.

- The child who needs to learn English needs a group with a high ratio of adults, one of whom can at least understand him.

- The handicapped child needs a group where he can have a special helper to himself or where the adult/child ratio is very high.

There is a case for doing some personal consumer research. Anyone who goes to look at a group carrying a clipboard and felt pen will get some very odd looks, but just bearing points in mind as we look around and watch what is happening can mean we look more closely at what we see and can sort it out later when we get home (see Fig. 13).

Having done this sorting out, we can work out if, on balance, this is the nearest we are going to get to what we are looking for. Or we may decide that the disadvantages will outweigh any slight advantage there may be, and that we will have to look further.

Obviously a tremendous number of parents *do* find what they are looking for.

Some mothers have found companionship and shared interest in mother and baby clubs, and parents and toddlers have found something for both of them in the parent and toddler groups. Anyone who does not share this need would be appalled by the amount of sheer noise and apparent chaos of these groups, but for mothers who are looking for somewhere warm where they can chat with friends and where their toddlers can meet other children, where someone else will make them a cup of tea and which is within pram-pushing distance, this is all they ask. Some groups do more. Ideas often evolve from the mothers themselves as to how this experience could be extended.

In spite of the impression we may have gained from what we read and hear about the number of under-5s who need care because their mothers work, the only increase in registered provision during the last decade has been in childminding.

**Figure 13** *Personal consumer survey for parents looking for extra experience for their child*

Cost (*Can I afford it?*) ☐   Distance (*Can I get there?*) ☐
Times (*Can I make it?*) ☐   Commitment, e.g. helping (*Can I meet it?*) ☐

|  | What to look for | What is my impression? | | | |
|---|---|---|---|---|---|
|  | (*How important is this to my child?*) *e.g. \* or \*\* or \*\*\** | Not accept-able | Fair | Satis-factory | Good |
|  | No. of sessions offered |  |  |  |  |
|  | Premises: *General impression* *Outside space and equipment* *Size of playroom* *Warm* *Reasonably clean* |  |  |  |  |
|  | Staff: *Attitude to children* *Quantity* *Apparent quality* |  |  |  |  |
|  | Atmosphere: *Relaxed and free* *or very formal* *Noise level* *Age of other children* |  |  |  |  |
|  | Play Activities: *Basic, e.g. sand/water* *Paint/dough* *Table toys e.g. jigsaws, construction sets* *Home corner, dressing up* *Books and things to talk about* *Stories, rhymes and music* *Opportunity for physical activity* |  |  |  |  |
|  | Anything else parent would like to see |  |  |  |  |

One would suspect that if as many mothers were as desperate to work as we are led to believe, the figures would be much higher.

If we have a look at where our children are at different ages, there are some interesting conclusions to be drawn about what it is that mothers want for their children.

## Where are the children?

We know 5–7-year-olds are in full-time school because 5 years is the legal age for formal education to begin. Some children may be in private schools, a very few may be being educated at home, but the vast majority are in state infant schools.

There is no definitive picture of where younger children are, since no one authority has responsibility for children under 5 years. However, by using 1975 and 1985 statistics collected by the National Children's Bureau (which, they point out, should be treated with some caution since some children may attend two groups and may have been counted twice – and in some cases England, Scotland and Wales arrange their figures differently so they cannot be added together), and cross-checking these figures with what is known from other sources, plus cross-checking with what was happening in 1975 (as recorded by the CHES study, see page 271), it is possible to get a good indication as to where our children probably are, even if one or two have not been counted at all and a few have been counted twice.

We know some under-5s are in 'proper' infant school classes – but since they will not be offered places there until they are 4 years and 1 day old, these figures have to relate to the 4–5-year-olds. In 1985 some 92.5 per cent of the 4-year-olds in infant schools attended full-time, five whole days each week.

We know that some 3–5-year-old children are in nursery classes in infant schools. These may or may not be more like infant classes. In 1985, 86 per cent of these children were attending part-time, i.e. either five mornings or five afternoons a week. 14 per cent were attending full-time, i.e. five days a week.

If the 'pattern of intake' remains as it was at the time of the CHES study, about 55 per cent of these children will start there at some time between 3 and 4 years. About 43 per cent will start there at the age of 4, and will probably have been in another group (probably a playgroup) before then. A few children may start before the age of 3.

We know some 3–5-year-old children are in nursery schools. In 1985, 24 per cent of children in nursery schools attended full-time, i.e. five full days per week, and 76 per cent attended either five mornings or five afternoons per week. If the 'pattern of intake' remains as it was at the time of the CHES study, about 65 per cent of these children would start at the age of 3 + years and about 27 per cent would start after the age of 4 years. A few may start before 3 years.

We know that some 3–5-year-old children are in playgroups because playgroup places have to be registered. The National Association of Pre-School Playgroups estimates that each registered place is used by 1.8 children. Most playgroups are open for less than five full days, and many are open for less than five half days, so very few children attending playgroups will have more than three sessions each week.

We can calculate (see Appendix 2, page 299) that some 2–3-year-olds are in playgroups because more playgroup places are being used than can be accounted for by the 3–5-year-olds.

We know how many children are in day nurseries and with childminders, because their premises have to be registered and the number of children they take has to be approved by a local DHSS officer. There are no separate statistics for some of the newer and more flexible forms of day care in nursery centres, family centres, community nurseries and workplace nurseries, but they will be included in the general figures because they too have to be registered.

We do not know how many children attend mother and baby groups, parent and toddler groups, toy libraries, drop-in centres or crèches which look after children for less than two hours, as they do not have to be registered and no one has records for them.

The following sections are based on such known information as there is, and refer to England, Scotland and Wales unless they are labelled 'England only'.

# Alternative care in local authority day nurseries, private day nurseries and with registered childminders

BABIES AND TODDLERS

The vast majority of babies and toddlers (more than 90 per cent) appear to be being cared for at home. There may be some children who do not show in the figures, even though their mothers work, because fathers or relatives are relied on to look after children or because they have an au pair or nanny living in – or because they use unregistered childminders.

The main increase in alternative care places has been with registered childminders. If mothers wanted to work while their children were very young these figures could have been larger, since childminding does not involve statutory training qualifications nor does it involve capital investment in special premises. In recent years childminders have been given increasing support by local authorities and they have also formed their own support group. This area of alternative care could easily have increased to meet demand – if demand was there.

Even good quality alternative care is poorly rewarded for the people who provide it, in terms of how much they are paid for their work (about half as much as the hourly rate for cleaning). Nevertheless, many working women would find that by the time they had paid for their children to be childminded plus the other expenses of working, there was very little or no financial gain to themselves or their families unless the salary they could earn was relatively high. For any increase in alternative care to happen or be demanded in the future it is likely there would be other factors at issue, such as career prospects, to persuade women to leave their young children to the care of someone outside the family.

ALTERNATIVE CARE FOR 3–5-YEAR-OLDS

This is more difficult to track down. Some children from this age group will be in day nurseries or with childminders. There will be others whose mothers use the five half days or five full days when their youngest child goes to nursery class, nursery school or early infant school as an opportunity for them to do some part-time work. Nursery classes, nursery schools, and

**Figure 14** *Percentage of 0–5-year-old population in registered alternative care*

| Placement: | 1975 | 1985 |
|---|---|---|
| In local authority day nurseries | 0.78% | 0.95% |
| In private day nurseries | 0.72% | 0.76% |
| With registered child minders | 2.3% | 4.0% |
| **Total** | 3.8% | 5.71% |

infant schools are free, so childminding costs are nil.

Certainly the figures involved (see Fig. 15) show that this is the most likely explanation for the discrepancies between the figures of mothers of under-5s who are 'economically active' and the figures for who looks after under-5s while mothers work.

**Figure 15** *Percentage of 3–5 population in LEA classes (England only)*

| Placement: | 1975 | 1985 |
|---|---|---|
| Nursery schools and classes | 10.0% | 22.5% |
| Infant school classes | 18.9% | 20.7% |
| **Total** | 28.9% | 43.2% |

## Where do children play away from home?

### CHILDREN OF 0–2 YEARS

There are no figures for play opportunities for this age range, since groups do not have to be registered if parents remain responsible for their children, if the children are there for less than two hours, or if no payment is made.

There is known to be an increase in mother and baby clubs of various kinds since 1975, so some babies may meet other babies at these groups.

There are no official figures for parent and toddler groups (where we would expect to find mobile children) for the same reason as given above. The experience of playgroup leaders, however, is that the vast majority of children entering play-groups have had some experience in a parent and toddler group or at some other centre where young children and parents are welcomed. Indeed, many playgroups are actively concerned with parent and toddler groups directly attached to them.

Children 0–2 years who are in nursery care or being childminded may also be involved in some kind of group play experience.

It seems reasonable to assume, therefore, that many children under 2 years are having some group play experience, even if it is only for two hours a week, even if it is not specially geared to the play needs of their specific age group and even if the play provision is not extensive.

### CHILDREN OF 2–3 YEARS

By calculating all the figures (see Appendix 2, page 299), it is clear that in 1985 some 2–3-year-olds were in playgroups. It is possible that a very few 2–3-year-olds are in nursery schools or nursery classes. The 2–3-year-olds who are not in playgroups or nursery schools or nursery classes may well attend a parent and toddler group or play centre, and some nearly-3-year-olds may be 'settled in' to a playgroup with their mother or childminder. See Fig. 16.

### CHILDREN OF 3–4 YEARS

There are enough places in playgroups, nursery schools, nursery classes and independent schools to accommodate all these children even if they share a playgroup place with another child and have only two or three sessions each week. However, this holds good only if the available places are in the same area as the children who need them – or if parents can afford any necessary fees. Fig. 17 shows the best approximation possible using such figures as there are (see Appendix 2, p. 299).

Whether or not children have free play experience in nursery classes and independent schools will vary depending on the type of group and the resources available to them. The ratio of adults to children will be less than in other types of groups.

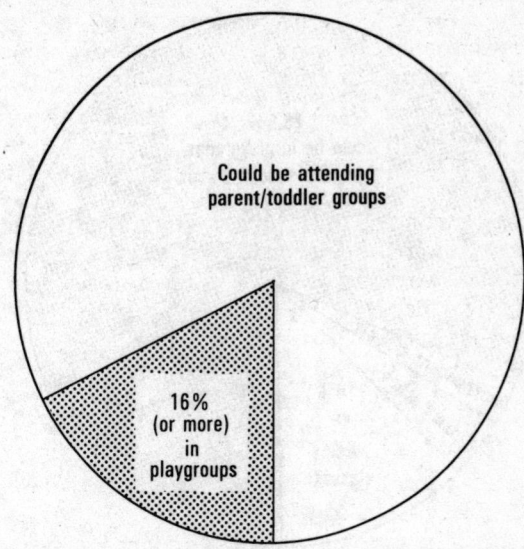

*Figure 16* 2–3-year-old children, 1985 (England only)

### CHILDREN OF 4–5 YEARS

The percentage of children entering formal infant school early is 41.5 per cent of the 4–5-year age range which is a very large number. Whether or not all these children are mature enough to benefit from being taught as opposed to learning for themselves is open to question. The ratio of adults to children could be one adult for thirty or more children.

The only increase in State nursery education places during the period between 1975 and 1985 is in nursery classes attached to infant schools. In England the number of places went up by 130 per cent. This happened largely as the result of the drop in the birth rate, which left empty space in the infant schools. The resources provided to equip and staff these empty rooms have been meagre in the extreme. Money for educational resources generally has been diminishing, and no one claimed the under-5s (for whom there was no statutory

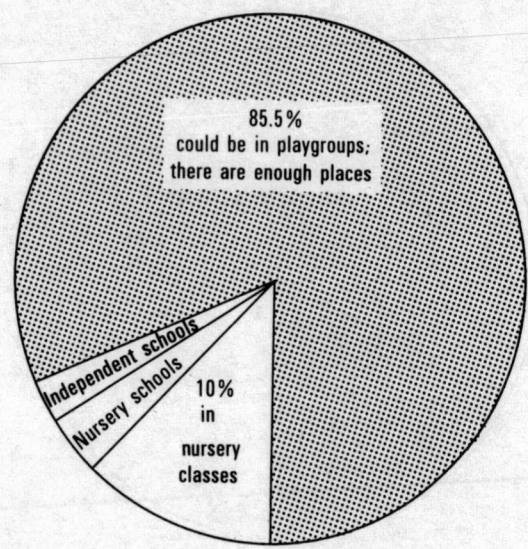

**85.5%**
could be in playgroups;
there are enough places

Independent schools

Nursery schools

10%
in
nursery
classes

*Figure 17* *3–4-year-old children, 1985 (England only)*

duty to provide) as a priority – except perhaps inner London and other very large cities with great problems of deprivation. As Fig. 18 shows, it is mainly 4–5-year-olds who have been affected by this change.

Whether or not children in these new nursery classes are in a teaching situation or a 'learning through play' situation will depend on the resources available. Certainly the ratio of adults to children will be far less than in other groups, though it ought to be more than in infant classes.

## Effects of changes arising from new nursery classes

The provision of more places in nursery classes, particularly where these places were offered to 4-year-olds, had a skittle (or knock-on) effect:

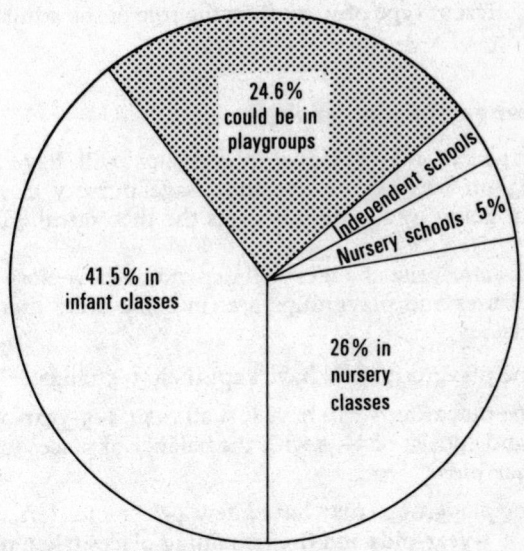

*Figure 18* 4–5-year-old children, 1985 (England only)

**1** Many playgroups lost their 4-year-olds to nursery classes and so had more space for 3-year-olds. In addition, playgroups increased their places by 24 per cent. This left some extra space, which was taken up by 2-year-olds in various ways. Some entered playgroups if their mothers stayed with them, some stayed in playgroups without their mothers, some playgroups used spare sessions for parent and toddler group activities

**2** The age profile of many playgroups has changed, and this will affect the quality of play experience for many 3–4-year-olds and for the fewer 4–5-year-olds who are still in playgroups.

**3** The adults who work in playgroups may well be working with a younger age range of children than before – they may have to do more 'mothering' with the youngest children and more 'leading' with the 3–4-year-olds if there are no 4–5-year-olds left to set an example. There may be a quicker turnover of children, so the mothering and leading starts all over again. This is a very different type of work than the role of the adult in a settled group of 3–5-year-old children.

## Changes in playgroups

The age profile in individual playgroups will have changed depending on whether or not they have nursery classes near them. Just going by the figures gives the theoretical effect – see Fig. 19.

In practice, the changes will depend on how close together nursery classes and playgroups are (in some areas there are no nursery classes):

- Some playgroups will have kept their 3–5 range.

- Some playgroups will have lost all their 4–5-year-old children and consist of 3–4s with the balance of places taken up by 2–3-year-olds.

- Some playgroups may have a few 4-year-olds left, a majority of 3-year-olds and the remaining places taken up by 2-year-olds.

- Some playgroups may consist of only 3–4-year-old children.

The net result is that many 3-year-olds have lost the opportunity to learn from 4–5-year-olds. They may also be being hampered by the presence of a large number of 2-year-olds.

### 2-year-olds in playgroups

Two-year-olds are delightful, but they are hard work. In the playgroup they need a lot of mothering, and if their mothers are not there the staff will have to give them a good deal of time and effort, which leaves less for the older children.

They can't play at the level of the 3-year-olds and they can be very disruptive. A 3-year-old gradually learns to listen to longer stories at story time if he sees older children doing so – the 2-year-old virtually has to be nailed down (if we look carefully at the adult who appears to be cuddling him on the edge of the ring of children, we can see just how tightly she is

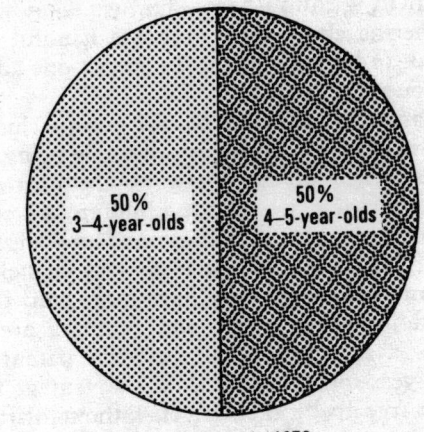

*Typical group in 1970*

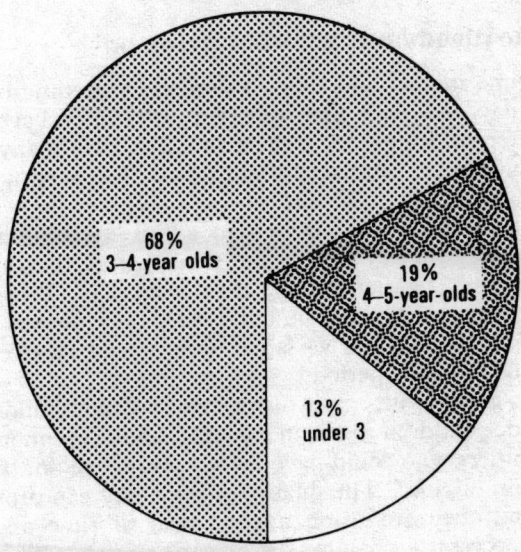

*Possible group in 1985*

**Figure 19** *Playgroup profile (England only)*

holding him). The 3-year-old will quietly watch what other children are doing or wait for his turn. The 2-year-old will join in like a bull in a china shop – he just takes what he wants without bothering about turns. He is a handful even at home with one adult to himself. He needs almost one adult to himself in the playgroup.

There are some very successful groups (judging by how the mothers using them appreciate what is being done) of just 2–3-year-olds which do not show on the charts. They have short regular sessions where the children are provided with carefully structured play activities, and the adults there play the same part and give the same amount of help as mothers do in the home situation. They have more staff than the usual playgroup staff/children ratio, and mothers are welcome to stay. This is a half-way house between parent and toddler group and 3-year-old playgroup. The advantage is that the 2-year-olds are free to be themselves without disrupting the 3-year-olds.

## The disadvantages of 'moving on'

By the time many children go to school, sometime between 4 years 1 day and their fifth birthday, they may have been in three different groups for a short time. In 1975 many children would have been put in just one group for very nearly two years.

It takes time for children to adjust to being in a new group. If they move two or three times before they are 5 (e.g. from a parent toddler group, to a playgroup, then on to a nursery class and/or early infant class), they do not have the opportunity to progress as far as they would have done in a continuous two-year period.

In a group with a fast turnover of younger children there are no older children to set an example, and if the more experienced mothers who could have helped also move on, this puts a great strain on staff. The quality of play they can provide may suffer, and they are using a good deal of time and energy without necessarily having the reward of job satisfaction in seeing results of their early efforts.

Parents whose children move on several times may also lose out, as they do not have the opportunity to progress to the deepest kind of involvement and participation in any of the groups their children attend (see page 274).

A reduction in the quantity and quality of play in early years may mean that children entering infant classes are not as competent and confident as they might have been, and this may slow down the group as a whole – and almost certainly makes the task of the infant teacher more difficult.

# Chapter 24

# The Benefits of Playing Away from Home for Children and Parents

Many people, first of all the experts and educationalists concerned with young children, and later the parents responsible for the phenomenon of the growth of pre-school playgroups, have always been convinced that suitable pre-school experience brings more long-term benefits than those which show at the age of 5. They have also been convinced that disadvantaged children could benefit more from help given before school age than from more intensive help provided during school years.

Isolated research projects in the past showed different results. It was not clear that there was any educational benefit, or which aspects of pre-school experience were the ones which brought any lasting benefit.

To quote from the second (1975) edition of *Play with a Purpose for Under-Sevens:*

> ... no one knows if truly widespread nursery education really works and pays dividends and if so what works best. It could well be that what we gain on the nursery swings we lose on the home roundabouts ...

> ... the people with the most to lose or gain are the children. From their point of view the first question to ask is 'do they need an upward extension of home or a downward extension of school ... enriched play or watered down education?' ...

> ... if the needs of young children have to be ignored or pushed to one side in order to make nursery education fit into existing schemes and patterns which have evolved to

suit older children, we may be doing something as damaging as making young children wear older children's shoes . . .

. . . the present provision of nursery education is rich in diversity – or a mess – depending on the view one takes.

## Some questions answered

In 1985, exactly ten years after these points were made, the report was published on a massive piece of research: *The Effects of Early Education.*\* The Child Health and Education Study research team which carried out the work drew its information from records kept on all the children born in England, Scotland and Wales during one week in 1970. Thus every area and every type of group of children were represented.

There was also a census of all pre-school education institutions in 1975, so every type of nursery group was represented.

All these children were tested at the age of 5 – and it was found that those children who had some nursery education showed higher test scores than those children who had not. They were tested again at the age of 10 and the report states

After taking account of many differences in the social and family circumstances of the children, it was found that those children who had attended L E A nursery schools or playgroups achieved higher scores in tests of general ability, reading and mathematics at ten years than children with no pre-school experience. However, L E A nursery class attendance was not associated with increased scores in all these tests.

This is an answer to one of the questions of 1975. Nursery education does work, and the long-term benefits still show at the age of ten. Five years' worth of formal education in primary school had neither diminished the benefits nor had it made up the lack of these benefits to children who did not have some nursery education before they started school.

---

\* A. F. Osborn and J. E. Millbank, *The Effects of Early Education*, Clarendon Press, Oxford, 1985.

The conclusions reached by the research team also give some very important leads.*

**1** The pre-school education available in 1975 was found to be successful in terms of lasting, measurable, educational benefit at the age of 10 years, i.e. at least five years after children left these pre-school places.

All children gained. Socially disadvantaged children gained slightly more than other children but the difference was small. The biggest difference in gain was between children who had some pre-school education and those who had none.

**2** Slight differences showed in the degree of benefit, depending on which type of pre-school experience children had . . .

■ Home playgroups appeared to give the most long-term benefit.

■ L E A nursery schools and hall playgroups were very similar in terms of long-term gain.

■ The scores of children who had attended L E A nursery classes were only higher than those for non-attenders in two of the seven tests used. For the other tests the children's scores were indistinguishable from those for children who had no nursery experience. The point is made that L E A nursery classes may not be very much different from infant school reception classes – and early entry to reception classes did not show long-lasting benefit . . . there is an urgent need to check that these children are indeed receiving an educational experience appropriate to the under-5 age group.

■ Children starting full-time infant school early (before the age of 5) showed no long-term benefit.

■ But the lowest scoring was associated with children who had no pre-school experience.

■ Comparisons of different groups which took the same proportion of disadvantaged children still showed differences in gain which related to the type of group.

**3** Another difference between the various types of groups was

* See *The Effects of Early Education*, op. cit., pp. 237–42, 226, 212–18, 156–7, 228–9, 239–40, 153, 142, 151, 156, 237, 92, 110–14, 196–9, 238–9.

the number of sessions they offered. This could vary between five full days or five half days in a nursery school or nursery class, five full days and long hours in a day nursery to perhaps just one or two sessions per week in a playgroup. It might be thought that if pre-school education is such a good thing then the more of it the better – but this did not prove to be the case. There was no significant difference in benefit shown between children attending one or two sessions a week and those attending more than five sessions a week.

4 Socially disadvantaged children . . . one interesting result of investigation showed that the children most likely to need pre-school education were also the least likely to get it. Socially disadvantaged children attending home playgroups did better than expected, and there was some indication that attending hall playgroups and LEA nursery schools did help these children. In contrast, those attending a nursery class tended to perform less well than average for this group.

5 Parent involvement . . . was a very familiar term in 1975. Analysis of test scores showed that those children whose parents were interested in their education, and whose own mothers helped in some way, achieved slightly higher test scores than those with less interested parents who did not take part. The use of parent helpers was not found to be detrimental, and the point is made that parent helpers are mothers who have natural skills.

6 The main conclusion was that provided a child receives proper care, has interesting activities and other children to play with (which the majority of groups have as a common element) the actual type of pre-school experience matters very little.

Some of the questions being asked in 1975 as to the most appropriate style of nursery education appear to have been answered. Time moves on, however. The picture of nursery provision has changed a good deal since 1975, as a quick glance back at the charts of where our children are will show. Whether the number of groups a child may now attend will reduce the benefit because each time he has to start again – whether the mutual benefit society of 3-5-year-olds which often used to exist was significant – remains to be seen.

The main conclusions will inevitably hold good. Our children do benefit from nursery education, disadvantaged children benefit from nursery education and, in a nutshell, the word education is not appropriate. It is indeed, the 'enriched play', rather than the 'watered-down education' which appears to work best.

Hopefully mothers and providers of and planners for the pre-school years will take note – which brings us to the adults involved in groups for under-7s.

## Parent involvement

Over the last twenty-five years or more the words 'parent involvement' have become very familiar. The phrase actually originated within the playgroup movement, but it is now widely used in many areas of provision for children. Unfortunately it is used in different ways to mean different things, depending on who is using it:

- It may mean informing parents about what is going on (sending home letters, which don't always get there – putting notices on the notice board, which not everybody sees).

- It may mean letting parents have some say in what is planned (which can vary between token parent governors or representatives and a hard-working meeting where all the parents help hammer out what needs to be done).

- It may mean using parents to provide resources (raising money, providing transport, helping with events or special activities).

- It may mean actually using parents for the day-to-day activities of the group (as helpers to staff or in addition to staff or as part of the adult/children ratio as in many playgroups).

- It can mean self-help groups, where parents whose children have a specific problem come together to provide support for each other and perhaps campaign for the resources they need for their children.

Most parents first become 'involved' when they take their child to a group, depending on how much participation they can undertake (i.e. if the group will let them and if they have the time/inclination to do so). The benefits can be fivefold:

1 *To their own children* – a parent who knows what goes on

in a group can talk to her child about what goes on there and carry back to the home some of the activities she sees. The parent who helps increase resources for the group, whether by raising money, helping with equipment or other chores, bringing in her extra personal skills, fresh ideas and interests or is an extra pair of hands and eyes when needed, enriches the group for her own child in a very practical way.

Children can take great pleasure and pride in feeling and seeing that their mother or father (or granny or grandad for that matter) is a valuable and valued part of the group.

The CHES study also indicates that there is a lasting benefit which shows up as better performance on the part of the child in later years.

**2** *To the other children in the group*, because they benefit from the increased resources. It also provides children with another adult to get to know and add to their collection of role models.

**3** *To the parents themselves* – immediate benefits are that they meet other adults with whom they share a common interest. Parents can learn more about children generally, how they develop, how wide the bounds of normality are. This can make life at home easier as they become more comfortable and confident as parents.

Longer-term benefits arise if parents gradually increase their participation. Most parents enjoy this, and it provides them with an interest on which they can spend time, effort and sometimes money without feeling selfish, since their children are benefiting too.

**4** *To the group*, because parent help increases their resources. It provides support for the people doing the day-to-day work of the group by leaving them free to get on with the job they do best. Not least, the more that parents know about what staff are doing and trying to do, the more likely they are to appreciate and cooperate with staff.

In the long term, parent involvement may make the group more secure, as it may well provide a continuity factor when there are frequent changes of staff. In a situation where a group is threatened, parents can and do make great efforts to ensure that it survives.

**5** *To the community* – parents can and will concentrate on a particular need for their own immediate area, which statutory bodies such as district or county or regional or national departments may not have the resources or powers to deal with. Parents can also have a more flexible approach, since once a need has been met or a problem has been solved they can quickly move on to the next thing that needs attention. Statutory bodies cannot react so quickly or so efficiently.

There is nothing magic about how parent involvement happens – it does not come about just because someone says it should. There is a distinct pattern which has to evolve, stages to be reached, obstacles to overcome.

## The bumpy road to parent involvement

STAGE 1 DEPENDS ON NEED...

> *The parent* needs/desires a group/class/school for the child and finds a suitable one which has a place to offer. OR – the parent is directed to send the child to a group and may have little or no choice about which it is to be ... This leads to SIMPLE INVOLVEMENT, which may be as little as the parent taking, or sending, the child to the group and complying with requests by the group, e.g. paying fees, providing aprons or plimsolls. The involvement ends at the group door. There is not necessarily any appreciation of the group beyond the fact that it is providing a service. The quality of the service will be judged on the short-term reaction of the child. If the child is legally obliged to be in the group (as at legal school age) the parent may not even think about the quality of the service.

STAGE 2 DEPENDS ON PERSONAL CONTACT...

> *IF the parent* goes into the group (the mother who works may not be able to do this).
> *IF the parent* talks to staff and other parents and vice versa (the shy or non-English speaking parent may have some difficulty) ...
> the parent develops some FAMILIARITY with the methods of the group.

**STAGE 3 DEPENDS ON OPPORTUNITY...**

*IF the group* can offer the parent some simple opportunity to help, e.g. with fund-raising or doing a simple chore and

*IF the parent* is able and willing (some can't and some aren't)

*IF the group* takes the time to show the parent what is needed (she is not a thought reader)

IF the SIMPLE PARTICIPATION is successful (it isn't always, and it may be nothing to do with the parent)

IF the group appears to appreciate her efforts (some forget to say thank you)... the parent starts to PARTICIPATE as a person in her own right, not just as a shadowy figure who provides the group with one of its quota of children.

**STAGE 4 DEPENDS ON TIME...**

As the parent gains confidence she may be willing to do more...

*IF the group* can offer more difficult work to be done (some don't and some can't)

*IF the parent and child* are in the group long enough for the parent to become COMPETENT and CONFIDENT (some aren't)... the group can use the parent as a RELIABLE RE-SOURCE.

Some groups who lose their children to other groups after a short time, or operate in an area where for some reason parents are not able to participate, will never have parents who have reached this stage. These are the groups which can be under great pressure unless they receive help and support from outside agencies.

**STAGE 5 LEADS TO MUTUAL BENEFIT...**

Once a parent has been used as a reliable resource over a period of time... the parent gains SELF-CONFIDENCE and SELF-IMAGE as a valued, valuable and essential part of the group and develops a SENSE OF RESPONSIBILITY for and LOYALTY to the group. Along with this goes RESPECT AND

UNDERSTANDING for the staff and what they are doing, and APPROVAL AND SUPPORT for the long-term aims of the group.

*The staff* can benefit from the PRACTICAL COMMITMENT of the parents, and gain JOB SATISFACTION from the feedback of approval and support of this parent and other parents, because once this system starts to operate it is SELF-PERPETUATING.

*The group* also benefits in both the short term and the long term, since there can be TRUE CONSULTATION between INFORMED PARTIES who are aware of each other's problems and long-term goals.

Any changes arising from consultation will have the full approval and commitment of everyone concerned, so they are more likely to be the 'right' changes and have more chance of being made to work.

*The child* benefits from the parent's involvement both at home and in the group, in all aspects and at all stages.

STAGE 6 DEPENDS ON THE SYSTEM . . .

*The parent's* full participation in the group leads to SKILL, ABILITY, SELF-CONFIDENCE and WILLINGNESS TO LEARN which are TRANSFERABLE to the next group she and her children join . . .

*IF that new group* is able and willing to offer the opportunity, this succeeding group benefits from the experience which was achieved elsewhere and they may not have to go through the very early stages of 'learning together'.

*IF the new group* does not or cannot use the parent's skills she can still use them in other ways for the benefit of herself, the family or the community.

It is obvious that there can be many points at which parents do not or cannot progress any further, either because there is no opportunity to do so or because there is no time to do so. The parent of a child who changes groups several times is never going to make enough progress to have been really useful to the group that is left behind, nor will she be useful to the new group until she, like her child, has settled in.

If, on the other hand, she is never able to contribute because the clique who have been there for years are reluctant to move over and let in someone new and fresh, there arises the situation where the old hands start to be resentful that 'no one else will help – new parents these days are just not interested'.

Apart from immediate and practical advantages, the long-term benefit is that when group and parent come to understand each other the staff will get more cooperation and respect, which leads to job satisfaction. This applies to every kind of work with children – but more particularly to the field of working with young children. These workers need all the cooperation and respect they can get, because they will certainly not get job satisfaction from the very low wages that go with child care and teaching.

# Chapter 25

# Living and Working with Young Children

Working with children is seen by many people as an attractive and worthwhile career. It is a socially acceptable thing to do – a statement like 'I want to work with children' or 'I work with people' immediately gives the impression of someone who cares, who has warmth, is competent. It evokes in the person who hears it a feeling of trust, reliability and security.

We tend to assume that everyone who works with children has had special training to meet children's needs. The training for different types of work with children is such a muddle, however, that quite often the people who do these jobs have had very little relevant or extensive training and experience in the normal needs and development of the children they care for.

### Choosing a career

Most people at the stage of choosing a career have to consider the practicalities of the training – the age at which training starts, any entrance qualifications needed, the length of training and the form it takes. All these details will be available from local careers advice centres for both school-leavers and more mature people.

They may find it more difficult to discover exactly what skills they will be taught and the amount of 'hands on' learning opportunity there will be for actually working with children. Very often training will concentrate on the specific tasks of the job, without giving students much experience of the individuals on whom these tasks are to be performed. Some newly qualified people find that they are proficient at the technical skills but not very good at relating to their 'clients' or 'pupils' or 'patients', and the difficulties they encounter make them – and the recipients of their efforts – very miserable.

People who find they do enjoy working with children and are good at it (the two usually go together) may discover that in order to progress up the career ladder to achieve more responsibility and adequate financial reward, they have to move right away from the people they care for, because promotion means more administrative duties.

## Training, rewards and career structure for work with children

All too often it is not the 'caring for and working with children' element of a job which receives adequate training or brings financial reward, or offers professional kudos and career prospects.

Parents receive no training, no salary and very little credit for their skills. Yet they have total responsibility and receive no support. They set their own goals, they provide, they manage, they administrate, they cooperate and sometimes they direct and employ other people. The people who provide alternative care and those who provide play experience are in much the same boat.

There are some avenues of informal training open to parents as carers and enablers, such as playgroup training courses, and short courses for childminders which adults can take if they wish – if they are available – if they can get to them – if they can afford the fees. These courses are usually relaxed, highly enjoyable and often achieve a big increase in personal learning for each individual because students are highly motivated. Most adults attend only when they are in an in-service situation already living or working with children, so they all bring and share knowledge of real children and real situations. There are no entrance qualifications, so anyone can join – but nor are there any leaving qualifications except a certificate of attendance. The only recognition is that some Social Services departments insist that this certificate is obtained before accepting someone as a play leader when considering registration of a playgroup.

There are some avenues of training, such as NNEB and

the newer City and Guilds and B. Tech courses, which involve varying amounts of practical training. Traditionally NNEBs are the young girls to be found caring for children in day nurseries under supervision of more senior staff, who themselves may be NNEBs who stayed in the nursery world – or they may be acting as assistants in nursery schools, nursery classes and infant schools, working under the supervision of teachers – or they may work as nannies under the supervision of parents. Career prospects go only as far as becoming a matron in a day nursery – and there are very few day nurseries, therefore very few day nursery matrons posts. Because of the nature of the work, there are few social opportunities to mix with other young people during working hours. The financial rewards are very poor in comparison with the degree of responsibility and the long-term benefits to the children with whom they work. If they wish to take more training to increase their qualifications, then the NNEB certificate carries no academic recognition towards entrance qualifications.

There are one or two new courses for play workers but they are very few, and as yet it is not clear how they will fit into any career structure or how the qualification will be regarded.

Teachers, in the main, start their training very young and often progress from school to college and then back into school as teachers. Their training will include some teaching practice, but their efforts during these short supervised periods will be directed towards successfully completing a specified project to further their own skills rather than to benefit the children on whom they practise. Very few teachers can remember anything they learned about children on their teaching practice, most cannot remember much of what they were taught about children as individuals during their training course, and very few, if any, will remember being taught anything about children, parents and families. It is not surprising, therefore, that many teachers do not see parents or families as having any connection with the work that they do with the children of parents and families.

Only specifically trained nursery teachers receive training relevant to under-5s, although some teachers in charge of nursery classes are able to take short conversion courses and some in-service training is available. The very few Advanced Diploma courses for post-qualified students are more likely to be seen as a means of advancement of career prospects than in terms of staying at the 'working with young children' level.

The rewards and job satisfaction of teaching have diminished rapidly over the last decades, and the career structure means having to move away from class contact to do more administration. Many of the teachers who are good at their job and enjoy being with children simply cannot afford to stay with them.

The same points would apply to the other fields of expertise which can involve work with young children.

## Losing out

Unfortunately there is sometimes a side effect to this lack of direct experience with children and families in professional training programmes.

It can lead to situations where professionals are slightly patronizing to parents and carers because they are judging them in the context of their own specialist skill. If the 'professionals' knew more about the unacknowledged and unrewarded skills needed and developed by carers and enablers, they would realize that these same people are, in fact, extremely competent and successful in their own field of responsibility.

There are also situations where carers and enablers are equally scathing about the lack of knowledge, the comparative youth and the inexperience of the 'so-called expert' who becomes involved with their children without being able to put the specific problem and the solution they are considering into the context of the life or the situation of the family group.

There is certainly a case to be made for everyone who wishes to work with children to start with a solid foundation of experience with normal children in normal situations (whatever that may mean, since situations vary wildly). Specific skills could be grafted on to this common core of experience, which would make professional training faster and more efficient and would lead to confident competence at the point of qualification, rather than the more usual vulnerable probationary period needing supervision.

## Hope for the future for carers and enablers

The National Council for Vocational Qualifications, set up by the Government in 1987, has been given the task of monitoring a new system of education and training qualifications for the 'caring industry' in general and for the under-5s as a separate group.

The aim is to achieve a simple system of qualifications which everyone can understand, which should be open to more people, including mature people, and which may cross the present professional boundaries of health, education and social work.

One of the objectives is to increase access to qualifications by recognizing competence in work activities however and whenever it was acquired, without insisting on that competence arising from special training methods or specific training courses which provide a traditional qualification. This should open the door to people who might previously have been barred from formal training.

Short courses, open learning and learning by experience will be considered acceptable if they have led to demonstrable competence.

'Assessment' procedures will consider the outcome of learning (what people can actually do) rather than the input of training courses (what is supposed to have been learned). Special arrangements could be made for people undergoing informal training to ask for assessment of their competence at various levels. It should be possible to work through the various levels and stages of qualification by completing separate units, so that training – and achieving qualifications – can be an on-going process rather than a once-and-for-all full-time training course ending with a pass or fail judgement at the end of the designated time.

An opportunity for mature people to undertake the more traditional routes to professional qualifications is looming on the horizon. The drop in the birth rate has worked its way through the schools year by year, starting with the infant schools (who made up their complement of spaces for 5-year-olds by admitting some 4-year-olds and opening nursery classes).

The educational area to be affected during the next few years will be higher education – and it is anticipated that there will be a 25 per cent shortfall in the number of young people applying to train for some of the professions which involve 'working with people'. The birth rate went on decreasing, so this situation will not improve for some while, if ever. In addition, poor remuneration and job satisfaction in the teaching and caring professions is not an incentive to young people, so other sources will have to be tapped to provide enough personnel to staff necessary services. This is the point at which the traditional training establishments may open their doors to the mature student, who can offer practical experience rather than academic qualifications.

We may therefore, in time, see a situation where 'people who work with children' do have experience with children and do merit the response we give and the respect in which we automatically hold them. Not least, the people who have the skills and responsibilities may be actually acknowledged, rewarded and respected for the 'caring' part of the work they do.

# Chapter 26
# The Last Word

The last words in the 1975 edition of *Play with a Purpose for Under-Sevens* were in a short chapter entitled 'Last Word'. It is interesting to look back and see what was thought to be important then, what the problems appeared to be, what the hopes for the future were – and to see how much progress has been made.

In some areas progress has been made, in others the situation has worsened – and some new problems have arisen. Which under-7s have benefited and which have lost out has been a lottery depending mainly on where they live.

### The family

In 1975 the strains and stress of divorce had only just begun to filter through to affect the lives of under-7s. Now we have a situation in which one child in eight will live with one parent or in a reconstituted family. Many adults, not just parents, who are legal relatives rather than blood relatives are having to work out for themselves a role which is unfamiliar not only to them but to society in general. We cannot be as confident as we used to be that children will start their social development in a group in which they have an unassailable place as 'my son', 'my grandson', 'my brother', 'my nephew'. Children have been given an additional set of relationships to which they have to adjust. This is a problem previous generations did not have – so they may not be able to help. A supportive atmosphere in a nursery group could help these children.

There is violence within some families. This may also have been the case generations ago, but the extended family of grandparents, aunts, uncles and cousins living nearby who could have supported children in this situation has gone. A secure, safe, stable nursery group could be an important support for children in present-day families where there is violence and abuse – and it could also support the adult members of the family by reducing some of the strain which leads to violence.

## The world outside

There is violence in the world immediately outside the front door which limits opportunities for outside play. There is real violence to be seen on television which far outshadows the simulated violence in programmes made for children. Perhaps our children are becoming so accustomed to violence that they will grow up to be adults who regard it as not only inevitable but also acceptable behaviour. Hopefully the opportunity to develop social skills and to adjust to a peer group without having to resort to physical violence can be given at an early, impressionable age through secure, stable nursery groups.

There have been economic upheavals which in some areas have led to widespread, long-term unemployment. The misery and deprivation that inevitably comes in its wake affects children just as deeply as parents. Supportive nursery experience may help these children, but unless it is free it will not be accessible. Parents with very little or no money coming in cannot afford to pay for this relief for the younger members of their families.

In 1975 the plight of children living in high-rise blocks was suggested as something which needed attention and as creating a priority need for pre-school provision for the children who lived in them. Some of those blocks have been knocked down, some have simply fallen down, but some remain. In addition we now have the problem of children who have no home at all, and the same priority need for nursery provision is still there.

Some of the schemes involving care of young children set up to provide training and employment for young people were less than satisfactory for the young children who were being used in this way. Some of the provison made to 'look after' young children while parents do something else, such as shopping or leisure activities or educational courses, have been of very poor quality. Young children need good nursery provision with mature responsible adults.

## Home accidents to under-7s

The very high recording of accidents to children who attend the large, overburdened, understaffed accident and emergency departments of large hospitals, where children have to wait for attention sometimes for hours, where there is not always anywhere to sit while waiting, among all the other road accidents, fire accidents, emergency accidents, industrial accidents . . . and are then found to need no treatment would not have happened twenty years ago.

Children would have been taken a short distance to the small casualty department of a cottage hospital or local hospital. The sister in charge would have dealt with any minor injury if she could, and perhaps called in a local doctor. The child could have been back in his home, pronounced safe or, if necessary, stitched up and bandaged within an hour, secure with his family and recovering from the incident. If the problem had been more than local resources could have dealt with, the sister or doctor at the local casualty department would have telephoned to a larger hospital to say the child was being sent there, told them what the problem appeared to be, and the staff would have been prepared to treat the child immediately he arrived. Even with the detour the child could well have received attention faster than he does in the new system.

## Pre-school provision for under-5s

There were high and confident hopes in 1975 for pre-school provision to expand, to improve and to be subsidized – but these hopes were not realized.

The drop in the birth rate, plus diminished resources, led to the only increase in free state provision being the use of empty school space to provide nursery classes which were under-funded and under-resourced – leaving the teachers there without enough assistance, materials and support to do the job they would have liked to do. Playgroups expanded their provision but were not able to make it free provision.

Playgroups and the work they had been doing were affected where state nursery classes creamed off their 4-year-olds and many children moved from one group to another in relatively rapid succession.

Money, time and effort has undoubtedly been spent on under-5s – but because no one agency has been given all the responsibility and all the resources, a good deal of these precious commodities have been mopped up by expensive and time-consuming coordinating and liaising exercises which have achieved very little. Each agency, whether voluntary or state-supported, has been concerned with protecting its own position and has seen provision for under-5s in terms of what it can provide rather than in the open-ended terms of what under-5s need. This has led to overlapping in some areas and gaps in others, where under-5s have been provided with what they didn't want rather than provided with what they did need.

The time is clearly ripe for one independent agency with no particular position to protect – except that of the children themselves – to find out what is needed. The cost of the exercise would probably be less than the cost which fragmented efforts are presently costing now.

## Provision for 5–7-year-olds

In schools under-7s have suffered from diminished and in-adequate resources just as every other area of education has suffered. In some areas parents have done wonders in providing primary schools with both essentials and extras, but this can happen only when parents are in a financial position to do this, so the lottery of where children live and in which kind of family applies here too.

Outside the home and school very little progress has been made in providing play areas for children – and some play areas which were there in 1975 are now not safe for under-7s either alone or with whoever takes them there, because of the possibility of violent attacks either for money, sexual assault or sheer mindless aggression.

## There are some bright spots . . .

Business interests have seen in children a means to create a market for toys and consumer goods which has received the full force of hard-selling techniques. A recent report indicates that these same aggressive marketing techniques have caused severe problems and left toy retailers 'jostling for position in a fragmented market'. Maybe, therefore, there is some hope that this kind of exploitation of children will die a natural death.

A very bright spot has been the CHES study into the effects of early education, which gives some very valuable and convincing pointers as to what sort of pre-school experience leads to long-term benefits. Even if short-term needs and benefits are ignored, presumably long-term educational benefits will be added into the balance sheet of cost-effectiveness on the grounds that less money spent earlier may lead to more money being saved later on.

## And the brightest spots of all . . .

The lack of educational resources for pre-school education may have been a blessing in disguise – had there been enough money perhaps all our children would have been taken into school at the age of 3, which is not what is wanted or needed. The voluntary and self-help sectors could have disappeared altogether and that would have been a great loss, as nursery groups clearly have a supportive social role to play in addition to extending play experience for children.

The door should soon be open for mature, experienced people to train for jobs with children which cut across the limits and barriers of teaching, social work and health care and where the deceptively simple caring and enabling role can be recognized, acknowledged and rewarded.

The door is open for parents to become involved and participate in decision-making about their children. If parents make politicians actually take note of what they have to say rather than allowing parents' unwelcome answers to politicians' rhetorical questions to be brushed aside, it could help education generally to provide a better service.

Meanwhile what is needed is for everyone concerned with under-7s to look at the total situation – without losing sight of individual children – and to re-think what it is that under-7s need to enable them to play purposefully and learn confidently.

# Appendix 1

# Organizations of Interest and Help to Parents

The groups listed below offer a variety of ways for members to contribute to and benefit from the organization. Some can provide advice and information, some can provide resources, support and training. Up-to-date information, addresses and telephone numbers can be found in the reference section of local libraries, in current copies of *Directory of British Associations*; *Councils, Committees and Boards*; *Centres and Bureaux*; *Charities Digest*; and *Atlas of British Charities*. Local libraries, Health Centres, Social Services departments will have lists of groups offering local activities.

**Action for Children**
(*previously National Children's Home*)

**Action for Sick Children**
(*previously NAWCH – National Association for the Welfare of Children in Hosiptal*)

**Association for all Speech Impaired Children (AFASIC)**

**Association of Parents of Vaccine Damaged Children**

**Association for Spina Bifida and Hydrocephalus**

**Barnardo's**

**British Activity Holiday Association**

**British Diabetic Association**

**British Epilepsy Association**

**Brittle Bone Society**

**Child Protection Helpline (NSPCC)**
(*Tel: 0800 800500*)

**Children's Legal Centre Ltd.**

**Citizens' Advice Bureaux (CAB)**
*local branches*

**Community Relations Council (CRC)**
*local branches*

**Cystic Fibrosis Research Trust**

**Down's Syndrome Association**

**Gingerbread**
(*one-parent family support groups*) *local branches*

**Hyperactive Children's Support Group**

**ICAN**
(*Invalid Children's Aid Nationwide*)

**Kids' Clubs Network (KCN)**
(*previously National Out of School Alliance*)

**Muscular Dystrophy Group of Great Britain**

**National Association for Gifted Children**

**National Association for Special Educational Needs**

**National Autistic Society (NAS)**

**National Association for Mental Health (MIND)**

**National Association for the Support of Small Schools**

**National Association of Toy and Leisure Libraries**
*local branches*

**National Campaign for Nursery Education (NCNE)**

**National Childbirth Trust (NCT)**
*local branches*

**National Childminding Association (NCMA)**

**National Children's Bureau (NCB)**

**National Council for Vocational Qualifications**

**National Council of Voluntary Childcare
Organizations (NCVCCO)**

**National Deaf Children's Society**

**National Eczema Society**

**National Foster Care Association**

**National Playbus Association**

**National Playing Fields Association**

**National Society for the Prevention of Cruelty to
Children (NSPCC)**

**Network 81**
*(help and advice on Special Needs procedures)*

**Parents against Injustice**
*(relating to legal procedures concerning abuse)*

**Pre-School Learning Alliance**
*(previously Pre-School Playgroups Association)*

**Pre-School Playgroups Association (PPA)**
*local groups (see above)*

**Royal Association for Disability and Rehabilitation (RADAR)**
*local groups*

**Royal National Institute for the Blind (Education and Leisure) (RNIB)**

**Royal National Institute for the Deaf (RNID)**
*local branches*

**Royal Society for Mentally Handicapped Children and Adults (MENCAP)**

**Royal Society for the Prevention of Accidents (RoSPA)**

**Save the Children Fund (SCF)**

**The Children's Society**
(*Church of England Children's Society*)

**The Spastics Society**

**Voluntary Council for Handicapped Children**

**Volunteer Centre**
(*see telephone directory for local groups*)

**Working Mothers' Association**

# Appendix 2

## Some Facts and Some Estimated Figures

1 Use of NCB figures to show 1975 and 1985 utilization of places in nursery classes in infant schools, infant classes in infant schools, nursery schools and independent schools by 3–5-year-old children (England only) to deduce the number of 3–5-year-olds who could be in playgroup. (The relatively small number who could be in alternative care has been ignored.)

**Figure 20** 3–5-year-olds (England only)

|  | 1975 | 1985 |
|---|---|---|
| Population Total | 1,409,900 | 1,184,500 |
| In nursery schools | 43,517 | 49,613 |
| In nursery classes | 94,401 | 217,323 |
| In infant schools | 265,968 | 245,631 |
| In independent schools | 30,066 | 32,081 |
| Totals in above groups | 433,952 | 544,648 |
| No. who could be in playgroup* | 975,948* | 639,852 |

*Not all these children would have had a place available, as there would not have been enough playgroups in 1975 to provide for more than 60 per cent of this number even if places were shared as they were in 1985.

**2** Calculation to show numbers of under-3s in playgroups in 1985:

Number of registered playgroup places 409,379
Each place is used by 1.8 children
Total number of children using playgroups 736,882
Number of 3–5s available to use playgroups 639,852

Even if all the 3–5s who are not in infant school or nursery school are making use of playgroups, this still leaves 97,030 children on playgroup registers who must be under 3.

(a) Assuming playgroups do not take children until they are 2 years old: the percentage of all 2–3-year-olds in playgroups is at least 16 per cent of that age group
(b) Assuming playgroups do not take children until they are $2\frac{1}{2}$ years old: the percentage of all $2\frac{1}{2}$–3-year-olds in playgroups is at least 32 per cent of that age group.

**3** Calculation to show where 4–5-year-old children probably were in 1985 (assuming intake patterns have not changed since the CHES study – which is the only guide there is – and ignoring the very small number who may be in day nurseries).

INFANT CLASSES in infant schools:
All children would start after the age of 4 years, i.e. 245,631 children (see Fig. 20).

NURSERY CLASSES in infant schools:
42.8 per cent of the children started at 4 years, 55.5 per cent of the children started at the age of 3 years, and half this number would have reached the age of 4 in any one year, i.e. 27.75 per cent.

Thus the percentage of nursery class places being used by 4–5-year-olds at any one time was 70.55 per cent of 217,323 places – i.e. 153,321 children.

NURSERY SCHOOLS:
27.4 per cent of the children started after the age of 4 years, 65.4 per cent of the children started between 3 and 4 years old, and half this number would have reached the age of 4 in any one year, i.e. 32.7 per cent.

Thus the percentage of nursery school places being used by 4–5-year-olds at any one time was 60.1 per cent of 49,613 places – i.e. 29,817 children.

INDEPENDENT SCHOOLS:
25 per cent of the children started at 4 years.
62.5 per cent of the children started at 3 years, and half
this number would have reached the age of 4 in any one year,
i.e. 31.25 per cent.

Thus the percentage of independent school places being
used by 4–5-year-olds at any one time was 56.25 per cent of
32,081 places – i.e. 18,045 children.

4 Tables to show where 4–5-year-old children and 3–4-year-
old children probably were in 1985.

### Figure 21 *4–5-year-olds*

**Approximate population of 4–5-year-olds    592,250**

| | | |
|---|---|---|
| In INFANT CLASSES in infant school | 245,631 | 41.5% |
| In NURSERY CLASSES in infant school | 153,321 | 25.9% |
| In NURSERY SCHOOLS | 29,817 | 5.0% |
| In INDEPENDENT SCHOOLS | 18,045 | 3.0% |
| Totals in above groups | 446,814 | 75.4% |
| No. who could have been in playgroups | 145,436 | 24.6% |

### Figure 22 *3–4-year-olds*

**Approximate population of 3–4-year-olds    592,250**

| | | |
|---|---|---|
| In INFANT CLASSES in infant school | none | none |
| In NURSERY CLASSES in infant school | 60,307 | 10% |
| In NURSERY SCHOOLS | 16,223 | 2.75% |
| In INDEPENDENT SCHOOLS | 10,025 | 1.75% |
| Totals in above groups | 86,555 | 14.5% |
| No. who could have been in playgroups | 505,695 | 85.5% |

# Appendix 3

## Useful Sources of Ideas for Play Material

MAIL ORDER (SEND FOR CATALOGUES)
NES
Nottingham Education Supplies
Pre-School Customer Service
Ludlow Hill Road
West Bridgeford
Nottingham NG2 6HD

Galt's Educational
Culvert Street
Oldham OL4

SPECIAL NEEDS
Anything Left-Handed Ltd
57 Brewer Street
London W1R 3FB

MAGAZINE
*The Good Toy Guide* (£2.50 approx.)
Free to members of the National Association of Toy and Leisure Libraries or
from W. H. Smith and Menzies

LOCAL TOY LIBRARY
Ask about local groups at child welfare
clinic *or* local library *or* social services
department.

LOCAL PLAYGROUPS
Sometimes order in bulk and may be
willing to sell to or order for parents.

# Appendix 4

## Safety Informa

*Information and figures f
from the following:*
Statistics and reports by th
Trade and Industry; data o
Accident Surveillance Sys
*Safety in the Home* (198
gratefully acknowledged.

*Safety materials can be*
RoSPA
Cannon House, Priory Que
Extensive literature and
Can supply material for
Proficiency Scheme. Send

National Playing Fields A
25 Ovington Square, Lon
Send for publications
playground managemer
absorbing surfaces, play
wide range of very us
provision for outside pla

# PENGUIN ONLINE

# READ MORE IN PENGUIN

In every corner of the world, on every subject under the sun, Penguin represents quality and variety – the very best in publishing today.

For complete information about books available from Penguin – including Puffins, Penguin Classics and Arkana – and how to order them, write to us at the appropriate address below. Please note that for copyright reasons the selection of books varies from country to country.

**In the United Kingdom**: Please write to *Dept. EP, Penguin Books Ltd, Bath Road, Harmondsworth, West Drayton, Middlesex UB7 0DA*

**In the United States**: Please write to *Consumer Sales, Penguin Putnam Inc., P.O. Box 12289 Dept. B, Newark, New Jersey 07101-5289.* VISA and MasterCard holders call 1-800-788-6262 to order Penguin titles

**In Canada**: Please write to *Penguin Books Canada Ltd, 10 Alcorn Avenue, Suite 300, Toronto, Ontario M4V 3B2*

**In Australia**: Please write to *Penguin Books Australia Ltd, P.O. Box 257, Ringwood, Victoria 3134*

**In New Zealand**: Please write to *Penguin Books (NZ) Ltd, Private Bag 102902, North Shore Mail Centre, Auckland 10*

**In India**: Please write to *Penguin Books India Pvt Ltd, 11 Community Centre, Panchsheel Park, New Delhi 110017*

**In the Netherlands**: Please write to *Penguin Books Netherlands bv, Postbus 3507, NL-1001 AH Amsterdam*

**In Germany**: Please write to *Penguin Books Deutschland GmbH, Metzlerstrasse 26, 60594 Frankfurt am Main*

**In Spain**: Please write to *Penguin Books S. A., Bravo Murillo 19, 1° B, 28015 Madrid*

**In Italy**: Please write to *Penguin Italia s.r.l., Via Benedetto Croce 2, 20094 Corsico, Milano*

**In France**: Please write to *Penguin France, Le Carré Wilson, 62 rue Benjamin Baillaud, 31500 Toulouse*

**In Japan**: Please write to *Penguin Books Japan Ltd, Kaneko Building, 2-3-25 Koraku, Bunkyo-Ku, Tokyo 112*

**In South Africa**: Please write to *Penguin Books South Africa (Pty) Ltd, Private Bag X14, Parkview, 2122 Johannesburg*